Beyond Combat
Women and Gender in the Vietnam War Era

Beyond Combat: Women and Gender in the Vietnam War Era investigates how the Vietnam War both reinforced and challenged the gender roles that were key components of American Cold War ideology. Although popular memory of the Vietnam War centers on the "combat moment," refocusing attention onto women and gender paints a more complex and accurate picture of the war's far-reaching impact beyond the battlefields. Encounters between Americans and Vietnamese were shaped by a cluster of intertwined images used to make sense of and justify American intervention and use of force in Vietnam. These images included the girl next door, a wholesome reminder of why the United States was committed to defeating communism; the treacherous and mysterious "dragon lady," who served as a metaphor for Vietnamese women and South Vietnam; the John Wayne figure, entrusted with the duty of protecting civilization from savagery; and the gentle warrior, whose humanitarian efforts were intended to win the favor of the South Vietnamese. Heather Marie Stur also examines the ways in which ideas about masculinity shaped the American GI experience in Vietnam, and ultimately, how some American men and women returned from Vietnam to challenge home-front gender norms.

Heather Marie Stur is an Assistant Professor of history at the University of Southern Mississippi. Dr. Stur has won fellowships from the Society for Historians of American Foreign Relations, the Gerald R. Ford Foundation, the Doris G. Quinn Foundation, the Marine Corps Heritage Foundation, the University of Wisconsin, and Marquette University. She has published in several journals and collections, including *The Sixties: A Journal of History, Politics, and Culture*; *America and the Vietnam War: Re-examining the Culture and History of a Generation*; *Highway 61 Revisited: Bob Dylan from Minnesota to the World*; *Soul Soldiers: African Americans and the Vietnam Era*; and *Milwaukee History*.

Beyond Combat

Women and Gender in the Vietnam War Era

HEATHER MARIE STUR

University of Southern Mississippi

CAMBRIDGE UNIVERSITY PRESS
Cambridge, New York, Melbourne, Madrid, Cape Town,
Singapore, São Paulo, Delhi, Mexico City

Cambridge University Press
32 Avenue of the Americas, New York, NY 10013-2473, USA

www.cambridge.org
Information on this title: www.cambridge.org/9780521127417

© Heather Marie Stur 2011

First published 2011
Reprinted 2012

A catalog record for this publication is available from the British Library.

Library of Congress Cataloging in Publication Data
Stur, Heather Marie, 1975–
Beyond combat : women and gender in the Vietnam War era / Heather Marie Stur.
  p. cm.
Includes bibliographical references and index.
ISBN 978-0-521-76275-5 (hardback) – ISBN 978-0-521-12741-7 (pbk.)
1. Vietnam War, 1961–1975 – Women. 2. Vietnam War, 1961–1975 – Participation,
Female. 3. Vietnam War, 1961–1975 – Social aspects. 4. Women – United States –
History – 20th century. 5. Women – Vietnam – History – 20th century.
6. Sex role – United States – History – 20th century. 7. Sex role – Vietnam – History –
20th century. 8. Masculinity – United States – History – 20th century. 9. Masculinity –
Vietnam – History – 20th century. I. Title.
DS559.8.W6S78 2011
959.704'3082–dc22   2011015050

ISBN 978-0-521-76275-5 Hardback
ISBN 978-0-521-12741-7 Paperback

To Jay, who provides the music.
And to Angus, who makes us want to dance.

Contents

Acknowledgments

At the end of my dissertation defense, one of my committee members, Alfred W. McCoy, remarked that I seemed to have had a lot of fun in graduate school. Puzzled, I must have looked at him inquiringly because he continued by saying he had read my acknowledgments, in which I had mentioned Friday Night Music Club, the 5260 crew, and other groups of friends and family members who had clearly made my time in graduate school bearable, if not a downright blast. Professor McCoy's comments reminded me then – and still do now – that the journey of writing a book, like anything in life, is best made with fellow travelers who provide guidance, encouragement, comfort, love, and, yes, fun, along the way. Thanking them here is just a small gesture compared to how much my fellow travelers have enhanced my life and this book.

The project began as a dissertation, and my committee at the University of Wisconsin (UW) provided invaluable advice and support when it was in its earliest stages. I thank my adviser, Brenda Gayle Plummer, as well as Tracy Curtis, Susan Johnson, Alfred McCoy, and Craig Werner for helping me clarify my vision and write better. I also thank Steve Stern and Jeremi Suri, who offered help and encouragement at various points during my time at UW. The Doris G. Quinn Foundation, the Marine Corps Heritage Foundation, the University of Wisconsin Center for Southeast Asian Studies, and the University of Wisconsin Department of History provided me with generous fellowships and grants that allowed me to complete my studies and dissertation in a timely manner, and I thank those organizations for their support. As I worked to transform the project from a dissertation to a book, I was fortunate to receive a William Appleman Williams Junior Faculty Research Grant from the Society for Historians of American Foreign Relations, a Gerald R. Ford Foundation Research Travel Grant, and a research grant from the Committee on Services and Resources for Women at the University of Southern Mississippi. I am very grateful to these organizations for their generous financial support.

No dollar amount can match the value of the archivists and professional colleagues who have helped me along the way. I have had the pleasure of meeting and working with archivists who have made the act of research less solitary and more enjoyable. I thank Richard Boylan at the National Archives in College Park, Maryland; Stacy Davis and William McNitt at the Gerald R. Ford Presidential Library and Museum; and Steven Fisher at the University of Denver Penrose Library Special Collections. The Vietnam Archive at Texas Tech University is an outstanding resource for those of us who study the Vietnam War, and I greatly appreciate the kindness and generosity that Laura Calkins, Ty Lovelady, and Steve Maxner showed me when I did research there. Amy K. Mondt was especially helpful in walking me through the process of obtaining permission to use images from the Vietnam Archive. At the Wisconsin Historical Society (WHS), James Danky was enthusiastic and helpful when I was just beginning my research, and the collection of GI antiwar newspapers housed at WHS led me to the ideas that became the foundation for this book. I am also grateful to the archivists who photocopied many pages for me from the Marguerite Higgins Papers at the Syracuse University Library Special Collections. It is good to have friends in high places, and Sondra Zaharias, a fellow Marquette class of 1998 graduate now employed at Getty Images, helped me get the rights to publish an image of Madame Ngo Dinh Nhu, one of my earliest inspirations for this book. Without that photograph, the book would just not feel complete to me. As I tested my ideas and research at conferences, I received helpful and encouraging feedback from fellow participants at the annual meetings of the Society for Military History and the Organization of American Historians, as well as at Texas Tech's Vietnam Symposium and the War and American Identity Conference at University College Dublin. I especially thank Justin Hart, Steve Maxner, David Ryan, and Janet Valentine for their comments on my work.

Michael Foley saw promise in this project when it still seemed like a rough draft to me, and I am eternally grateful to him for pushing me to do my best work and for believing in its value. In his capacity as co-editor of *The Sixties: A Journal of History, Politics, and Culture*, Mike reached out to me, a new scholar, with respect and enthusiasm, and he has been a steadfast supporter ever since. His work on draft resistance during the Vietnam War is a model of scholarship, and through his peace activism, he lives the ideals that he teaches. Mike is also a dad, and our e-mail conversations have often turned to the joys and challenges of raising young children while trying to write books.

Closer to home, I am inspired and sustained daily by my amazing colleagues in the History Department at the University of Southern Mississippi. Not only am I surrounded by brilliant scholars and innovative teachers, but there is laughter in our hallways, as well as good music in the main office thanks to Shelia Smith, our extraordinary office administrator who knows the inner workings of the university better than anyone. For her patience and support, I owe Shelia way more thanks than I can express here. I am especially thankful to my friends in the Center for the Study of War and Society: Susannah Ural, Andrew Wiest, and Kyle Zelner, and I owe a deep debt of gratitude to my department chair, Phyllis Jestice, who somehow found time in her jam-packed schedule to read my entire manuscript and offer detailed comments that seemed to come from a specialist in modern U.S. history even though she is a medievalist. Phyllis is a visionary department chair, committed to cultivating a faculty of productive, successful, and happy scholar-teachers, and she makes special efforts to help junior faculty achieve their professional goals. I am one of the lucky recipients of her support. I also thank Michael Neiberg, now of the U.S. Army War College, who was my faculty mentor during my first year at Southern Miss. His guidance and encouragement were crucial as I learned the ropes of being a history professor, both at the university and in the profession at large.

At Cambridge University Press, I am grateful to my editor, Eric Crahan, who saw something worthwhile in this project and who patiently guided me through the publishing process. A constant advocate for me, Eric helped me focus the project and remained committed to helping me achieve its full potential. His assistant, Abigail Zorbaugh, and Paul Smolenski, senior production controller, worked hard to prepare the manuscript for publication, and I thank them for their support. I also thank senior project manager Peggy Rote and the copy editors at Aptara, Inc., for seeing the manuscript through the final stages of production. The two anonymous readers who commented on the manuscript offered wise insights and thoughtful suggestions that strengthened the book immensely. I am extremely grateful to the readers for the time they took with my work.

This book would not have been possible without the women and men who generously shared with me the stories of their service in Vietnam and after. I am indebted to Lynda Alexander, Doris "Lucki" Allen, Joan Barco, Doug Bradley, Nancy Calcese, Colleen Campbell, Carol Chapman, Jeanne Christie, Bill Davis, Judy Davis, Joyce Denke, Debra Drummond, Marj Dutilly, Shirley Fleischauer, Susan Franklin, Marj Graves, Dorris Heaston, Shirley Hines, Kathleen Huckabay, Kay Johnson, Rene Johnson, Ann Kelsey, Nancy Keough, Martha Maron, Linda McClenahan, Lola McGourty, Susan McLean, Jim Mifflin, Janie Miller, Eileen O'Neill, Sandra Pang, Dorothy Patterson, Nora Preston, Linda Pugsley, Paula Quindlen, Mary Robeck, Jim Roseberry, Anna Rybat, Emily Strange, Mike Subkoviak, Elton Tylenda, Nancy Warner, J. Holley Watts, Linda Wilson, Patty Wooldridge, and Jennifer Young for their openness and honesty. My friend, Doug Bradley, has been especially helpful and incisive. I hope this book does justice to their experiences.

My friends are blessings that I do not give thanks for nearly enough. A special shout-out goes to Story Matkin-Rawn and Tyina Steptoe, dear friends and dissertation writing group members. The feedback and encouragement they gave me during our weekly meetings at Angelic Brewery are evident in this book, and I raise a pint of Leinie's Summer Shandy to them. I love that we have continued on our academic journey together, now as professors, and though our meetings are much less frequent these days, I know there is some collaborating in store that is going to be awesome. I absolutely miss Friday Night Music Club, especially founding members Charles Hughes, Alexander Shashko, and Craig Werner . . . we may never completely agree about rock-n-roll, but man, the debates were so much fun. I thank Matt Blanton, Andrew Case, Dave Gilbert, Brenna Greer, Holly McGee, Jennie Miller, Leah Mirakhor, Will Shannon, Maia Surdam, Zoe Van Orsdol, Vanessa Walker, and Stephanie Westcott for their friendship during graduate school and since. Above all, I thank my old friends who knew me long before I was a historian, and whose constant love and support has kept me grounded and joyful. Kati Kreslins, Brigid Miller, Becky Rocker, Mark Shields, and Chris Toma are truly some of the most important people in my life, and their loyal friendship is priceless.

The enthusiasm of my wonderful family sustained me through the long process of writing this book. I owe a lifetime of love and thanks to my parents, Jeffrey and Michaline Stur, whose belief in me has never faltered, and who have supported me unconditionally in every possible way. My siblings, Erica Burg, Dave Burg, and Jeff Stur; and my goddaughter, Charlotte "Chachi" Burg, are constant sources of joy in my life, and I love them dearly. Much love and thanks to Grandma and Grandpa

Nalewski; Aunt Kathy Nalewski; Aunt Patti and Uncle Eddy Centkowski; Aunt Judith Rutovic; Aunt Tina and Uncle Rich Bronisz; Aunt Nina and Uncle Eric Stur; April Richwalski; Tricia Bronisz; Brent Bradford; BreAnne, Bob, and Mihaly Csernak; Mathew Richwalski; and Jonathan Bronisz. I also thank my in-laws, the Campbells and the Van Orsdols, for their love and support. My Grandma and Grandpa Stur did not live to see the completion of this project, but they were two of my biggest cheerleaders, and I love and miss them terribly. I know they are watching over me and beaming with pride.

Craig Werner has already been mentioned several times in these acknowledgments, and that is a testament to how important he is to me. Ever since we met at Borders in Madison, Wisconsin, one cold morning years ago and bonded over our shared love of Springsteen's "Incident on 57th Street," Craig has been a devoted mentor and a steadfast friend. He has believed in me when my own faith has faltered, and he pushes me to think more deeply, write more confidently, trust my instincts, and stay true to my convictions. For those reasons and more, Craig's imprint is all over this book. He has read every word many times and provided countless wise comments, graceful critiques, and empathetic pep talks as the project took shape and evolved over time. I am a better scholar, a better writer, and a better teacher because of Craig, and I hope that I can at least begin to repay him by channeling his energy when I mentor my own students. Muchas gracias, mi amigo.

Two people have brought the ultimate joy and purpose to my life. Jay Van Orsdol is my artist and my guitar man, and on more than one occasion he has turned our little house in Hattiesburg, Mississippi, into a juke joint. He is a patient problem-solver and an affectionate father, and he makes a mean red beans and rice. His kind-hearted smile has never stopped melting my heart. Angus "Cheeky Boy" Van Orsdol loves everything about this life (including the spicy red beans and rice), and he lets us know that with his big belly laugh and his happy dance. He is my sweet baby boy, and I hope he grows up to be just like his daddy. For the life that we have created, and for all that is yet to come, I dedicate this book to my guys with deepest love.

Introduction

Lily Lee Adams served as an Army nurse in Vietnam from 1969 to 1970 at the 12th Evacuation Hospital in Cu Chi. She was a twenty-year-old American girl, a New Yorker, the daughter of an Italian mother and a Chinese father. John F. Kennedy's call to young people – "Ask not what your country can do for you, ask what you can do for your country" – had inspired her to join the military. In many ways, Adams's story was typical of young Americans who volunteered for the armed services in the 1960s, but her Asian heritage resulted in some telling differences. Some of the U.S. servicemen she encountered in Vietnam assumed that Adams was a prostitute when she was not wearing her nurse's uniform. "When I was in civilian clothes and walking around with a guy, the other guys would just assume I was a whore," Adams said. "The Army used to truck in whores all the time." She learned to keep her military identification with her at all times. "It really hurt inside that I had just spent twelve hours treating their buddies, and they thought I was just some Vietnamese whore," Adams said. When GIs solicited her for sex, she would think, "You guys don't even know that if you came into my hospital I'd be taking care of you, giving you everything I have just to keep you alive." Even the Vietnamese guards at the post exchange (PX) where Adams was stationed assumed she was a prostitute and demanded her ID while waving other military staff through. Adams remembered a nurse from the Philippines who left Vietnam after a few months of service because of similar treatment. "She was not used to the sexual harassment and racial discrimination, and she asked me how I handled it," Adams said. "I told her I got used to it. I grew up with discrimination and learned how to deal with it."[1]

The troops' responses to Adams were grounded in a set of contradictory assumptions and images – passed down in basic training, popular culture, political speeches, and GI folklore – that assigned ideologically charged meanings to Asian and American women. Focusing on the tension between these images and the lived experiences of men and women in (and after) Vietnam, *Beyond Combat: Women and Gender in the Vietnam War Era* investigates the conflict, not just as a military maneuver, but also as a complex web of personal encounters between Americans and Vietnamese that took place in the hothouse environment of war. Although popular memory of the Vietnam War centers on the "combat moment," refocusing attention onto women and gender paints a more complex – and, ultimately, more accurate – picture of the war's far-reaching impact beyond the battlefields. A substantial majority of interactions between American men and various groups of women, whether American or Vietnamese, took place not in combat situations, but on bases in Long Binh and Qui Nhon, in brothels in An Khe and Cam Ranh Bay, and along the boulevards of cities such as Saigon and Da Nang. These encounters, which were grounded in the reality of American power and dominance even when individual GIs attempted to soften that reality through humanitarian outreach, were shaped by a cluster of intertwined images that Americans used to make sense of and justify intervention and use of force in Vietnam: the girl next door, a wholesome reminder of why the United States was committed to fighting communism; the dragon lady, at once treacherous and mysterious, a metaphor for both Vietnamese women and South Vietnam; the "John Wayne" figure protecting civilization against savagery; and the gentle warrior, whose humanitarian efforts were intended to win the favor of the South Vietnamese. A careful examination of these images reveals the ways in which home-front culture influenced American policymaking and propaganda regarding Vietnam, and how the actual lived experiences of the men and women on the ground both enforced and challenged the gender ideology deployed in military and diplomatic rhetoric.

---

[1] Victor Marina, "Fighting for your country," *Rice*, April 1988, 37; "'We saved lives in Vietnam,' recalls Adams. But racism, Agent Orange, left their scars." *Asian Week*, February 22, 1985, Lily Adams Collection, University of Denver Penrose Library, Box 1, Folder "Lily Adams." See also Kathryn Marshall, *In the Combat Zone: An Oral History of American Women in Vietnam* (Boston: Little, Brown, 1987), 222.

Even as they were being challenged on the home front, American Cold War ideas about manhood and womanhood shaped relations between U.S. military bases and surrounding Vietnamese communities; they were invoked to mobilize citizens for the war effort and played a role in humanitarian endeavors by U.S. troops in Vietnam. At times, South Vietnamese women were cast as "damsels in distress," representatives of a nascent democracy – a Southeast Asian mirror of American Cold War norms – in need of protection from Communist despoilers. At other times, Americans viewed Vietnamese women with suspicion, as new incarnations of the "dragon ladies" of the World War II era or, as Adams's experience demonstrates, sex objects whose purpose was to satiate the carnal desires of American troops.

In contrast to the dragon lady and the sex object, both of whom represented real and metaphorical threats to U.S. troops, the American "girl next door" – white, middle class, and pure – symbolized the way of life the United States had committed itself to defending against communism and a host of associated fears, including homosexuality, racial strife, the collapse of the nuclear family, and the disintegration of capitalist prosperity.[2] Faced with these anxieties, American women who ventured to Vietnam were expected to fulfill the conventional women's roles of caregivers, mothers, and virginal girlfriends, even as their concrete experiences told a different story. The images were pervasive, surfacing in U.S. policymakers' conversations, informational pamphlets published by the State and Defense departments, Army operations manuals, newspapers and magazines published for servicemen, and hundreds of popular songs, movies, and television shows. Combining the currents running through these images, Adams's experience highlights the misunderstandings they caused when applied to actual women. As an American woman in nurse's attire, she had an accepted, if marginal, role in a war zone, but her Chinese ethnicity activated the stereotypes that led some troops, both American and Vietnamese, to conclude that she was more likely a dragon lady than a girl next door.

The confusion surrounding women's roles in Vietnam played out in complicated ways in the experiences of male GIs as well. Like American and Vietnamese women, U.S. servicemen found themselves in situations that had been shaped by a set of gendered assumptions, articulated with

[2] Elaine Tyler May explores the links between home front gender ideology and Cold War containment in *Homeward Bound: American Families in the Cold War Era* (New York: Basic Books, 1999).

varying degrees of clarity and awareness, about America's place in the world. In U.S. popular culture, the girl next door's archetypal defender was John Wayne, who, as Richard Slotkin writes, symbolized the "perfection of soldierly masculinity" in the 1960s.[3] The John Wayne image, transmitted through generic cowboy and soldier characters in movies and on TV, as well as by Wayne himself, represented U.S. martial prowess along with a broader collection of American virtues, including patriotism, courage, Christian faith, and unremitting dedication to protecting the civilization embodied in the girl next door. Growing up in a militarized culture predicated on defending the American way of life, many of the young men who went to Vietnam, as Andrew Huebner has observed, considered John Wayne the embodiment of their "martial dreams."[4] Born during World War II and coming of age during the nebulous, nearly fifty-years-long event called the Cold War, they witnessed empires collapse and new nations emerge in the initial phases of the postcolonial struggle, which would define the second half of the twentieth century. The generation of American boys whose fathers had fought against Germany and Japan was encouraged to make sense of these circumstances not by looking ahead, but by looking back, beginning with their childhood games, playing cowboys and Indians and reenacting World War II.[5] As they approached and entered their teenage years, they listened to President John F. Kennedy's rhetoric about fighting tyranny and spreading democracy throughout the decolonizing world.[6]

When put into action in Vietnam, this dual mission – to battle communist insurgency while winning hearts and minds with modernization projects and humanitarian aid – gave rise to a variation on the John Wayne theme: the "gentle warrior." As depicted in both military and civilian media, the gentle warrior was to be the bearer of U.S. benevolence,

---

[3] Richard Slotkin, *Gunfighter Nation: The Myth of the Frontier in Twentieth-Century America* (Norman, OK: University of Oklahoma Press, 1992), 489–533.

[4] Andrew J. Huebner, *The Warrior Image: Soldiers in American Culture from the Second World War to the Vietnam Era* (Chapel Hill, NC: University of North Carolina Press, 2008), 250.

[5] Tom Engelhardt, *The End of Victory Culture: Cold War America and the Disillusioning of a Generation* (New York: Basic Books, 1995), 69–89.

[6] For a discussion of the Kennedy administration's modernization theories, see Michael E. Latham, *Modernization as Ideology: American Social Science and "Nation Building" in the Kennedy Era* (Chapel Hill, NC: University of North Carolina Press, 2000); Nils Gilman, *Mandarins of the Future: Modernization Theory in Cold War America* (Baltimore: Johns Hopkins University Press, 2007).

similar to organizations such as the Peace Corps and the U.S. Agency for International Development. Providing health care to Vietnamese families, building schools, and sponsoring orphanages, gentle warriors – a term used in *The Observer*, the official newspaper for the U.S. Military Assistance Command Vietnam (MACV) – represented an alternative to communist brutality as they deployed what Joseph Nye calls "soft power."[7] The dragon lady, the girl next door, John Wayne, and the gentle warrior reflected gendered, ultimately patriarchal, beliefs about national security and America's duty to weaker peoples and nations. The images illustrate how popular home-front beliefs about men's and women's appropriate roles were deployed in U.S. policies toward Vietnam, reflecting what Americans thought about themselves and about the U.S. position in the world. Like the depictions of women, though, the images of men circulating through military rhetoric and the mass media reflected irreconcilable tensions, not just in the images, but in the U.S. mission itself. Vietnamese men were notably absent from the American wartime imagery, and although some GIs acknowledged the martial fortitude of their enemies in the National Liberation Front and North Vietnamese Army, their allies in the Army of the Republic of Vietnam (ARVN) were rarely depicted in soldier folklore or home-front popular culture.[8]

The policies of Kennedy and his successor, Lyndon Johnson, were grounded in a pervasive and powerful gender ideology, which was often implied rather than explicit, in which John Wayne and the girl next door represented American power and civilization. These images would shape the experiences of the Americans who served in Vietnam, as well as the policies that sent them there. As Susan Jeffords writes in *The Remasculinization of America: Gender and the Vietnam War*, a book that profoundly influenced my work, the Vietnam War consisted not just of battlefields, but also "fields of gender," in which "enemies are depicted as feminine, wives and mothers and girl friends are justifications for fighting, and vocabularies are sexually motivated."[9] On these fields of gender, the irresolvable tensions in American ideology became clear.

---

[7] Joseph Nye, *Soft Power: The Means to Success in World Politics* (Cambridge, MA: Public Affairs, 2004).

[8] On ARVN, see Andrew Wiest, *Vietnam's Forgotten Army: Heroism and Betrayal in the ARVN* (New York: New York University Press, 2007).

[9] Susan Jeffords, *The Remasculinization of America: Gender and the Vietnam War* (Bloomington, IN: Indiana University Press, 1989), xi.

Vietnamese women were at once damsels in need of rescue and dragon ladies who must be slain, the American girl next door represented an ideal of white femininity that was under fire from the women's and civil rights movements, and the gentle warrior attempted to rebuild that which his comrades destroyed in combat, exposing the contradictory nature of soft power and ultimately failing to mask the war's devastating effects. For some individual U.S. servicemen, the time they spent teaching English to Vietnamese students or providing medical care to remote villages helped them feel human and offered a sense of purpose in what otherwise seemed to be a pointless war. In the larger context of U.S. policies, massive bombing, misguided operations, and atrocities negated much of the good that some GIs tried to do.

Juxtaposed with the realities of day-to-day experiences in Vietnam, the images together point to a fundamental contradiction in the American mission, which has been identified in James Gibson's *The Perfect War: Technowar in Vietnam* and Christian Appy's *Working-Class War: American Combat Soldiers and Vietnam*. Even as the United States presented itself as a benevolent entity protecting the American way of life from the insidious spread of communism and rescuing the Vietnamese from communist oppression, U.S. policies and actions damaged the infrastructure, economic system, and family structures that military humanitarian projects attempted to fix. Grounded in gendered and racialized beliefs about American power, the notion that the United States had to destroy Vietnam to save it – an idea based on a statement a U.S. Army major allegedly made to journalist Peter Arnett after a battle in the city of Ben Tre – fundamentally undermined official rhetoric about democracy building.[10]

Drawing on oral histories and extensive interviews, as well as foreign policy documents, military publications, civilian newspapers and magazines, and the literature of GIs and veterans, *Beyond Combat* pays special attention to the experiences of women, primarily American but also some Vietnamese, who until recently have remained relatively absent from Vietnam War scholarship. As psychiatrist Robert Jay Lifton wrote regarding his work with Vietnam veterans, although war primarily is about "male obligation and male glory," women – in symbol and in reality – are crucial to it, used to confirm the manhood of soldiers and positioned

[10] James Gibson, *The Perfect War: Technowar in Vietnam* (New York: Atlantic Monthly Press, 1986), 226; Christian Appy, *Working Class War: American Combat Soldiers and Vietnam* (Chapel Hill, NC: University of North Carolina Press, 1993), 207–8.

either as sources of "chivalric inspiration" or dehumanized justifications for brutality.[11] Vietnam was the descendant of a legacy of wars in which women were used to build troop morale and inspire political obligation among U.S. troops, as works by Ann Pfau, Sonya Michel, and Robert Westbrook illustrate.[12] Taking place at a historical moment when gender roles were undergoing challenges and changes on the home front, the Vietnam War differed from previous wars because the tensions and contradictions that had previously been veiled were exposed in a much clearer way.

Just as there was no typical GI in a war in which men were clerks, bakers, dog handlers, and journalists as well as combat soldiers, there was no generic story of the American woman in Vietnam. We can only estimate the numbers of women who served in the military in Vietnam – although the Defense Department did not keep accurate records on women, it has calculated that approximately 7,500 women served in Vietnam; the Veterans Administration has set the number at 11,000. More than 80 percent were nurses, most from the Army Nurse Corps. Among those who were not nurses, about 700 women were members of the Women's Army Corps (WAC), and much smaller numbers served in the Navy, Air Force, and Marines.[13] Pinning down the numbers of civilian women who worked in Vietnam is even more difficult; estimates have gone as high as 55,000.[14] Kathryn Marshall, a journalist who compiled an oral history anthology based on interviews with American military and civilian women who

[11] Robert Jay Lifton, *Home from the War: Learning from Vietnam Veterans* (Boston: Beacon Press, 1992), 245.

[12] Ann Pfau, *Miss Yourlovin: GIs, Gender, and Domesticity during World War II* (New York: Columbia University Press, 2008), via Gutenberg-e, www.gutenberg-e.org/pfau/; Sonya Michel, "American Women and the Discourse of the Democratic Family in World War II," in *Behind the Lines: Gender and the Two World Wars*, ed. by Margaret Randolph Higonnet, et al (New Haven, CT: Yale University Press, 1987), 154–67; Robert Westbrook, "'I Want a Girl, Just Like the Girl That Married Henry James': American Women and the Problem of Political Obligation in World War II," in *American Quarterly*, Vol. 42, No. 4 (December 1990), 587–614.

[13] Another 500 women served in the Air Force during the Vietnam War, but most of them were stationed in the Pacific and other parts of Southeast Asia, not in Vietnam. Fewer than thirty women Marines served in Vietnam. In addition to nurses, nine women Navy officers served tours of duty in Vietnam. See Marshall, 4; Ron Steinman, *Women in Vietnam* (New York: TV Books, 2000), 18–20; Susan H. Godson, *Serving Proudly: A History of Women in the U.S. Navy* (Annapolis, MD: Naval Institute Press, 2001), 213; Col. Mary V. Stremlow, *A History of the Women Marines, 1946–1977* (Washington, DC: History and Museums Division Headquarters, U.S. Marine Corps, 1986), 87.

[14] Marshall, 4; Milton J. Bates, *The Wars We Took to Vietnam: Cultural Conflict and Storytelling* (Berkeley, CA: University of California Press, 1996), 163.

served in Vietnam, notes that the lack of official records "both serves as a reminder of government mishandling of information during the Vietnam War and points to a more general belief that war is men's business."[15] Even though the number of American women who served was minuscule compared with the number of men, ideas about women and gender were, in fact, very present in foreign policy documents, policymakers' conversations, soldier folklore, and the rhetoric of basic training.

Although a few women went to Vietnam before the United States committed combat troops, the majority of American women who served in Vietnam in either military or civilian capacities arrived between 1965, the year of the first deployment of ground troops, and 1973, when the last U.S. combat troops departed. Women were exempt from the draft, and not all women who joined the armed services during the era wanted an assignment to Vietnam. When it came down to personnel needs, some who went did so only because they had received orders. In contrast, civilian women by and large chose to go to Vietnam, often because they desired to help the troops. Whether military or civilian, those who picked Vietnam went for a variety of reasons that depended on factors such as race, class, and religion. The Army Nurse Corps offered money for college and career opportunities that some female recruits viewed as a move toward independence. Some women thought service in Vietnam sounded like an adventure, with the chance to travel to an exotic locale while avoiding or delaying marriage and family life. Others felt guilty that conscription forced men to serve, and they wanted to do their part to help. Another group was answering President Kennedy's call to young Americans to go out into the world as missionaries of democracy. Whatever their motivations or backgrounds, all the American women who served in Vietnam had to deal with the tensions that came to a head with particular clarity for Lily Lee Adams.

Beyond Combat contributes to the growing body of scholarly literature on American women and the Vietnam War inspired by the oral histories compiled by Keith Walker, Ron Steinman, Kathryn Marshall, Olga Gruhzit-Hoyt, and Elizabeth Norman.[16] Kara Dixon Vuic's *Officer, Nurse, Woman: The Army Nurse Corps in the Vietnam War* examines

---

[15] Marshall, 4.

[16] Women's oral history collections include Keith Walker, *A Piece of My Heart: The Stories of Twenty-Six American Women Who Served in Vietnam* (New York: Ballantine Books, 1985); Kathryn Marshall, *In the Combat Zone*; Elizabeth Norman, *Women at War: The Story of Fifty Military Nurses Who Served in Vietnam* (Philadelphia: University of Pennsylvania Press, 1990); Olga Gruhzit-Hoyt, *A Time Remembered: American Women*

the Army Nurse Corps' efforts to recruit both female and male nurses amid increasing challenges to traditional gender roles. Vuic argues convincingly that even though the Army had to respond to gender changes to meet its wartime personnel needs, it ultimately did not reject the gendered structure in which men were fighters and women were caregivers.[17] Like Vuic's book and the aforementioned oral history collections, my work approaches the subjects of women and gender in the Vietnam War from American perspectives. Although I provide a glimpse of the war's impact on Vietnamese women through those viewpoints, I look forward to the continued work of scholars of Vietnamese history, some of whom, including Sandra Taylor, Nathalie Huynh Chau Nguyen, and Karen Gottschang Turner, have begun the process of telling the stories of women from both North and South Vietnam.[18]

As Elaine Tyler May outlined in the now-classic *Homeward Bound: American Families in the Cold War*, Americans used gender and sexuality to make sense of the Cold War world, linking private matters such as marriage and family life to U.S. foreign relations. Engaged in an ideological struggle with the Soviet Union for power and influence in the world, U.S. leaders portrayed capitalist democracy as the humane alternative to communism; in his "kitchen debates" with Soviet premier Nikita Khrushchev, then-Vice President Richard Nixon held up suburbia and its affluence as the epitome of American values. The heterosexual gender roles implicit in the image were strictly enforced, with the white, middle-class, suburban, nuclear family as the ultimate symbol of appropriate roles for men and women. Bringing the notion of "separate spheres" into the mid-twentieth century, politicians, sociologists, and medical doctors prescribed policies that once again placed women in charge of the home and childrearing and gave men financial and political responsibilities.[19]

---

in the Vietnam War (Novato, CA; Presidio Press, 1999); and Ron Steinman, *Women in Vietnam* (New York: TV Books, 2000).

[17] Kara Dixon Vuic, *Officer, Nurse, Woman: The Army Nurse Corps in the Vietnam War* (Baltimore: Johns Hopkins University Press, 2010).

[18] For studies devoted to various Vietnamese women's experiences in the war, see Sandra C. Taylor, *Vietnamese Women at War: Fighting for Ho Chi Minh and the Revolution* (Lawrence, KS: University Press of Kansas, 1999); Karen Gottschang Turner, *Even the Women Must Fight: Memories of War from North Vietnam* (Hoboken, NJ: John Wiley & Sons, 1999); Nathalie Huynh Chau Nguyen, *Memory is Another Country: Women of the Vietnamese Diaspora* (Santa Barbara, CA: ABC-CLIO, 2009). See also Le Ly Hayslip's memoir, *When Heaven and Earth Changed Places: A Vietnamese Woman's Journey from War to Peace* (New York: Plume, 1990).

[19] May, xxiv-xxv.

Whatever the theoretical expectations, the experiences of women in the Cold War era reflected the disconnects between the image of the suburban housewife and the realities for most American women, as Wini Breines, Susan Douglas, Alice Echols, Ruth Feldstein, Susan Hartmann, Joanne Meyerowitz, and Ruth Rosen have shown.[20] Married and middle-class women increasingly sought paying work outside the home, and groups such as the National Manpower Council and the President's Council on the Status of Women called for the incorporation of women into service for the nation's defense. Tracking the contradictions embedded in the situation, scholars including Robert Corber, K. A. Cuordileone, John D'Emilio, and Jane Sherron De Hart have shown how policymakers capitalized on the culture of fear and uncertainty in the Cold War world to demonize and persecute Americans – especially gays, lesbians, and African Americans – who defied or tried to live outside the boundaries of domesticity. Their work is part of a broader conversation concerning the transitions that were taking place in post-World War II American society, transitions that would ultimately redefine "traditional" gender roles.[21]

As Sara Evans and other women activists have written, those roles persisted even within the era's movements for social change; their experiences of marginalization within civil rights and antiwar organizations

---

[20] Wini Breines, *Young, White, and Miserable: Growing Up Female in the Fifties* (Chicago, University of Chicago Press, 1992); Susan J. Douglas, *Where the Girls Are: Growing Up Female with the Mass Media* (New York: Times Books, 1994); Alice Echols, *Shaky Ground: The Sixties and Its Aftershocks* (New York: Columbia University Press, 2002); Susan M. Hartmann, *From Margin to Mainstream: American Women and Politics since 1960* (New York: Alfred A. Knopf, 1989); Hartmann, "Women's Employment and the Domestic Ideal in the Early Cold War Years," in *Not June Cleaver: Women and Gender in Postwar America, 1945–1960*, ed. Joanne Meyerowitz (Philadelphia: Temple University Press, 1994); Joanne Meyerowitz, "Beyond the Feminine Mystique: A Reassessment of Postwar Mass Culture, 1946–1958," in *Not June Cleaver*; Ruth Feldstein, *Motherhood in Black and White: Race and Sex in American Liberalism, 1930–1965* (Ithaca, NY: Cornell University Press, 2000); Ruth Rosen, *The World Split Open: How the Modern Women's Movement Changed America* (New York: Penguin, 2006).

[21] John D'Emilio, *Sexual Politics, Sexual Communities: The Making of a Homosexual Minority in the United States, 1940–1970* (Chicago: University of Chicago Press, 1983). See also Robert J. Corber, *Homosexuality in Cold War America: Resistance and the Crisis of Masculinity* (Durham, NC: Duke University Press, 1997); K.A. Cuordileone, *Manhood and American Political Culture in the Cold War* (New York: Routledge, 2005); Jane Sherron De Hart, "Containment at Home: Gender, Sexuality, and National Identity in Cold War America," in *Rethinking Cold War Culture*, ed. Peter J. Kuznick (Washington, DC: Smithsonian Books, 2001); Michael Kimmel, *Manhood in America: A Cultural History* (New York: The Free Press, 1996), 236–37, 241–42.

motivated them to fight for women's equality.[22] In his work on draft resistance, Michael Foley has shown that although male chauvinism was part of the culture, as it was in most New Left movements, some women found empowerment in the work they did to oppose the draft, even if they did not hold leadership positions. Foley demonstrates how complex – and, ultimately, individual – conceptions of gender and power could be. For women such as Evans, draft resistance marked "the point of ultimate indignity" because it was, by definition, male-centered, and thus often relegated women to subservient, sexually stereotyped roles. For others, anti-draft activism provided the first opportunity to do something they felt was truly important.[23] Inside and outside the movements, gender was in flux during the Cold War, and challenges to traditional modes of thinking took form in a variety of ways that were not always apparent to the men and women involved.

In addition to addressing these issues, *Beyond Combat* responds to historian Joan Scott's challenge to diplomatic historians to examine the gender politics that have shaped foreign relations and wars.[24] Following the lead of Scott and Emily Rosenberg, scholars such as Seth Jacobs, Christina Klein, Melani McAlister, Andrew Rotter, and Naoko Shibusawa have provided a foundation for understanding how these gender roles influenced U.S. foreign policymaking in the early Cold War, and their works offer context for decisions regarding Vietnam.[25] Shibusawa describes how U.S. military and political leaders, journalists, authors, and

[22] Sara Evans, *Personal Politics: The Roots of Women's Liberation in the Civil Rights Movement and the New Left* (New York: Vintage, 1980).

[23] Michael Foley, "'The Point of Ultimate Indignity' or a 'Beloved Community'? The Draft Resistance Movement and New Left Gender Dynamics," in *The New Left Revisited*, ed. John McMillian and Paul Buhle (Philadelphia, Temple University Press, 2003), 178–98; see also Foley, *Confronting the War Machine: Draft Resistance during the Vietnam War* (Chapel Hill, NC: University of North Carolina Press, 2003).

[24] Joan W. Scott, *Gender and the Politics of History* (New York: Columbia University Press, 1988); Emily S. Rosenberg, "Gender," *Journal of American History*, 77 (June 1990), 116–24; Rosenberg, "Walking the Borders," *Diplomatic History*, 14 (Fall 1990), 565–73.

[25] Naoko Shibusawa, *America's Geisha Ally: Reimagining the Japanese Enemy* (Cambridge, MA: Harvard University Press, 2006); Christina Klein, *Cold War Orientalism: Asia in the Middlebrow Imagination, 1945–1961* (Berkeley, CA; University of California Press, 2003); Andrew Rotter, "Gender Relations, Foreign Relations: The United States and South Asia, 1947–1964, *Journal of American History*, Vol. 81, No. 2 (Sept. 1994), 518–42; Rotter, *Comrades at Odds: The United States and India, 1947–1964* (Ithaca, NY: Cornell University Press, 2000); Seth Jacobs, *America's Miracle Man in Vietnam: Ngo Dinh Diem, Religion, Race, and U.S. Intervention in Southeast Asia* (Durham, NC: Duke University Press, 2005).

Hollywood executives cast Japan as a submissive woman – a "geisha" – during the post-World War II occupation to shift American public opinion of Japan, formerly a hated enemy, toward acceptance as a Cold War ally. Efforts to cultivate warm, patriarchal feelings among Americans for Asia continued throughout the 1950s, Klein explains, to foster support for U.S. involvement in the affairs of allies and potential allies in Asia. Rotter shows that beliefs about masculinity and femininity shaped U.S. policymakers' attempts to understand the newly independent India, which they cast as effeminate, and therefore indecisive and weak, based on their assumptions about Indian men.

The gendering of power that cast the United States as a global father figure influenced American relations with the Middle East, Melani McAlister explains, writing that U.S. policymakers "used a complex and pernicious language of gender to suggest that American power would produce a well-ordered international family."[26] Jacobs traces these cultural approaches to America's prewar involvement in Vietnam, where the United States supported Ngo Dinh Diem as leader of South Vietnam. A Catholic and staunch anti-communist, Diem was the "miracle man" for U.S. policymakers in an otherwise untrustworthy, less manly, Asian nation, Jacobs writes. Central to these foreign policy approaches was an American self-perception that linked power with heterosexual masculinity, as Robert Dean and Donald Mrozek have shown. Dean notes that the "lavender scare" that targeted gays in the State Department and other federal government institutions in the 1950s created a climate in which political weakness was equated with effeminacy and, worse, homosexuality. This mindset had a profound impact on both Kennedy and Johnson, who assessed U.S. foreign relations in general, and American intervention in Vietnam in particular, in gendered and sexualized terms.[27] For them, a tough, prepared, aggressive U.S. military must be on hand to rescue nations from the grip of communism.

Bringing together discussions of gender and foreign policymaking, Cynthia Enloe's work on gender, militarization, and international relations has demonstrated that women long have been crucial to the

---

[26] Melani McAlister, *Epic Encounters: Culture, Media, and U.S. Interests in the Middle East Since 1945* (Berkeley, CA: University of California Press, 2005), 47.

[27] Robert Dean, *Imperial Brotherhood: Gender and the Making of Cold War Foreign Policy* (Amherst, MA: University of Massachusetts Press, 2001); Donald Mrozek, "The Cult and Ritual of Toughness in Cold War America," in *Rituals and Ceremonies in Popular Culture*, ed. Ray B. Browne (Bowling Green, OH: Bowling Green University Popular Press, 1980), 178–91.

military's image as a powerful masculine institution even while they are required to occupy subordinate positions in martial hierarchies. Enloe's writings reveal how militaries rely on and sustain gender, from the state sanctioning of prostitution at the request of an occupying military to the enforcement of specific images of masculine sexuality. Hierarchical gender constructions were, and continue to be, perpetuated on stateside and overseas bases, where military policies have shaped men's and women's sexuality, determined entrepreneurial and women's economic opportunities, regulated public health, and controlled entertainment. Women who signed up for the armed services, Enloe notes, were required to "behave like the gender 'woman'" so as not to disrupt the masculine image of the military.[28]

Leisa Meyer demonstrates how these patterns were present when the Women's Army Corps (WAC) was created during World War II. Both critics and supporters relied on long-established discourses about race, gender, and citizenship when building their cases for or against women's incorporation into the Army. Meyer points out that some opponents of bringing women into the Army feared it would upset the long-standing belief that military service is the ultimate measure of masculinity. Others considered the WAC a hideout for promiscuous heterosexual women and for lesbians, endangering traditional values regarding family and domesticity.[29] These anxieties did not disappear after World War II, and the WAC leadership continued its attempts to calm them into the Vietnam era even as the Army requested the deployment of WACs to join the war effort in Vietnam. The presence of American women in Vietnam muddled the gendered image of war – fighting men doing America's business overseas, wives and girlfriends waiting back home, and local women providing the outlet for the pent-up sexual energy of virile servicemen. These images and corresponding assumptions fed into the already tense environment of war and undermined the ideals the United States claimed to defend.

Over the course of the war, a growing number of soldiers and homefront activists came to recognize these contradictions, and some actively

[28] Cynthia Enloe, *Does Khaki Become You? The Militarization of Women's Lives* (London: Pandora, 1988); See also Enloe, *The Morning After: Sexual Politics at the End of the Cold War* (Berkeley, CA: University of California Press, 1993) and Enloe, *Bananas, Beaches, and Bases: Making Feminist Sense of International Politics* (Berkeley, CA: University of California Press, 2000).
[29] Leisa D. Meyer, *Creating G.I. Jane: Sexuality and Power in the Women's Army Corps During World War II* (New York: Columbia University Press, 1996).

challenged the warrior ethos. Histories of the GI antiwar movement –
notably Richard Moser's *The New Winter Soldiers: GI and Veteran
Dissent During the Vietnam Era*, Richard Stacewicz's *Winter Soldiers:
An Oral History of the Vietnam Veterans Against the War*, and David
Cortwright's *Soldiers in Revolt: GI Resistance During the Vietnam War* –
have shown how GIs' and veterans' rejection of the warrior myth was
a main component of their opposition to the Vietnam War.[30] Taken
together, Americans' Vietnam War experiences and the GI antiwar movement contributed to a multifaceted transformation of Cold War gender
ideology, affecting military culture, men's and women's familial roles,
constructions of gender and sexuality, and the symbolism buttressing
U.S. foreign policy.

The meanings embedded in the images of the male warrior, the girl next
door, and the abstract foreign woman continue to linger in U.S. relations
with the world, however. They also remain influential to Americans'
understandings of the armed services and which roles women and men
should hold in them. Beth Bailey's study of the Army's transition to an
all-volunteer force found that the post-Vietnam Army both responded to
demands for women's equality and attempted to maintain outdated gender stereotypes. Even as the Army redefined its image from emphasizing
male citizenship to a promise of educational and professional advancement for both men and women, debates about proper gender roles continued to influence it.[31]

Each of the chapters of *Beyond Combat* explores one aspect of the part
gender played in Vietnam and how the Vietnam experience influenced the
home front. Opening in Saigon, Chapter 1 sets up the gender ideology
current during the war and its use of images of Vietnamese women, highlighting the tension between Vietnamese women as symbols and the war's
impact on women's lives. If Vietnamese women symbolized the dragon

[30] On the GI and veteran antiwar movement, see Richard Moser, *The New Winter Soldiers:
GI and Veteran Dissent During the Vietnam Era* (New Brunswick, NJ: Rutgers Univer-
sity Press, 1996); Richard Stacewicz, *Winter Soldiers: An Oral History of the Vietnam
Veterans Against the War* (New York: Twayne Publishers, 1997); David Cortwright,
Soldiers in Revolt: GI Resistance During the Vietnam War (Chicago, IL: Haymarket
Books, 1975); Gerald Nicosia, *Home to War: A History of the Vietnam Veterans Move-
ment* (New York: Carroll & Graf, 2004); Andrew Hunt, *The Turning: A History of
Vietnam Veterans Against the War* (New York: New York University Press, 1999);
and Robert Jay Lifton, *Home from the War: Learning from Vietnam Veterans* (Boston:
Beacon Press, 1992).
[31] Beth Bailey, *America's Army: Making the All-Volunteer Force* (Cambridge, MA: The
Belknap Press of Harvard University Press, 2009).

lady to be tamed or slain, volunteers in the Red Cross Supplemental Recreational Activities Overseas (SRAO) program, the subjects of Chapter 2, were their antithesis, the girl next door. Known as "donut dollies," SRAO women went to Vietnam as morale boosters. They were the embodiments of the wives, sisters, and girlfriends waiting for the troops back home, but the thick sexual tension in Vietnam made it difficult to impose rules forbidding physical intimacy between donut dollies and troops. Donut dollies were symbols of middle-class domesticity, but by going to Vietnam, women escaped or postponed marriage and lived what the women's movement was calling for, even though many did not identify with the women's movement. Chapter 3 examines the experiences of nurses and Women's Army Corps personnel. Despite their military status, WACs and nurses faced the same tensions and assumptions as donut dollies. Nurses' regular dealings with wounded and dying servicemen challenged what it means to "see combat." Because of the meanings embedded in their experiences, military women in Vietnam played a bigger role than their numbers imply. American women served in Vietnam in many other capacities, including flight attendants, entertainers, journalists, and civilian employees of the armed services, but I focus on donut dollies, WACs, and nurses because they had a day-to-day experience in Vietnam, often working alongside male troops.

Chapter 4 turns the focus to male troops, who grappled with the contradiction between love and violence as they carried out their ambivalent roles as both gentle warriors and gunslingers. The tensions in what American servicemen were supposed to be shaped their interactions with Vietnamese and American women in Vietnam. Chapter 5 discusses the GI antiwar movement that issued a rejection of the sexism, racism, and hypersexual masculinity that defined the Vietnam soldier experience. Some antiwar GIs and vets demanded a reassessment of gender roles that did not link masculinity with the warrior myth, and they called on their fellow servicemen to join with women in a struggle for gender liberation. As the connection between military service and manhood lost credibility in the wake of the Vietnam War, and the draft ended, the branches of the military reached out to women to fill the ranks of the all-volunteer force. The conclusion examines the responses to the opening of the services to women, which reveal both gender changes and resistance to transformations of established gender roles.

Although *Beyond Combat* draws on a variety of theories and methodologies, its center lies in the images reflecting American diplomatic, military, and popular attitudes toward Vietnam, and the stories of the women and men whose daily lives revealed the tensions in those images. Each account contained herein reflects one person's individual experience and is important to my telling of the Vietnam War story because it illustrates either an aspect of America's gendered war ideology or a challenge to it. As is the case with any event as far-reaching as the Vietnam War, there are as many narratives as there are lives touched by it, so the continued work of collecting Vietnam-era oral histories will only help us paint a more complete picture of the war's impact and legacies. What I offer here are some select portraits that depict the tensions and contradictions in the war's central imagery for Americans.

Everyday encounters and images that seemingly lack significance in ordinary life were charged with meaning in Vietnam, not only for the individuals who experienced them but also for those of us who are trying to come to a deeper understanding of how the United States entered the war, the war itself, and the war's profound impact on American society. A cartoon drawing of a Vietnamese woman with a dagger strapped to her shapely leg; an American woman applying lipstick before heading out to the Red Cross recreation center where she was stationed; a U.S. serviceman hugging a Vietnamese baby – taken at face value, these are simple images and moments. Read in the context of the war, though, they underscore the importance of both women and gender to Americans' attempts to make sense of and justify U.S. intervention, while illuminating the contradictions in the American mission and the beliefs that motivated it.

Vietnamese Women in the American Mind

Gender, Race, and the Vietnam War

Beauty queen candidates decked out in sequins, black lace gloves, false eyelashes, and padded bras, cloaked in the scent of hairspray, filled the Rex Movie Hall in Saigon on a May evening in 1971. As electric fans tried in vain to cool the packed room, young Vietnamese women, their made-up faces glistening, paraded across a catwalk for audience members who drank Pepsi, smoked, and ate ice cream.[1] The spectacle was Saigon's first beauty pageant, attended by a crowd of Saigon's small but influential middle class, along with American diplomats. The high ticket prices kept most soldiers – American or Vietnamese – from going. Rejecting the miniskirt, which had become one of the symbols of an American cultural invasion, the women in the pageant wore the *ao dai*, a traditional Vietnamese outfit consisting of a long dress with thigh-high slits on either side, worn over loose-fitting pants. As one of the promoters of the pageant put it, "Saigon is invaded by miniskirts and hot pants, and we are opposed to it. We think the Vietnamese women are so beautiful in their own dress they do not need to vulgarly display their charms." Despite the attempts to stress Vietnamese cultural autonomy, the pageant blatantly signified Saigon's Westernization, from the audience members' consumption of American soft drinks to contestants' desires to become Hollywood stars.[2] It was a pageant of contradictions with Vietnamese women at the center, and it encapsulated a set of images and ideas that had become hallmarks of U.S. intervention in

---

[1] Gloria Emerson, "A beauty contest with a difference: Saigon's first, and girls didn't weep." *New York Times*, May 29, 1971, 8.
[2] Ibid.

Vietnam. The women were emblems of exotic sexuality, but also of Vietnamese modernity, objects of desire whose superficial familiarity masked
their intractable otherness. Those contradictions reflected the contentious
notions of masculinity and femininity that shaped women's roles during
the Vietnam War, pointing to the unresolved ideological tensions that
would play a crucial role in the unraveling of the American military
mission.

By 1971, the United States, deeply entrenched in the Vietnam War, was
slowly extricating itself from the conflict. The ideology that had influenced American intervention in Vietnam had become embedded in the
culture of the war, reflected in a series of images of Vietnamese women,
which dictated their daily interactions with American soldiers. U.S. policymakers, as well as many ordinary citizens influenced by newspaper and
magazine coverage, viewed Vietnam through the lenses of gender and
race, seeing a land and a people that were at once alluring and dangerous. Three images, each with a long history in western attitudes toward
Asia, were particularly important in relation to Vietnamese women. First,
the women represented the dangerous Asia that threatened U.S. interests
in the Cold War world. Second, they were damsels in distress who needed
to be protected. Third, they were sexual objects to be dominated and pos-
sessed. The contradiction between the image of protection and the reality
of domination, justified by the need to ward off the "dragon lady," completed a contradictory loop in which the United States dominated what it
was protecting.

Motivated by the Cold War imperative to shape the development
of newly independent nations and draw them into the Western sphere
before the Soviet Union staked its claim on them, U.S. policymakers,
from the Truman administration on, committed money and materiel
in hopes of preventing a communist takeover of Vietnam. The largely
unknown backwater was important not in itself, but as part of a larger
picture. Throughout the decolonizing world, Cold War tensions threatened to erupt into "hot wars" as colonized peoples first fought for independence and then struggled to implement stable governments. For the
United States, the decolonizing world posed an opportunity to gain allies
as well as a challenge to prevent communist insurgencies from taking
power in newly independent nations. Throughout the Cold War, U.S.
policymakers repeatedly interpreted local independence movements as
Soviet-backed uprisings. The misunderstandings were further complicated by attitudes toward race and gender that led American policymakers

to see Third World leaders as being incapable of handling their own affairs.[3]

When Vietnam declared its independence in 1945 after a defeated Japan relinquished control, Ho Chi Minh, leader of the nationalist, communist Viet Minh, reached out to President Truman for recognition and assistance. Viewing Ho as a communist rather than a freedom fighter, Truman and his advisers, concerned over political instability in Western Europe, chose to support France, which sought to reinstate the political and economic control it had established in Vietnam in the 1850s. War between the French and the Viet Minh broke out in 1946; by the end of 1950, the Truman administration authorized $100 million to bolster the French cause. By the time French forces surrendered at Dien Bien Phu in 1954, ending what is sometimes called the first Indochina war,

---

[3] A sample of the growing body of literature on decolonization during the Cold War includes Matthew Connelly, *A Diplomatic Revolution: Algeria's Fight for Independence and the Origins of the Post-Cold War Era* (Oxford: Oxford University Press, 2002); David Ekbladh, *The Great American Mission: Modernization and the Construction of an American World Order* (Princeton, NJ: Princeton University Press, 2009); Michael Latham, *Modernization as Ideology: American Social Science and 'Nation Building' in the Kennedy Era* (Chapel Hill, NC: University of North Carolina Press, 2000); Christopher J. Lee, *Making a World After Empire: The Bandung Moment and Its Political Afterlives* (Ohio University Press, 2010); Jonathan Nashel, *Edward Lansdale's Cold War* (Amherst, MA: University of Massachusetts Press, 2005); David F. Schmitz, *The United States and Right-Wing Dictatorships* (Cambridge: Cambridge University Press, 2006); Schmitz, *Thank God They're on Our Side: The United States and Right-Wing Dictatorships, 1921–1965* (Chapel Hill, NC: University of North Carolina Press, 1999); Jeremi Suri, *Power and Protest: Global Revolution and the Rise of Détente* (Cambridge, MA: Harvard University Press, 2003); Odd Arne Westad, *The Global Cold War* (Cambridge: Cambridge University Press, 2005). Scholars who have focused specifically on race and gender in the history of decolonization include Thomas Borstelmann, *The Cold War and the Color Line: American Race Relations in the Global Arena* (Cambridge, MA: Harvard University Press, 2003); Mark Bradley, *Imagining Vietnam and America: The Making of Postcolonial Vietnam, 1919–1950* (Chapel Hill, NC: University of North Carolina Press, 2000); Mary L. Dudziak, *Cold War Civil Rights: Race and the Image of American Democracy* (Princeton, NJ: Princeton University Press, 2002); Van Gosse, *Where the Boys Are: Cuba, Cold War America, and the Making of a New Left* (London: Verso, 1993); Michael Hunt, *Ideology and U.S. Foreign Policy* (New Haven, CT: Yale University Press, 1987); James H. Meriwether, *Proudly We Can Be Africans: Black Americans and Africa, 1935–1961* (Chapel Hill, NC: University of North Carolina Press, 2001); Brenda Gayle Plummer, *Rising Wind: Black Americans and U.S. Foreign Affairs, 1935–1960* (Chapel Hill, NC: University of North Carolina Press, 1996); Penny Von Eschen, *Race Against Empire: Black Americans and Anticolonialism, 1937–1957* (Ithaca, NY: Cornell University Press, 1997); *Window on Freedom: Race, Civil Rights, and Foreign Affairs, 1945–1988*, ed. Brenda Gayle Plummer (Chapel Hill, NC: University of North Carolina Press, 2003).

the United States had spent approximately $1 billion, footing the bill for nearly 80 percent of the war's cost.[4] In the wake of the Viet Minh's decisive victory, the Geneva Accords divided Vietnam into two temporary nations, the Republic of Vietnam (or South Vietnam), a non-communist state headed first by former emperor Bao Dai and then by Ngo Dinh Diem, and the Democratic Republic of Vietnam (or North Vietnam), a communist-controlled nation led by Ho Chi Minh. An election was scheduled for 1956 to reunite the two halves of Vietnam, but, aware that Ho would certainly have won, the United States and the South Vietnamese canceled the election. Determined to contain communism above the 17th parallel, the United States assumed responsibility for the development and support of South Vietnam.[5]

Efforts by the Eisenhower and Kennedy administrations to build a noncommunist alternative to Ho Chi Minh's North Vietnam centered on Ngo Dinh Diem, South Vietnam's president from 1955 to 1963. Diem's appeal to the United States was not simply political. As historian Seth Jacobs has demonstrated, Secretary of State John Foster Dulles and other important members of the Eisenhower administration committed U.S. support to Diem because he seemed less "Asian" than other potential South Vietnamese leaders who were equally opposed to communism. In a primarily Buddhist nation, Diem was Catholic at a time when Catholic church membership was on the rise in the United States. He had lived at seminaries in New Jersey and New York under the sponsorship of Francis Cardinal Spellman, who became one of Diem's staunchest allies. Most importantly, he seemed comfortable among the men responsible for U.S. foreign policy. Support for Diem continued into the Kennedy era, with then-Vice President Lyndon Johnson calling him "the Winston Churchill of Southeast Asia." In anticipation of Johnson's trip to Saigon in 1961, Colonel Edward Lansdale, another major Diem supporter, described him this way: "Diem's feet barely seem to reach the floor when he is seated. However, he is not defensive about his short stature and is at ease around tall Americans. He has a very positive approach to Westerners, not the least bit concerned about differences such as Asian-Caucasian background. When the vice president sees him, he will find

---

[4] Mark Philip Bradley, *Vietnam at War* (Oxford: Oxford University Press, 2009), 56.
[5] For surveys of the Vietnam War, see George Herring, *America's Longest War: The United States and Vietnam, 1950–1975* (New York: McGraw-Hill, 2001); Stanley Karnow, *Vietnam: A History* (New York: Penguin, 1997); and Marilyn B. Young, *The Vietnam Wars, 1945–1990* (New York: Harper Perennial, 1991).

him as interested in cattle an any Texan, and as interested in freedom as Sam Houston." Although U.S. policymakers viewed a generalized Asia as untrustworthy and effeminate, Diem was a *man*.[6] As U.S. relations with South Vietnam soured during Kennedy's presidency, the image of Diem changed. Conversations and correspondence between Kennedy and his advisers increasingly cast Diem as weak, ineffective, and too easily swayed by his brother, Ngo Dinh Nhu, and sister-in-law, Madame Nhu.

The evolution of Diem's image was part of a larger pattern of political discussions, media coverage, and government propaganda, in which Vietnamese women, presented in both positive and negative images, became the symbols of South Vietnam. In the "positive" scenario, as depicted in magazine features about economic development in urban South Vietnam, young, educated Vietnamese women working in modern office buildings in Saigon represented a nation flourishing under the guidance of the United States. The danger lay in the alternative – the "dragon lady" – a cunning, beautiful Asian woman who transformed from seeming friend to deadly foe at a moment's notice. From Madame Nhu – the most publicly visible member of Diem's family – to prostitutes and bar girls, women symbolized South Vietnam in the American mind. The images of them circulating in the media and in the minds of policymakers were deeply embedded in the justifications for U.S. policies. Even when women were not explicitly part of references to South Vietnam, descriptions of its relationship with the United States were explained using sexual metaphors. Undersecretary of State George Ball described American fascination with South Vietnam this way: "As I knew from experience with my French friends, there was something about Vietnam that seduced the toughest military minds into fantasy."[7]

Those images were interwoven with anxieties about gender relations in the United States during a time of rapid social change. Emerging from, and part of, Cold War culture, the Vietnam War coincided with a period in which anxieties about acceptable expressions of masculinity and femininity informed foreign as well as domestic policymaking. John F. Kennedy and Lyndon Johnson perceived foreign relations in gendered terms, linking military strength with masculine power. Kennedy was particularly concerned about the softening effects of suburban comforts on

[6] Jacobs, 16.
[7] Howard Jones, *Death of a Generation: How the Assassinations of Diem and JFK Prolonged the Vietnam War* (New York: Oxford University Press, 2003), 114.

middle-class American men; his well-publicized physical fitness agenda was designed in part to ensure that America's future soldiers would be physically ready for combat in Third World jungles. In this context, American and Vietnamese women played symbolic roles in the implementation and conduct of U.S. diplomatic and military policy in South Vietnam. As the nation was recruited into the Western sphere, American men became both defenders against the threat of the dragon lady and protectors of Vietnamese women as representatives of an American-style femininity, even though that gender label was undergoing change at home.

Dragon Ladies, Geishas, and Roses

These images marked extensions of a tradition of feminizing Asia that had been particularly clear during the recent reconstruction of Japan, and that was intensified by South Vietnam's role as a testing ground for America's Cold War policy. From the highest levels of policymaking to the masses of ordinary citizens, Americans viewed South Vietnam through stereotypes of Asians that had been part of American culture since the nineteenth century. Robert G. Lee has described how American definitions of "Asian" and "Oriental" related to economic imperatives, immigration issues, and diplomatic concerns which presented Asian nations or peoples of Asian descent as threats to America's domestic status quo or its international interests. Images such as the Chinese "coolie" laborer developed in the late nineteenth century amid class and race tensions stemming from industrialization, immigration, and emancipation. Designating Chinese immigrants as a racial "other" allowed working-class European immigrants to claim a white – and thus American – identity, raising themselves up on America's racial hierarchy above Chinese workers of the same economic status.

Ambiguous sexuality, at once taboo and alluring, characterized white, middle-class views of Asian men and women, classifying them as offering an alternative to the strictly contained Victorian heterosexuality. As the United States became increasingly interested in Pacific markets and concerned about the rise of Japanese power at the turn of the twentieth century, the racial and sexual threats were combined in the notion of the "Yellow Peril." Although the male villain Fu Manchu of the Sax Rohmer novels was the most common articulation of the Yellow Peril in the early twentieth century, Fu Manchu aspired to bring the entire globe under the rule of an "Asian empress." The success of this insidious plot would disrupt both the international political/economic order and the

Anglo-American gender structure that linked whiteness, masculinity, and power.[8]

Constructions of Asia as feminine, sexualized, and dangerous were staples of twentieth-century popular culture. In the 1930s, the "Dragon Lady" debuted to American mass audiences through Milton Caniff's syndicated comic strip, "Terry and the Pirates." When Caniff approached Joseph Patterson, editor of the *Chicago Tribune–New York Daily News* syndicate, with some samples of his work in 1934, Patterson suggested that Caniff draw a strip about Asia, musing that "adventure can still happen out there. There could be a beautiful lady pirate, the kind men fall for," an embodiment of the mysteries of the Orient. With that, "Terry and the Pirates" – and the Dragon Lady character, the first villain Caniff drew for the strip – were born.[9] The Dragon Lady's real name in the strip was Lai Choi San. She was a Chinese pirate, a villain Caniff believed to be "ten times more interesting" because she was a woman. Caniff described her as "the strongest of all because she had the double weapon of beauty and absolute ruthlessness, which everybody, man and woman, dreads and anticipates with shuddering pleasure." By 1940, Caniff had transformed the Dragon Lady from a pirate to a guerrilla fighter, creating one of the definitive images of the conflict some thirty years before the Vietnam War.[10]

A second image of Asian women, as helpless damsels in need of protection, existed in uneasy proximity to that of the dragon lady. The contradictions between and within these images can be seen in the American media's treatment of Madame Chiang Kai-Shek. When the United States supported China in the 1930s and in World War II, American supporters of Chinese leader Chiang Kai-Shek often lauded his wife as well, comparing her to Joan of Arc and Florence Nightingale for her work with Chinese orphans. In a July 1942 *Life* magazine article, Clare Booth Luce, wife of publisher Henry Luce, called Madame Chiang the world's "greatest living woman." Several months later, Texas Representative Sam Rayburn praised her as "one of the outstanding women of all the earth." Focusing on her physical beauty, media coverage of Madame Chiang set her up as a contrast to her American counterpart Eleanor Roosevelt, a

---

[8] Robert G. Lee, *Orientals: Asian Americans in Popular Culture* (Philadelphia, Temple University Press, 1999).

[9] "Escape artist," *Time*, Jan. 13, 1947, http://www.time.com/time/magazine/article/0,9171,855598-1,00.html.

[10] *Milton Caniff: Conversations*, ed. Robert C. Harvey (Jackson, MS: University Press of Mississippi, 2002), ix, 20, 162.

woman known for her brains more than her looks and suspected of leftist leanings. In the symbolic imagery of the relationship between the United States and China, Madame Chiang was, as Laura Tyson Li writes, "a mysterious and exotic Asian female. She projected the image of a tiny woman, frail yet valiant, being rescued by tall, strong, chivalrous male senators. China was the damsel in distress and America the knight in shining armor."[11]

During the occupation of Japan after World War II, the images of both the dragon lady and the damsel were deployed to justify military and diplomatic policies. The gendering of Japan as female – a geisha, as Naoko Shibusawa explains it – was a key element in the postwar relationship between Japan and the United States, its occupier. Whereas the face of wartime Japan in American media was that of a vicious, bloodthirsty man, Japanese women symbolized the defeated postwar nation. Feminizing Japan allowed the U.S. occupation to appear benevolent and paternal, but the sexual stereotyping of Japanese women suggests that the benevolence masked the desire for and reality of domination. The Far East edition of *Navy Times* regularly published a cartoon that featured "Baby-san," a curvaceous, sexually-suggestive Japanese woman who symbolized the fantasy of some American servicemen. At the same time, the idealized Japanese woman – shy, pliant, submissive – represented an alternative to the increasingly politically active American woman. Anxieties about women who had entered the workforce during the war and refused to go quietly back into the home played out in articles that depicted Japanese women as preferable to American women, who were the "white man's burden," in the words of photographer Carl Mydans.[12] As would be the case in Vietnam, the gendered images connected with the U.S. occupation of Japan reflected both the tensions between men and women on the home front and the contradiction between protection and domination at the core of U.S. foreign policy.

The best known incarnation of the dragon lady was Tokyo Rose, the name U.S. troops gave to the group of Japanese women who broadcast propaganda aimed at demoralizing American servicemen. The best-known Tokyo Rose was Iva Toguri d'Aquino, an American of Japanese descent who was living in Japan when the war started. D'Aquino

[11] Laura Tyson Li, *Madame Chiang Kai-Shek: China's Eternal First Lady* (New York: Atlantic Monthly Press, 2006), 180–204.
[12] Naoko Shibusawa, *America's Geisha Ally: Reimagining the Japanese Enemy* (Cambridge, MA: Harvard University Press, 2006), 4–5, 26, 36, 42.

became the human face of Tokyo Rose when she was convicted of treason in 1949 and imprisoned for six years for disseminating enemy propaganda.[13] Like the Dragon Lady of Milton Caniff's cartoons, the fictional Tokyo Rose represented a dangerous yet alluring Asia whom the United States must tame or slay to protect its power and security in the world. Although d'Aquino herself was a slightly bookish, plain-looking woman, portrayals of Tokyo Rose in American media presented her as an "oriental Ava Gardner," fulfilling the expectation that the source of the voice broadcast to U.S. troops in Japan was a mysterious, sexually alluring woman. As journalist Russell Warren Howe has written, in the context of American sexual anxieties at the dawn of the Cold War, it was nearly inevitable for "the little typist to become a dragon lady."

The image of Tokyo Rose, as that of the dragon lady, feminized the Asian threat and justified the masculine power of U.S. occupation troops' political mission.[14] Attitudes toward race, gender, and sexuality, which had little or no relation to the lives of actual Asian women, converged to create a character that bolstered U.S. diplomatic and military endeavors, a pattern that recurred as the United States became embroiled in Vietnam. There was no better embodiment of the contradictions than Madame Nhu.

Madame Nhu – "Joan of Arc or Dragon Lady?"

When the October 1962 issue of *Life* magazine hit the stands, readers encountered a picture, taken by English photojournalist Larry Burrows, that depicted a fascinating evolution in the Dragon Lady's political history. Clad in a pale satin *ao dai* and flanked by Vietnamese women in military uniforms, Madame Ngo Dinh Nhu raised a gun and, with one eye closed as she focused on her target, pointed it as if she were prepared to shoot (Figure 1). Her face bore the calm confidence of a seasoned gunslinger, and the crucifix that hung from a chain around her neck dared her critics – and the majority-Buddhist Vietnamese population – to attack her, a member of South Vietnam's most prominent Catholic family. The object of her aim could have been the philandering husband of a fellow Vietnamese woman; a Buddhist protesting the government of

---

[13] Caroline Chung Simpson, *An Absent Presence: Japanese Americans in Postwar American Culture, 1945–1960* (Durham, NC: Duke University Press, 2001), 76–112.
[14] Ibid., 85, 111.

FIGURE 1. Madame Ngo Dinh Nhu fires a .38 pistol as members of her women's paramilitary force look on. The photograph, taken by Larry Burrows, ran in the October 26, 1962 issue *of Life*. Getty Images.

her brother-in-law, Ngo Dinh Diem; or an American man attempting "to seduce Vietnamese women into decadent paths."[15] Describing her style of dress, a French journalist described Madame Nhu as "molded into her . . . dress like a dagger in its sheath."[16] Although this imagery echoes that surrounding the stereotypical dragon lady, Madame Nhu attempted to redefine the role as one of protector, adding to the confusion U.S. diplomats and soldiers experienced when trying to categorize Asian women.

The photograph of Madame Nhu with a gun illustrated one of the ways in which gender shaped U.S. encounters with South Vietnam. Similar to the Asian woman in the "Terry and the Pirates" comic strip, Madame Nhu appeared both seductive and dangerous – a metaphor for Vietnam. In the early 1960s, she graced the covers of *Time* and *Life* magazines, highlighting the American public's fascination with her. Even Diem did not receive such exposure in the U.S. media. Foreign policy documents

[15] Telegram from the Embassy in Vietnam to the Department of State, Saigon, April 13, 1963, *Foreign Relations of the United States, 1961–1963* (Washington, DC: U.S. Government Printing Office, 1991), 3: 225 [Hereafter *FRUS*, followed by year and volume].
[16] Howard Jones, *Death of a Generation: How the Assassinations of Diem and JFK Prolonged the Vietnam War* (Oxford: Oxford University Press, 2003), 293.

make it clear that U.S. political leaders during Kennedy's presidency monitored Madame Nhu's media appearances and were acutely aware of her influence on Vietnamese relations with the United States. It is unclear how much power Madame Nhu actually had in shaping South Vietnam's policies, but Kennedy administration records and U.S. media coverage reflect a belief that she did.

As one of nine women in the National Assembly of the Republic of Vietnam in the early 1960s while Diem was president of South Vietnam, Madame Nhu considered herself part of a long tradition of Vietnamese women warriors who fought invaders and oppressors throughout Vietnam's two-thousand-year history.[17] She commissioned a statue of the Trung sisters – Vietnamese heroines from a war with China in the year 40 AD – to be built in her likeness in Saigon. In the late 1950s, she established the Women's Paramilitary Corps, and when her daughter, Le Thuy, turned eighteen, Madame Nhu attempted to make her a warrior by giving her a gun – "the better to shoot Viet Cong with."[18] Although Madame Nhu positioned herself in the history of Vietnamese fighting women, she also represented a modernizing South Vietnam, one that the Kennedy administration hoped would develop into a stable, capitalist democracy with American guidance. As someone who both charmed and angered Americans, Madame Nhu stood for the tensions in U.S. modernization efforts. The Kennedy administration cast the United States as protector of South Vietnam against communism, but Madame Nhu had already claimed the role of protector for herself, the legacy of the Trung sisters. She did not fit into America's ideological vision, and U.S. media portrayals gradually shifted from damsel to dragon lady in their largely unsuccessful efforts to understand her.

The *Life* magazine picture of Madame Nhu aiming a gun was just one of several photographs that manifested the contradictions. In January 1959, *Time* called Madame Nhu a "dainty emancipator" in explaining her work in the National Assembly regarding women's issues. The article noted that Madame Nhu, "a Christian, is not only the first lady of a Buddhist land; she is also the most determined feminist since the late Emmeline Goulden Pankhurst," a comparison to the leader of the British women's suffrage movement. The article used Madame Nhu as the symbol of a free South Vietnam under the leadership of Diem, stating that although Vietnamese women had few rights in the past, "when

---

[17] Milton Orshefsky, "Joan of Arc or Dragon Lady?" *Life*, October 26, 1962, 55.
[18] "Girls Under Fire," *Time*, July 23, 1965, 23.

South Vietnam became independent, the women found a champion" in Madame Nhu. As a member of South Vietnam's first family, she handled "a bewildering assortment of visitors and letters asking every sort of favor, from help in curbing an abusive husband to advice on a Latin essay."[19] Overall, the article portrayed Madame Nhu as an industrious, devoted member of the Ngo family and a concerned citizen of Vietnam, characteristics that also defined a good American woman in the Cold War era. Just as they had used *Time* and *Life* to support Madame Chiang Kai-Shek, Henry and Clare Booth Luce published laudatory coverage of the Catholic, anticommunist Madame Nhu. As time went on and U.S. relations with the Diem regime grew strained, the tone of media coverage of Madame Nhu shifted from supportive to suspicious to hostile.

Throughout the course of Diem's presidency, American policymakers and journalists were at a loss regarding how to deal with Madame Nhu. Magazine articles revealed fascination with this "fragile, exciting beauty who stands only 5 ft. 2 in. in high heels."[20] In contrast to the damsel image, the media at times presented her as a threat to gender norms. An article in *Time* declared that she "rules the men who rule the nation," and the reporter deemed her a "flaming" feminist.[21] Kennedy's advisers called her everything from "beautiful" to "bitchy" to "brutal." As relations between the Kennedy and Diem administrations deteriorated, assessments of Madame Nhu became more hostile, and the agenda underlying the U.S. role as benevolent protector became clearer. Edward Lansdale and Maxwell Taylor, prominent U.S. advisers to Diem, accused her of alienating Saigon's educated and professional classes – the very groups on which Diem should have been relying for political support – by speaking out against Diem's critics and rivals and attempting to push legislation without going through the National Assembly's official procedures.[22] State Department officials noted that Madame Nhu's public comments attracted attention because she was "unfortunately too beautiful to ignore," and officials at the U.S. Embassy in Saigon called for her complete removal "from the public eye in view of the adverse effects . . . of

[19] "Dainty Emancipator," *Time*, January 26, 1959, http://www.time.com/time/magazine/article/0,9171,892087,00.html.
[20] Charles Mohr, "The Queen Bee," *Time*, August 9, 1963, 21.
[21] Ibid.
[22] Briefing Paper Prepared by the Embassy in Vietnam: "Possible Actions by GVN as Quid Pro Quo for Additional U.S. Support," Saigon, October 17, 1961, *FRUS, 1961–1963*, 1:387.

her activities on the political standing of the (Diem) government."²³ Even her supporters chafed at the way she disrupted the U.S. agenda. Wesley Fishel, head of the Michigan State University Vietnam Advisory Group, a consulting organization to the Diem regime, described Madame Nhu as "brilliant, vivacious, bitchy, and brutal . . . and with the purest of intentions she is succeeding in alienating substantial segments of the population from her brother-in-law's regime at a time when it needs the enthusiastic support of everyone."²⁴

American policymakers' concerns were not necessarily unjustified, given the importance they placed on maintaining a positive international image in hopes of obtaining Third World allies. In addition to speaking out against Diem's critics, especially Buddhists, Madame Nhu did not hesitate to attack the U.S. government, military, and media. She charged the Kennedy administration with not providing enough military and financial aid, and she accused U.S. servicemen of attempting to "seduce Vietnamese women into decadent paths."²⁵ She regularly clashed with reporters and eventually banned *Newsweek* entirely from South Vietnam.²⁶ As the Kennedy administration attempted to mold Diem's South Vietnam into a model of U.S. Cold War success in the Third World, Madame Nhu's public presence threatened the American mission by making it look as though the United States supported an antidemocratic, oppressive regime.

Conversations about Madame Nhu frequently were connected to talk of Diem's masculinity, which implied his inadequacy as a representative of the United States' masculine power. Letters, records of conversations, and other foreign policy documents indicate that American advisors to Vietnam were preoccupied with Diem's sexuality. They fixated on his unmarried status, often referring to him as the "bachelor president." Major General Tran Van Don, acting chief of South Vietnam's Joint General Staff, told American advisors that Diem had never engaged in a sexual

²³ Memorandum From the Assistant Secretary of State for International Organization Affairs (Cleveland) to the Assistant Secretary of State for Far Eastern Affairs (Hilsman), Washington, October 2, 1963, *FRUS, 1961–1963*, 4:335–36. Memorandum from the Counselor of the Embassy in Vietnam (Mendenhall) to the Public Affairs Officer in Vietnam (Anspacher), Saigon, November 22, 1961, *FRUS, 1961–1963*, 1:659.

²⁴ Letter from Wesley R. Fishel of the Michigan State University Group in Vietnam to President John A. Hannah of Michigan State University, Rangoon, February 17, 1962, *FRUS, 1961–1963*, 2:150–51.

²⁵ Telegram from the Embassy in Vietnam to the Department of State, Saigon, April 13, 1963, *FRUS, 1961–1963*, 3:225–26.

²⁶ John Mecklin, *Mission in Torment: An Intimate Account of the U.S. Role in Vietnam* (New York: Doubleday, 1965).

relationship with anyone.[27] That Diem's sexual activity – or lack thereof –
was a topic of conversation in policymaking circles is itself revealing.
U.S. officials closely scrutinized Diem's relationship with Madame Nhu.
Because Diem had no wife, his sister-in-law became known as the unofficial first lady of his administration. In describing the personal relationships among the Ngo family members living in the presidential palace,
Tran Van Don explained to American advisors that "for the past nine
years, Diem has Madame Nhu to comfort him after day's work is done.
She is charming, talks to him, relieves his tension, argues with him, nee-
dles him, and, like a Vietnamese wife, she is dominant in the household."
However, Don stressed, Diem and Madame Nhu did not have a sexual relationship. She was Diem's "platonic wife." Noting that "Madame
Nhu can be extremely charming," Don explained that she was able to
charm Diem into saying "yes when he wants to say no." Therefore, Don
warned that it would be "practically impossible" to remove Madame
Nhu from Saigon, which Secretary of State Dean Rusk, U.S. Ambassador
Henry Cabot Lodge, and other Kennedy administration officials considered repeatedly as political conditions in Saigon collapsed.[28]

The descriptions of Madame Nhu's role in the presidential household
and her relationship with Diem echo the explanation of Vietnamese family
structure in a handbook published for U.S. Army personnel deployed
to Vietnam. In describing the status of men and women in Vietnamese
families, the handbook notes that although custom required wives to
respect and submit to their husbands and in-laws, "many Vietnamese
wives are in fact extremely powerful and exercise a strong formative
influence on their husbands' opinions and actions." Both village women
and urban educated women typically managed the family income, and
some owned land or businesses. The handbook states that village women
often worked harder than their male counterparts, and an urban wife
usually was "accepted as an intellectual equal by her husband, entering
into literary discussions with him and listening as he recites poetry."[29]
A pamphlet published by the U.S. Information Agency (USIA) stated

[27] Telegram from the Central Intelligence Agency Station in Saigon to the Agency, Saigon,
    August 24, 1963, *FRUS, 1961–1963,* 3:615.
[28] Telegram from the Central Intelligence Agency Station in Saigon to the Agency, Saigon,
    August 24, 1963; Further Rusk Cable to Lodge on Diem-Nhu Relationship, *New York
    Times,* July 1, 1971, 9; Memo on Washington Meeting in Aftermath of August Plot,
    New York Times, July 1, 1971, 10.
[29] Harvey H. Smith et al., *Area Handbook for South Vietnam* (Washington, D.C.: U.S.
    Government Printing Office, 1967), 115.

that "the philosopher-king or poet-king is still the basic masculine ideal" for Vietnamese men.[30] Engaged in pursuits such as poetry, which did not fit the mainstream American definition of masculinity, Vietnamese husbands such as Diem were not necessarily masters of their households, or even of their thoughts. Contradicting Cold War American ideas about the husband's role within a family, this set of characteristics allowed U.S. policymakers to define American power in opposition to perceived Vietnamese social and cultural inadequacies. As part of a framework that established a patriarchal relationship between the United States and South Vietnam, the Army handbook depicted Vietnamese men as unmasculine and thus in need of protection.

American perceptions of Vietnamese gender were intertwined with attitudes grounded in Cold War sexual anxieties and deep-seated Orientalist images. Obsessions over "proper" expressions of heterosexual masculinity and femininity revealed themselves in foreign relations metaphors that linked deviant sexuality to race. Robert Lee maintains that the "combination of submissive innocence and assertive sexuality is the epitome of Orientalist fantasy."[31] Analyzing portrayals of Asians in film and literature, Lee notes a common pattern in American popular culture, in which Americanization transforms Oriental women from "dangerously transgressive into a symbol of domesticity.... Meanwhile, Asian men remained outside the American family, marginalized, invisible, and racially Other."[32] This pattern played out clearly in relation to Madame Nhu, who represented the domesticated nation being brought into the American sphere while Diem was relegated to the shadows. At the same time, Madame Nhu symbolized the "dangerously transgressive" aspect of Asia – not only did she appear sexually suggestive, but her outspokenness was also dangerous to the American mission in South Vietnam and international perceptions of the United States–South Vietnam alliance. Part of the dilemma Kennedy's advisors faced was how to contain Madame Nhu, symbolically domesticating her and placing her in a space that would not disrupt America's nation-building efforts. Ultimately, the attempt would fail, and she would be removed from the public eye.[33]

---

[30] Chester Baines, "Vietnamese Individual Behavior, the Family, and Social Values," U.S. Army Civil Affairs School, Fort Gordon, GA, December 1968, Glenn Helm Collection, Folder 08, Box 12, The Vietnam Archive, Texas Tech University.

[31] Lee, *Orientals*, 169.

[32] Ibid., 162.

[33] Throughout Diem's regime, articles and photographs in U.S. media expressed fascination with Madame Nhu as someone inherently foreign and enigmatic. The continued

By the time American voters elected John F. Kennedy to the presidency in 1960, U.S. support for Diem had begun to falter as a result of a variety of factors, including antagonisms between the Diem government and Buddhists, disagreements between Diem and his American advisers, and Diem's unwillingness to remove the Nhus from their positions of political influence. In that year, some members of the American Friends of Vietnam (AFV), a lobby group dedicated to the conviction that "the U.S. had a unique ability, even an obligation, to lead the peoples of Asia into a modern, democratic world," had begun to lose faith in Diem. They blamed Diem's increasing unwillingness to listen to them on Ngo Dinh Nhu and Madame Nhu, who they said had alienated much of South Vietnam's population and created what critics claimed to be a "family dictatorship.[34] Undoubtedly, Madame Nhu played a significant role in creating disaffection among the South Vietnamese population by accusing Buddhists of being communists who deserved persecution by the Diem government. In 1962, Wesley Fishel of Michigan State University lamented that the "evil influences" of the Nhus had rendered Diem unable to build a democracy in South Vietnam. In a letter to John B. Hannah, president of Michigan State, Fishel wrote that "unless what I have termed the 'evil influences' are removed from the scene, in one way or another, Ngo Dinh Diem's government is not going to make the grade."[35] It was as though the problem was not Diem, the man U.S. policymakers had anointed to head an anti-communist South Vietnam, but rather the irresistible influence of Madame Nhu that prevented Diem from

interest in Vietnam was a legacy of what Christina Klein describes regarding Americans' attraction to Asia in the early Cold War. In the late 1940s and through the 1950s, Asian-themed novels, plays, news articles, and other cultural forms aimed to foster fond feelings among Americans for Asians, with a broader purpose of garnering public support for the expansion of U.S. power into the Pacific. Klein ends her study in 1961, stating that at that time Vietnam began to be the Asia focal point for U.S. policymakers at the expense of the rest of the Far East. This led to a lessening of cultural productions depicting sentimental images of Asia, but it did not disappear from the American psyche. Media depictions of Madame Nhu illustrate the transition from sentimental images Klein describes to the animosity between Kennedy administration officials and the Diem regime that marked the end of America's attempt to build an ally and the beginning of full-scale war. See Christina Klein, *Cold War Orientalism: Asia in the Middlebrow Imagination, 1945–1961* (Berkeley, CA: University of California Press, 2003).

[34] Morgan, *The Vietnam Lobby: The American Friends of Vietnam, 1955–1975* (Chapel Hill, NC: University of North Carolina Press, 2009), xiii, 62; George C. Herring, *America's Longest War: The United States and Vietnam, 1950–1975* (New York: McGraw-Hill, 2002), 82.

[35] Ibid., 84.

developing his political regime along the lines designated by the United States.[36]

The author of a March 1962 article in *Time* wondered if Madame Nhu were more akin to an "Asian Joan of Arc" or an "Oriental Lucrezia Borgia," a reference to a powerful and corrupt Catholic Italian family of the Renaissance era. No longer viewed as an emancipator, Madame Nhu had become a "puritanical feminist" and "South Vietnam's most bitterly debated female," the reason Diem's regime was so oppressive. By that point, she had begun to criticize the United States for not doing enough to stop the spread of communism in Vietnam, and it is clear that her outspokenness had a negative impact on media coverage.[37] Later in 1962, *Life* published a feature about Madame Nhu titled "Joan of Arc or Dragon Lady?" with accompanying photographs illustrating her various personalities. The lead image depicted Madame Nhu standing beneath a statue of the Trung sisters, situating her in the tradition of the Vietnamese independence struggle, but the accompanying caption included a quote from Madame Nhu that indicated that she, in a way, rejected the sisters' work in favor a type of heroism rooted in Catholic ideology – "Getting on an elephant and putting on a suit of armor as old heroines did doesn't attract me at all. I prefer the silent, everyday struggle of the saints." The reporter described Madame Nhu as "the most controversial, powerful, unloved, devious, single-minded, interesting, difficult beauty not only in southeast Asia but anywhere east of the Suez." A photo spread showed her talking with the press, interacting with government officials, and teaching members of the Women's Paramilitary Corps how to shoot a gun. In contrasting photos, Madame Nhu played darts with her husband and two children in what appeared to be a pleasant day out for a nuclear family. The final picture showed Madame Nhu praying during Mass in a Catholic church.[38]

The images of Madame Nhu in the U.S. media in the months leading up to the assassination of Diem in November 1963 reflect the increasing difficulty of resolving her symbolic functions. *Time* placed Madame Nhu on the cover of its August 9, 1963 issue. She was seated for a portrait, with what appears to be the stained glass window of a church behind her. Her hands are folded in front of her, displaying her long, polished

[36] Morgan, 93.
[37] "Joan or Lucrezia," *Time*, March 23, 1962, http://www.time.com/time/magazine/article/0,9171,829109,00.html?promoid=googlep.
[38] Orshefsky, 55–64.

fingernails. Facing the camera, she looks directly at the reader, her face difficult to decipher – neither smiling nor frowning nor blank. A picture accompanying the article shows Madame Nhu inspecting the cadets in the Women's Paramilitary Corps, her pale *ao dai* a sharp contrast to the cadets' dark uniforms. The picture's caption notes that "a rap of her fan is the roll of kettledrums."[39] The next month, *Time* ran another article about Madame Nhu, referring to her as "Dragon Lady." The reporter stated that, at a press conference, she "displayed an incredibly fascinating feminine charm. Whether twirling a parasol or hiding shyly behind an ivory fan, she both attracted and annoyed." A French reporter told the *Time* writer, "I had a strong desire to slap her, but from very, very close."[40]

A few journalist friends remained supportive of Madame Nhu, including Clare Booth Luce; Marguerite Higgins, a veteran war correspondent; and Eugene Gregory, an officer in the U.S. Information Service (USIS) who, along with his wife, Ann, edited the *Times of Vietnam*, an English-language newspaper published in Saigon. However, as Diem continued to fall out of favor with the Kennedy administration, Madame Nhu's relationship with most American reporters grew openly hostile, a pattern exacerbated by the arrival of young journalists such as David Halberstam, Neil Sheehan, and Malcolm Browne, who went to Vietnam expecting full access to military and government intelligence while also being unafraid to criticize U.S. policies or the Saigon regime. Halberstam described Madame Nhu:

Madame Nhu was a strikingly beautiful woman, and she was well-aware of it. Yet she looked too perfectly manicured ... to be leading a country at war. Her speeches rang with appeals to sacrifice, but there was nothing about her that gave any indication of sacrifice. To me she always resembled an Ian Fleming character come to life; the anti-goddess, the beautiful but diabolical sex-dictatress who masterminds some secret apparatus that James Bond is out to destroy. She liked power and it showed.... In contrast to Diem, who was shy and ill at ease in public, and Nhu, who often seemed indifferent, Madame Nhu had a real zest for the ceremonies of leadership. She was the only one of the family who walked the way a dictator should walk – with the flair and obvious enjoyment, trailed by a line of attendants – turning first to the right, then to the left in acknowledging the crowd. It was always a virtuoso performance, and a reporter watching felt this was the way Mussolini must have done it.[41]

39 Mohr, 21–25.
40 "Dragon Lady, Dragonfly," *Time*, September 20, 1963, 33.
41 Antoinette May, *Witness to War: A Biography of Marguerite Higgins* (New York: Penguin Books, 1983), 240.

James Bond was an international Cold War hero who combined John Wayne's independence in the fight with the smoothness of a 1960s playboy. In the 007 movies, Bond frequently had to outsmart beautiful, sexually alluring women to accomplish his mission; Halberstam's description of Madame Nhu highlighted her sexuality and physical appearance as that which was dangerous about her. Calling her a "sex-dictatress" likely was tongue-in-cheek, but it was revealing in the context of American perceptions of the Diem regime. Diem did not carry himself as a powerful head of state, and the fact that Madame Nhu did disrupted the image of America's traditional allies while also perpetuating the notion of a mysterious Asia that U.S. power had to tame or slay.

The new reporters joined veteran newsmen François Sully of *Newsweek* and James Robinson of NBC, both of whom had raised the ire of Diem, his family, and his government with their critical coverage. In September 1962, Diem banished Sully from Saigon, but before Sully left Vietnam, he filed a scathing report on the Diem regime with the U.S. embassy. Calling Diem disconnected from life in Vietnam and his secret police "amateurish," Sully asserted that "the most extraordinary personality in the Ngo dynasty" was Madame Nhu, "a beautiful, gifted, and charming woman" who was "also grasping, conceited, and obsessed with a drive for power that far surpasses that of even her husband." Sully continued, "It is no exaggeration to say that Madame Nhu is the most detested personality in South Vietnam." A month after Sully departed from Saigon, Diem expelled NBC's Robinson because he had criticized Madame Nhu in a news piece.[42] For her part, Madame Nhu accused journalists of being "intoxicated by Communism."[43] She echoed the contempt Diem and Nhu held for the American journalists, whom they accused of working to overthrow Diem's government.[44] Referring repeatedly to Madame Nhu as a dictator, Halberstam suggested that South Vietnam could not be a democracy while Diem – and, by association, Madame Nhu – held power.

Faced with increasing criticism, Madame Nhu tried to show that she did wield power in the Diem regime. She portrayed herself as a champion of Vietnamese women's rights, organizing the Women's Solidarity

---

[42] Jones, *Death of a Generation*, 195–96, 206–8, 305–6.
[43] Memorandum from the Public Affairs Officer of the Embassy in Vietnam (Mecklin) to the Ambassador in Vietnam (Nolting), Saigon, November 27, 1962, *FRUS, 1961–1963*, 2:745.
[44] Report from the Assistant Secretary of State for Public Affairs (Manning) to the President, Washington, undated. *FRUS, 1961–1963*, 3:535.

Movement and Women's Paramilitary Corps of Saigon, an armed force of women soldiers not affiliated with the Army of the Republic of South Vietnam (ARVN). She also sponsored legislation outlawing divorce and dancing, in both cases arguing that she was protecting the rights of Vietnamese women. Her ban on divorce was meant to overturn a law allowing husbands to leave their wives for a number of reasons but forbidding women from filing for divorce for any reason unless approved by the president.[45] Linking social restraint with military toughness, Madame Nhu sponsored a resolution "To Make Society Healthier and Reinforce the National Forces." The twofold bill, introduced in 1962, aimed to eliminate economic opportunities for "bar girls" and instead funnel women into the military. The law specifically targeted "taxi dancers" – women who worked in bars and nightclubs as dance partners for patrons. Expressing her disdain for taxi dancers, Madame Nhu told a *Life* magazine reporter that the women "left their homes in the country attracted by that stupid profession. Now we need them back there, if necessary by starving them into more useful jobs like teaching or nursing."[46] In keeping with Madame Nhu's morality crusade, General Paul Harkins forbade departing GIs from kissing their Vietnamese girlfriends at the airport because it would anger the Diem government.[47]

Madame Nhu's critics blamed her Catholicism for these policies, but it is unclear what her true motives were. The Catholic Church of the 1950s and 1960s did not forbid dancing, boxing, or beauty contests. Madame Nhu's laws, particularly those aimed at women's sexuality, were at least in part a criticism of the U.S. presence in South Vietnam. The bar girls and taxi dancers who made a living serving American men stationed in Saigon were not far removed from prostitution, providing evidence for Madame Nhu's assertion that American men corrupted Vietnamese women.[48] Long after Diem and the Nhus were gone from South Vietnam, the war would have devastating effects on Vietnamese women, forcing many into the sex trade or jobs at seedy bars and nightclubs, so perhaps in some ways, Madame Nhu's policies were prescient. Madame Nhu's approach to the problem illustrates the tension between traditional values and attempts at modernization. Perceived as both a feminist and an oppressor by

---

[45] Orshefsky, "Joan of Arc or Dragon Lady?" 58.
[46] Orshefsky, 63.
[47] Mecklin, *Mission in Torment*, 63.
[48] Telegram from the Embassy in Vietnam to the Department of State, Saigon, April 13, 1963, *FRUS, 1961–1963*, 3:225–26.

Americans and Vietnamese, Madame Nhu symbolized the ideological struggle embedded in U.S. policy toward Southeast Asia. Although she viewed herself as a protector of Vietnamese women, many Americans saw an intrusive Dragon Lady making decisions about her society without the blessing of American advisers.[49]

Although at one time publications described Madame Nhu as a progressive champion of women's rights, as Diem's reign neared its end, American journalists named her as one of the main reasons the United States could no longer support Diem. In a September 1963 article, *New York Times* reporter James Reston wrote that Americans could not "see Asia for Madame Nhu," suggesting that her words and behavior were obscuring American objectives regarding South Vietnam.[50] On October 11, 1963, Madame Nhu, along with her teenaged daughter, Le Thuy, found herself on the cover of *Life* for the last time. The tone of the accompanying article reflects the erosion of her "positive" symbolic function, referring to her as "tactless" and "talkative" and implicating her in the growing discontent among the population of South Vietnam over Diem's administration. The article blamed the crisis in Diem's government in part on "the talk of his acid-tongued sister-in-law Madame Nhu," indicating a belief that she was more than just a nuisance. Describing Diem's road to ruin, the author continued that "it was Diem's tough sister-in-law, Madame Nhu, who pushed through a series of blue laws that abolished what little freedom there was in Vietnamese life by banning everything from dancing to divorce."[51] Yet even then, Madame Nhu remained "a study in bewitchery," still captivating, still able to cast a spell on Americans, just as Vietnam would hypnotize the United States and keep it entranced for a decade.

The final act of the drama surrounding Madame Nhu began during the 1963 Buddhist crisis, when the monk Thich Quang Duc immolated himself in the middle of a busy Saigon street. Speaking in a voice that expressed neither "feminine" softness nor a modern Western attitude, Madame Nhu became Diem's spokesperson, denouncing South Vietnam's Buddhist leadership and referred to the self-immolation as a "barbeque."

---

[49] On November 2, 1963, Diem and Nhu were assassinated while Madame Nhu was in Beverly Hills, California, on a U.S. speaking tour. A string of corrupt leaders rotated through Saigon's presidential palace. America's role in Vietnam shifted from advisory to combat in March 1965, when the first Marine combat units landed at Da Nang.

[50] James Reston, "The Problem of Perspective in Public Affairs," *New York Times*, September 15, 1963, 196.

[51] "Mac Finds Out What's Gone Wrong," *Life*, October 11, 1963, 23–25.

Her comments drew the ire of African and Asian delegates to the United Nations, causing Kennedy administration officials to begin to fear that the American alliance with the Diem regime endangered U.S. relations with other newly independent nations.[52] A *New York Times* editorial suggested that Madame Nhu's prominence and outspokenness were harming an otherwise successful U.S. mission.[53] Congress threatened to cut funding for South Vietnam; Kennedy and his advisers pushed Diem to send Madame Nhu out of the country, lest the world view him as "being led around by apron strings."[54] In response, she accused the U.S. embassy of threatening and blackmailing her to prevent her from speaking out against South Vietnam's Buddhist leaders.[55] Bringing the U.S. relationship with the Ngo brothers to a brutal end, Ambassador Lodge and the C.I.A. encouraged a coup that removed them from power and assassinated them on November 2, 1963. Madame Nhu, who had been in the United States when the coup occurred, was exiled to Europe. After that point, the focus of the gender and sexual tensions that characterized U.S. intervention would shift from the exotic dragon lady to ordinary Vietnamese women.

Images of Vietnamese Women in GI Folklore

The idea of the dragon lady took on new forms after large numbers of American combat troops arrived in South Vietnam beginning in March 1965; the gender ideology that linked Asian women to foreign relations issues had a significant impact on the lives of Vietnamese women in Saigon and the southern countryside. As with Madame Nhu, these ordinary women were viewed through lenses that ultimately revealed the contradiction at the heart of the gender ideology that informed American policy toward South Vietnam. A cluster of images propagated in U.S. soldier folklore served to justify the targeting of Vietnamese women as both enemy combatants and sexual playthings, whereas tales and rumors about the women often characterized their sexuality as a weapon,

---

[52] Telegram from the Embassy in Vietnam to the Department of State, Saigon, September 7, 1963, *FRUS, 1961–1963*, 4:132; "Inquiry by U.N. Rejected," *New York Times*, September 14, 1963, 2.

[53] "Mrs. Nhu Speaks Out," *New York Times*, August 9, 1963, 22.

[54] Telegram from the Department of State to the Embassy in Vietnam, Washington, August 8, 1963, *FRUS, 1961–1963*, 3:557.

[55] David Halberstam, "Charges Threat by Embassy," *New York Times*, August 8, 1963, 1.

blurring the line between sex and violence. The very women the United States was supposed to protect became targets – and the images, especially that of the dragon lady, in effect blamed them for their own victimization. An economy organized around sex developed as the number of troops increased; the war's destruction of South Vietnam's countryside left many young women with few choices other than to go to the cities, where jobs as hostesses, bar girls, and prostitutes awaited them. The portrayals of South Vietnamese women and the effects of the war on them illustrate another side of the contradiction between the ideology of protection and the reality of domination. As Cynthia Enloe has described, houses of prostitution transacting business near U.S. military bases allowed American servicemen to prove that they conformed to the standards of masculinity that defined military strength.[56] Jim Roseberry went to Vietnam with the Army at the age of twenty-two and was stationed in Can Tho and Long Binh during his tour of duty from July 1969 to July 1970. He learned that the combination of racism and misogyny rendered Vietnamese women "the lowest people on the planet."[57]

Drill instructors and other servicemen enforced the notion that Vietnamese women functioned to accommodate the sexual needs of U.S. troops.[58] References to women in the language of basic training were used to denigrate recruits and define the enemy. In his study of U.S. combat troops sent to Vietnam, Christian Appy writes that throughout basic training, drill instructors repeatedly used pejorative terms about women to accuse recruits of showing weakness. To be called a woman – or, usually more crudely, a "cunt" or "pussy" – was to be pegged as lacking manhood. Appy quotes novelist Tim O'Brien, who wrote that during basic training, "women are dinks. Women are villains. They are creatures akin to Communists and yellow-skinned people and hippies." Additionally, references to women and femininity were synonyms for homosexuality, an even more damaging accusation because military law prohibited homosexual relations. Recruits who were called "faggots" or "queers" by drill instructors faced more vicious treatment.[59] In this climate, proving masculinity through aggressive displays of heterosexuality became part of the rite of passage. Some U.S. servicemen in Vietnam

---

[56] Enloe, *Does Khaki Become You?*, 35.
[57] Author's interview with Jim Roseberry, April 2007, Madison, WI.
[58] Enloe, *Does Khaki Become You?*, 35.
[59] Christian Appy, *Working-Class War: American Combat Soldiers and Vietnam* (Chapel Hill, NC: University of North Carolina Press, 1993), 101–02.

combined dragon lady imagery and the heterosexual masculinity instilled in them in basic training with fears of the enemy's potential to maim or kill them. The long-standing gendering of Asia as female and the insistence on heterosexual displays of manhood made Vietnamese women the troops' symbolic adversary. The National Liberation Front's use of female troops further complicated the situation: in some cases, Vietnamese women *were* enemy combatants.[60]

Images of Vietnamese women in GI culture often portrayed them as deadly enemies, but in other contexts, they symbolized either the nation that the United States had committed to modernizing and protecting or the underside of the Western culture that accompanied the U.S. presence in Vietnam. U.S. military and government handbooks about South Vietnam often featured photographs or drawings of Vietnamese women wearing the *ao dai* on their covers, as if the image were the country's national symbol. By contrast, members of Saigon's Vietnamese educated and professional class often pointed to prostitutes and miniskirt-wearing bar girls to criticize the social and cultural impact of the U.S. presence, and they attempted to assert Vietnamese culture in ways that might slow the spread of American influence. Positioning women as symbols of South Vietnam as well as potential enemies enforced the partially conscious assumptions about American masculinity and power that infiltrated foreign policymaking and found expression in sexual metaphors created – and sometimes acted on – by troops on the ground. The image of modernity presented South Vietnam as a worthy ally, but the dragon lady signified the dangerous "other" whom the United States must dominate. Even when this was not articulated in the political vocabulary of the time, the images that circulated among troops, policymakers, and the American public indicate the presence of the contradictions in the American mind.

A common image in G.I. folklore was that of the sexually alluring yet dangerous Vietnamese woman, whose danger was precisely her sexuality. Urban legends cautioned U.S. servicemen against engaging in sexual intercourse with Vietnamese prostitutes. *Vagina dentata* – "toothed vagina" – myths circulated among soldiers, warning that Vietnamese women sympathetic to the Viet Cong put razor blades, broken glass, sand, and other materials in their vaginas to injure unsuspecting male customers.

---

[60] On women in the NLF and North Vietnamese Army, see Sandra C. Taylor, *Vietnamese Women at War: Fighting for Ho Chi Minh and the Revolution* (Lawrence, KS: University Press of Kansas, 1999); Karen Gottschang Turner, *Even the Women Must Fight: Memories of War from North Vietnam* (New York: John Wiley & Sons, 1998).

In addition to legends about women who could literally tear a penis apart, tales about Vietnamese women carrying incurable venereal disease circulated among American soldiers. In the five years following the end of the Vietnam War, Monte Gulzow and Carol Mitchell interviewed thirty-five Vietnam veterans about *vagina dentata* myths. Some believed that their military superiors created the rumors to scare GIs into avoiding prostitutes. Others said that soldiers swapping tall tales had made up the legends.[61] Whatever their basis in fact, the legends embodied fears related to an inability to tell friend from foe, racism against Vietnamese women, fear of castration, and underlying anxiety concerning the vulnerability of American power.

The ideology that gendered South Vietnam as feminine was predicated on belief in the masculine power of the United States, but those thoughts played out in soldiers' minds in ways that demonstrate the tenuous nature of the ideas. Soldier-produced cartoons, anecdotes, and images provide a glance into the cluster of attitudes toward Vietnamese women. *Sorry 'Bout That* and *Be Nice*, two books written by Ken Melvin, a pseudonym for "a couple of guys who have been in Vietnam long enough to remember when there were four taxis, two apartments, six girls, and only one VC assassination squad assigned to each American in Saigon,"[62] include clear examples of the dragon lady ideology. Surviving Vietnam meant fending off gold-digging bar girls in addition to dodging bullets and shrapnel. The hapless GI who trusted a Vietnamese woman – or worse, fell in love – was likely to wake up one day stripped of his wallet and his pride. In these accounts, American manhood was fragile, and Vietnamese women were calculating.

The cover of *Sorry 'Bout That*, published in 1966, features a drawing of a Vietnamese woman wearing the dress part of the *ao dai* but not the pants, so her legs are bare all the way up to her hips. The neckline of the dress is cut wide to reveal her collarbone and the top of her chest in the style popularized by Madame Nhu. On the cover of *Be Nice*, published a year later, a Vietnamese woman wears a much more provocative version of the *ao dai* – the dress is short rather than floor length, and, similarly to the woman on the cover of *Sorry 'Bout That*,

---

[61] Monte Gulzow and Carol Mitchell, "'Vagina Dentata' and 'Incurable Venereal Disease': Legends from the Vietnam War." *Western Folklore*, Vol. 39, No. 4 (Oct. 1980), 306–16.
[62] Ken Melvin, *Sorry 'Bout That: Cartoons, Limericks, and Other Diversions of GI Vietnam* (Tokyo: The Wayward Press, 1966), back jacket flap. See also Melvin, *Be Nice: More Cartoons and Capers of GI Vietnam* (Tokyo: The Wayward Press, 1967).

the woman is not wearing the traditional pants. The dress's neckline is cut so low that the woman's ample breasts spill over it. With shiny, black stiletto heels completing the outfit, the woman looks at the reader, beckoning with her finger. As symbols of the Vietnam War, the cartoon women demonstrate the prominent and threatening place of sexuality in many soldiers' imaginations.[63]

The sexually suggestive appearance of a Vietnamese woman often masked danger, a central aspect of the dragon lady myth (Figure 2). Both *Sorry 'Bout That* and *Be Nice* include pictures of Vietnamese women equipped with weapons to harm a U.S. GI. A limerick in *Sorry 'Bout That* tells the tale of a woman who had a "killer" bosom. "A bar girl wore 38 D's / Rather much for a Vietnamese / So they searched her, with pleasure / And discovered this treasure / One grenade, one plastique, two punjis."[64] Plastique is a soft, malleable explosive material; a punji stick is a bamboo or wood stake with a sharpened edge, often used in Viet Cong booby traps. In *Be Nice*, a two-page spread shows a couple of American soldiers hiding behind some reeds with a sound-detecting machine while a Vietnamese woman in a tiny bikini strolls down a nearby path. The caption under the picture states, "There's an enemy ambush up ahead. The wheezer machine detects the sound of heavy breathing."[65] The sexy Vietnamese woman was a pied piper attempting to lure U.S. troops out of hiding. A few pages later, a cartoon bird warns, "Man who seek Oriental flower sometimes stung by honey bee."[66] Read as a metaphor for the war, the woman is South Vietnam itself, wounding the American man who chases her.

Frequently, the images created by soldiers grant Viet Cong women credit for their fighter potential. The National Liberation Front (NLF) was known for employing women soldiers as well as men, reinforcing the image of Vietnamese women as enemy combatants. A cartoon drawing depicted a Vietnamese woman with hand grenades on her breasts asking a GI, "What give you idea I Viet Cong girl?" The accompanying limerick described a Viet Cong woman. "They called her sweet Victor Charlene / The cutest VC they had seen / But she kicked when they tackled her / Clawed when they shackled her / And cussed like a salty Marine."[67] These

[63] Ibid.
[64] Melvin, *Sorry 'Bout That*, 30.
[65] Melvin, *Be Nice*, 8–9.
[66] Ibid., p. 13.
[67] Melvin, *Sorry 'Bout That*, 58.

FIGURE 2. The cover of *A Pocket Guide to Vietnam*, a guidebook published in multiple editions throughout the 1960s by the Defense Department, featured a young Vietnamese woman as the symbol of South Vietnam. U.S. Government Printing Office.

depictions of Vietnamese women using their sexuality to lure American troops and then murder them with the weapons of war raise questions about the conduct of the Vietnam War and U.S. servicemen's perceptions of their power and manhood. Judging by the tone of the anecdotes in *Sorry 'Bout That* and *Be Nice*, fearing or being wary of Vietnamese women did not render GIs cowardly. Only a foolish soldier would take up with a Vietnamese woman without ensuring that she did not have tricks up her sleeve or grenades under her skirt. This warning followed American servicemen from the countryside to the cities, where many displaced Vietnamese women found work in the sex economy that catered to foreigners.

The South Vietnamese press occasionally played into these fears, as when the English-language *Vietnam Inquirer* published a rumor about how to identify an undercover Viet Cong woman. In its June 4, 1968 issue, the newspaper reported in an article titled "Long-Haired Army" that VC women spies were known for wearing a watch on their right wrist, a dark blue *ao dai*, and no brassiere. The writer took note of the fact that a bra was supposedly the place where spies hid their weapons, so its absence in this case was curious. Nonetheless, the reporter observed, "if the story was true, the Communists have given the police of Saigon a most pleasant task amid many more arduous ones – watching the contours of women while trying to reshape the course of events."[68] Whether a true account or the perpetuation of a myth, the story illustrates the pervasiveness of the untrustworthy Vietnamese woman in the wartime culture.

The contradiction between the images of women as threats and victims had an impact on American perceptions of Vietnamese male soldiers as well. U.S. personnel often viewed Viet Cong fighters, male and female, as masculine competitors – "well-equipped and highly skilled in both conventional and subversive warfare."[69] Members of Lyndon Johnson's administration, such as McGeorge Bundy, Dean Rusk, and Maxwell Taylor, characterized the NLF as "well-motivated," "highly disciplined," and a "tough enemy both physically and morally."[70] On the other hand, U.S. soldiers' descriptions of the male troops of the ARVN repeatedly characterized them as lazy, passive, immature, fearful, and unskilled in the art of war.[71] In Vietnam, the U.S. military engaged in a masculine "contest" of "military power" with the NLF, whereas many American GIs considered ARVN men "faggots." Conversely, they agreed that "the VC have a lot

---

[68] "Long-Haired Army," *Vietnam Inquirer*, Vol. 1, No. 7, June 4, 1968, Glenn Helm Collection, Folder 01, Box 10, The Vietnam Archive, Texas Tech University.

[69] Stated by William Bundy in a speech on January 23, 1965. Quoted in Jennifer Milliken and David Sylvan, "Soft Bodies, Hard Targets, and Chic Theories: U.S. Bombing Policy in Indochina," *Journal of International Studies*, 1996, 25(2): 321–59.

[70] Milliken and Sylvan, "Soft Bodies, Hard Targets."

[71] Ibid., 328.

of balls."[72] An article in *Uptight*, a magazine the U.S. Army published for its troops in Vietnam, described a program that aimed to transform ARVN recruits into "Vietnamese fighting men." To ease the loneliness of adjusting to military life, "pretty young Vietnamese women" visited as morale boosters.[73] To fight alongside U.S. forces, South Vietnamese servicemen had to prove that they were prepared, which was linked directly to masculinity.

Not all Vietnamese women U.S. servicemen encountered were prostitutes or VC sympathizers. They were business owners, secretaries, and maids who worked for the U.S. military or made money serving Americans stationed in Vietnam. The Vietnam Council on Foreign Relations, a Vietnamese-run organization based in Saigon, published a booklet in 1969 or 1970 about the various roles women played in South Vietnam's war effort. Opening with a case study, the booklet told the story of Nguyen Thi Nam, a twenty-seven-year-old mother of four who gave up her comfortable job as a secretary in a government office to become a medic with a Revolutionary Development team in Long An, a province south of Saigon that had been heavily infiltrated with Viet Cong. Revolutionary Development was part of the U.S. CORDS program – Civil Operations and Revolutionary Development Support – implemented beginning in 1967 to secure territory from Viet Cong insurgency and stimulate support for the United States and the government of South Vietnam.

In her job as medic, Nam walked to houses throughout the province handing out medicine, examining wounds, and teaching residents about sanitation and personal hygiene. Explaining her decision to join the Revolutionary Development team, Nam said: "When I was a secretary, I wore a long, flowered *ao dai* every day, but I wasn't helping anyone. Now, in my black uniform, I am doing something for my people. I like being able to share both their sickness and happiness."[74] It was yet another example of how the actual lives of Vietnamese women did not reflect the images of them. Even those women who worked with U.S. forces did not always look the part that was portrayed in magazines and keepsakes. The author of the story, a reporter named Phung Thi Hanh, wrote that the circumstances of war had pushed many Vietnamese women into

---

[72] Lifton, *Home from the War*, 196.
[73] "The ARVN Recruit," *Uptight*, United States Army, Vietnam. Summer, 1971, 31–33.
[74] Phung Thi Hanh, "South Vietnam's Women in Uniform," Vietnam Council on Foreign Relations, Saigon (No date), 3, Douglas Pike Collection: Unit 11 – Monographs, Folder 21, Box 05, The Vietnam Archive, Texas Tech University.

national defense roles; at the end of 1969, about four thousand women
had joined the Women's Armed Forces Corps, three thousand worked
for the National Police, and 365 were members of Revolutionary Development teams, as was Nguyen Thi Nam.

In addition, the story reported that more than one million Vietnamese
women had volunteered for the People's Self-Defense Forces, armed civilian teams tasked with protecting villages at the local level from Viet
Cong infiltration. In total, 20 percent of the population of South Vietnam was involved in national defense, the reporter wrote, and of that, at
least 30 percent were women.[75] The importance of Vietnamese women
in the fight against VC infiltration was related to women's stature in
rural communities. Writing about Vietnamese family relations for the
U.S. Army Civil Affairs School, United States Information Agency (USIA)
associate Chester Baines described peasant women as powerful members
of rural communities, often the main business owners and local organizers despite the conventional expectation that women were subservient to
men. Because of peasant women's authority in their communities, U.S.
intelligence agents believed that if they could get the women on their side,
they could then reach peasant men.[76]

Women also worked for South Vietnam's National Police. By 1970,
the 85,000-officer force included 3,000 women. As did their male counterparts, women officers completed a basic training course in which they
learned traffic control, the use of weapons, and the techniques of psychological warfare. Although most women officers did secretarial work,
some conducted undercover work for the National Police Special Branch.
Others interrogated female captives and staffed checkpoints along busy
routes throughout the country. Hanh's article told the story of Mrs.
Huynh Thi Trang, a thirty-one-year-old widow who joined the force to
support her three children. As an officer, she worked a checkpoint on
Route One between Saigon and Tay Ninh, and she learned how to spot
illegal identification carried by male and female Viet Cong insurgents.[77]
Contrary to both the image of the dragon lady and that of the *ao dai*-clad
woman in need of protection, some Vietnamese women worked directly
with the American war effort.

Mike Subkoviak, a twenty-seven-year-old married serviceman, spent
much of his tour in Vietnam working alongside Vietnamese women. Stationed there in 1971, Subkoviak managed Army offices in Long Binh and

[75] Hanh, 5–7, 11–13.
[76] Chester Baines, "Vietnamese Individual Behavior, the Family, and Social Values."
[77] Hanh, 15.

Binh Thuy, a village in the Mekong Delta. Many of the employees in his offices were Vietnamese women who worked as secretaries and typists. At any given time, there were about a half-dozen Vietnamese women working for him. They spoke English – the language skill was required to do the jobs – and Subkoviak trusted their loyalty. His superiors never warned him to think otherwise, and most of the work the women did was routine paperwork – processing passes for soldiers going on leave, handling reassignment forms, and administering passes to go off base. He also knew Vietnamese women who were maids for the barracks and servers in the mess hall. Subkoviak had "much more contact with Vietnamese women than American women," rarely seeing Red Cross women, WACs, or USO entertainers. Most of the American women he saw were nurses working at one of the Long Binh medical facilities. He never worked with any Vietnamese men. "We would see Vietnamese men in the military once in a while or Vietnamese business men," Subkoviak said, but none worked with him directly.[78]

Although Vietnamese women outnumbered their American counterparts in Subkoviak's Vietnam experience, "both female entities were on some kind of pedestal because there were so many men and so few women." He enjoyed having women around, in a nonsexual way. "I was married, but it was nice to have the feminine touch, to have that be part of your life," Subkoviak said. "There's something that's really missing. Even if you didn't have your hair fixed or have makeup on, it's nice that you're a woman, and that you have a woman's voice and a woman's perspective." He would have preferred to see more American women – "familiarity of culture and even race" – but the presence of any women made the war zone "seem a little more normal."[79]

In some cases, U.S. servicemen married Vietnamese women and chose to make Vietnam their home. Bill Davis, an Army helicopter mechanic, observed some former Special Forces soldiers who became maitre d's and bodyguards at officers' clubs. Many had married Vietnamese women, and others had opened businesses in villages and cities. Davis discovered an American expatriate enclave in Cholon, Saigon's Chinese neighborhood. Davis did not meet any American women during his tour of duty, but he has photographs of three Vietnamese women he knew during the war. One picture is of Hoa, a woman he lived with for a while in Vung Tau, a coastal town that once was a resort destination for French colonists and wealthy Vietnamese. U.S. forces built a base there, and Vung Tau

[78] Author's interview with Mike Subkoviak, March 2006, Madison, WI.
[79] Ibid.

became an in-country R&R spot. Davis met Hoa at the beach, and they fell for each other. She had children, one of whom Davis thought an American GI might have fathered. Living with Hoa was difficult because of the curfew ordering servicemen out of the town by nightfall. "She was paying incredible bribes to the local police so I could be there, and she was very upset that I kept a gun there," Davis said. "It just couldn't work. Establishing relationships in Vietnam was very difficult because everyone is under a lot of pressure. Everybody knows what everyone else is doing."[80]

Davis's other pictures are of two Vietnamese sisters who ran a steam bath and massage parlor that doubled as a bar in Vung Tau. The women and Davis became good friends; several of his pictures show the three of them smiling and laughing together. "They took a liking to me, and I took a liking to them," Davis said. "I hung out there a lot." The sisters and Hoa were the only women with whom Davis had relationships while in Vietnam. He saw a few American women in Vung Tau, but other than the nurses and USO entertainers, he did not know what they were doing there. What he did know was that enlisted men "weren't allowed to interact with [American] women." The belief among GIs was that American women were in Vietnam for the pleasure of the officers.[81]

Gender Ideology in Wartime Saigon

In the air-conditioned jungle of Saigon, the circumstances of the war buttressed a defense of American gendered power predicated on partially conscious assumptions about masculinity. Everyday interactions between American men and Vietnamese women took place in a sexualized context created by several intersecting forces. When President Lyndon Johnson evacuated all American dependents from Saigon in 1965 out of concern for civilian safety, he created a bachelor culture in which most Americans who worked in Saigon were single, living without wives or children while in Vietnam. The war in the countryside pushed Vietnamese women into the cities while sending able-bodied Vietnamese men into military service. In unintentional ways, American men and Vietnamese women became the living embodiments of the gender ideology that informed U.S. policy toward Vietnam. In both practical and symbolic terms, they reinforced the notion of American heterosexual masculinity, which informed U.S. intervention in Vietnam.

[80] Author's interview with Bill Davis, May 2007, Oak Park, IL.
[81] Ibid.

Prostitution was the most visible and obvious form of the pattern, but "women's work" performed by hostesses, bar girls, and maids was part of the same ideological and imagistic morass. In their miniskirts and red lipstick, bar girls who served American men represented one aspect of the militarization of women's lives in Vietnam, drawing the ire of South Vietnamese critics who saw in this a corruption not just of Vietnamese women, but also of middle-class Vietnamese values, which came to be symbolized in the *ao dai*. Whereas the war forced rural women into an urban working class – and into miniskirts – for the purpose of economic survival, it also affected middle-class women by imposing on them an expectation of purity reflecting American gender norms and positioning them as a representation of Vietnamese modernity. The struggle between the *ao dai* and the miniskirt fed class tensions, and although American ideology called for the protection of middle-class womanhood, the presence of Americans in Vietnam created an immense demand for exploited sex workers.

U.S. military and government personnel stationed in Vietnam might have turned to materials published for American readers by the State and Defense departments that attempted to explain the Vietnamese class structure. One such factbook, titled *Area Handbook for South Vietnam*, described a three-class structure in South Vietnam, and women occupied different places in each class. The upper class was a small group of elite government officials, professionals, owners of large businesses and estates, and religious leaders. The urban middle class, also small, consisted of small business owners and educated wage earners. The largest class consisted of rural peasants, urban wage laborers, small shopkeepers, and "individuals in personal service occupations," presumably housekeepers, cooks, and the like. Vietnamese women comprised "an unknown but large proportion of the labor force."[82] These handbooks for Americans undoubtedly failed to capture all the nuances and subtleties of Vietnamese class differences, but they matter because they help to explain Americans' perceptions of the Vietnamese, even if those perceptions did not reflect the realities.

The American presence caused changes to Vietnamese society that put all these roles under pressure. By 1969, Saigon's population had increased from about 400,000 at the start of World War II to more

[82] *Area Handbook for South Vietnam*, ed. Harvey H. Smith et al. (Washington, DC: U.S. Government Printing Office, 1967), 93, 349.

than 2.5 million.[83] Before 1964, 80 percent of Vietnamese were rural farmers. By 1970, 40 percent to 50 percent of the population of South Vietnam lived in cities. Some were refugees from the war-torn countryside, whereas others hoped to make money from the wartime economy. The population surge took its toll on the city. Traffic jammed Saigon's streets, and pollution threatened to destroy its plant life. Saigon and other cities suffered endemic breakdowns of sewage, garbage disposal, school, telephone, and electrical systems. By contrast, Saigon's wealthy families lived in "spacious villas solidly built of stone or brick and equipped with running water, electricity, and sanitary facilities."[84] Meanwhile, sheets of rolled beer cans were reused as siding for homes in the burgeoning slums. Aluminum shacks doubled as billboards for Miller High Life, Pabst Blue Ribbon, and Budweiser. Karen Offut, a stenographer in the Women's Army Corps who was stationed in Saigon for part of her tour of duty, noted that in Saigon, "there were just thousands and thousands of people and then there would be big mansions and right next to it would be these little three-sided houses or makeshift homes made out of flattened beer cans."[85] In 1970, about 158,000 Vietnamese worked for the U.S. military and civilian companies, and many others found income in war-related services, from housekeeping to brothels.[86]

The war drove both men and women into the city, but Vietnamese women were especially important to Saigon's wartime economy. All Vietnamese men between the ages of eighteen and thirty-seven were subject to the military draft and required to serve at least two years, which left Vietnamese women to fill factory and other urban employment positions. Women made up the majority of workers in textile, food processing, plastics manufacturing, and communications companies.[87] They also took their places operating heavy machinery, repairing automobiles, and holding jobs in engineering. Vietnamese intellectuals emphasized these opportunities for women in new industries. An article in the English- and French-language *Vietnam Observer*, whose Vietnamese-run staff was "a group of professors, political leaders, journalists," portrayed the women

---

[83] *Army Civilian Employment: Living and Working in Vietnam* (Washington, DC: U.S. Government Printing Office, 1969), 6.

[84] *Area Handbook for South Vietnam*, 121–24.

[85] Ron Steinman, *Women in Vietnam: The Oral History* (New York: TV Books, 2000), 263; see also *Area Handbook for South Vietnam*, 136–37.

[86] "The Urban Trend," *Time*, August 30, 1970, http://www.time.com/time/magazine/article/0,9171,876792,00.html.

[87] *Area Handbook for South Vietnam*, 349–50, 441.

workers as "more skillful than their male counterparts" and noted that
the women "demonstrated that the 'weaker' sex is capable of performing
a man's job."[88] Americans also pointed to Vietnamese women workers
as examples of successful modernization. In a 1968 training manual
designed to introduce U.S. foreign service workers to South Vietnam's
society, the Vietnam Training Center of the State Department's Foreign
Service Institute noted that Vietnamese women would soon outnumber
men in the population, owing in large part to the number of men killed in
combat.[89] Therefore, it concluded, "today's women are playing an active
role in deciding Vietnam's future – a role that is concerned with social,
economic, cultural, and political development in this Asian society."[90]
In 1968, of the 330,000 members of Saigon's labor force, about 250,000
were women.[91]

Opportunities in the workforce did not change the image of the ideal
Vietnamese woman in American propaganda. An article in the June 1970
issue of *Pipeline*, the newsletter of the Office in Charge of Construction
(OICC), the Defense Department agency responsible for civilian construction in Vietnam, provided a telling example of the gender ideology
at work. Titled "The Woman in Vietnam" and featuring a drawing of
a demure Vietnamese woman, it explained that her main focus was her
family, and that even though she considered "fame and fortune to be of
superficial, fleeting importance," she was expected to be "concerned with
her own beauty. She must know how to preserve her youthful beauty. She
must know how to dress pleasingly and properly." A Vietnamese woman
was to be quiet, gentle, and submissive to her parents until she got married, after which she then would be submissive to her husband. The article noted that although the requirements of a proper Vietnamese woman
"appear to be unfair, the resulting sacrifices have helped preserve balance in society." Although women's freedoms had expanded, "enabling
the woman to alter her role in society . . . she continues to embrace those
good qualities which have helped make her society strong."

---

[88] Nguyen Thuoc, "Miss Duong Drives a Bulldozer," *Vietnam Observer*, December 1968,
    29–30; see also *Vietnam Observer*, October and November 1968, John Cheney Collec-
    tion, Folder 01, Box 01, The Vietnam Archive, Texas Tech University.
[89] "Women in Vietnam," Study aid, Vietnam Training Center, October 1, 1968, Jackson
    Bosley Collection, Folder 03, Box 01, The Vietnam Archive.
[90] Ibid.
[91] "The Women," *Time*, November 8, 1968, http://www.time.com/time/magazine/article/
    0,9171,902501,00.html.

Because the war required able-bodied Vietnamese men to join the military, women's support of their communities meant leaving the home and
entering the workforce, but the article presented Vietnamese women as
emblems of Cold War domesticity: "the Vietnamese woman is still highly
respected for her devotion and sacrifice in the service of her husband and
her children. Most women who are working for foreign employers do
so because of their present economic situation." Vietnamese women's
entry into many fields of employment, "from the care and consolation
of their fellows in distress to administrative labor to heavy industry
and construction," the article argued, meant that they were part of "the
world movement for the advancement of women's rights." Juggling
child care and other domestic responsibilities with wage work in various
industries outside the home, Vietnamese women helped "to keep the
home front strong while their men are fighting on the battlefield."[92]

The article cast an image of Vietnamese women as the combination
of traditional yet modern that matched U.S. intentions for a developed
South Vietnam. A woman's proper place was primarily in the home, but
when called on in times of war or other crisis, women kept the nation
afloat while men went off to fight. The notion was familiar to Americans
who had called on Rosie the Riveter in times of need, then expected her
to return happily to the kitchen. That the accomplishments and character
of Vietnamese women stood for the nation as a whole further emphasized
that U.S. policy toward Vietnam gendered their ally as the feminine object
of masculine American power.

The paucity of Vietnamese men in the employment pool was a major
factor in the dominance of Vietnamese women in American-patronized
urban service industry jobs. The handbook for U.S. personnel noted that
Americans in Vietnam "increased the demand for cabdrivers, servants,
petty entrepreneurs, and entertainers," and Vietnamese women "of all
ages predominate among urban petty vendors."[93] Although American
women lived and worked in Saigon during the war, the vast majority of
Americans in Vietnam were men, and the services available in the city
played on their perceived desires. Advertisements for bars and nightclubs
in Saigon clearly catered to heterosexual men. For example, the Fuji Bar
trumpeted its ability to meet basic needs – "charming hostesses, cold beer,
reasonable prices." The nightclub Queen Bee advertised live music by two
different bands each night and a "corner to relax in the company of pretty

---

[92] "The Woman in Vietnam," *Pipeline*, June 1970, Vol. III, No. 6.
[93] *Area Handbook for South Vietnam*, 349.

hostesses."[94] In the economy of wartime Saigon, there was money to be made catering to the masculinity of American men.

The "hostesses" advertised by establishments such as Fuji Bar and Queen Bee were more commonly known as "bar girls." Most bar girls were members of the urban working class or rural peasants who came to the city during the war looking for work. Sometimes they tended bar, but often their real job at a bar, club, or restaurant was simply to wait for American men to come in, and then ask the male patrons if they wanted to buy "Saigon tea." The beverage itself usually was cola or some other ordinary drink, but it was more expensive than a can of soda. For the extra cost, the bar girl stayed and chatted with the man. Although the National Assembly had made prostitution illegal during Diem's presidency, thanks in part to lobbying by Madame Nhu, subsequent governments legalized the sex trade. Although some government officials and religious leaders denounced cabarets and Western dances, recalling a 1963 law that had outlawed the cabaret trade, there was no serious consideration of shutting down the activities.[95] By the mid- to late 1960s, both Americans and Vietnamese assumed that bar girls and prostitutes were one and the same.

One of the most visible markers of bar girls was the miniskirt, which itself became a source of conflict. Some members of Saigon's elite frowned on the miniskirt, viewing it as a symbol of the debauchery Americans brought to the city.[96] Vietnamese critics of American cultural infiltration used the miniskirt to link urban problems to U.S. intervention. In an effort to remedy the problem of pedestrians slowing vehicle traffic as throngs of people tried to cross downtown Saigon's busy streets, the city government in 1968 commissioned the building of two footbridges to lift walkers above the streets. However, the editors of *Vietnam Observer* worried that rather than alleviating traffic jams, "these bridges may become the scene of an exciting spectator sport – watching beautiful girls in miniskirts trip daintily across which could contribute to more traffic congestion, which surely is not why they are being built in the first place."[97]

The Saigon government officially condemned the miniskirt, and police harassed Vietnamese women who wore them in public. Middle-class Vietnamese condemned the economic climate in which bar girls could make

---

94 Tad Bartimus et al., *War Torn: Stories of War from the Women Reporters Who Covered Vietnam* (New York: Random House, 2002), 117.
95 *Area Handbook for South Vietnam*, 142.
96 "Footbridges and Miniskirts," *Vietnam Observer*, December 1968, 19, John Cheney Collection, Folder 01, Box 01, The Vietnam Archive.
97 "Footbridges and Miniskirts," 19.

more money than university professors.[98] A reporter for *Time* magazine observed, though, that elite Vietnamese criticized Western-style clothing out of concern for cultural traditions, not sexual morality. "The Thai or Vietnamese businessman who openly keeps several 'minor wives' or mistresses and regularly visits the local massage parlor frowns on miniskirts not because they are morally objectionable but because they represent a cultural intrusion."[99] To avoid attention on their commutes home from work, some bar girls chose to change out of their miniskirts and hot pants and put on *ao dais* after their shifts.[100] The women, many of whom undoubtedly worked in bars and nightclubs because they needed the income and had few, if any, other options, were caught in a hot war as well as a culture war, in which their clothing served as a moral barometer measuring Saigon's character.

Vietnamese critics of the miniskirt favored the *ao dai* as the type of clothing "respectable" women should wear.[101] Postcards, magazine covers, and promotional photos regularly featured young, attractive Vietnamese women wearing the *ao dai*.[102] A 1971 issue of *Vietnam Magazine*, published by the Saigon-based Vietnam Council on Foreign Relations, placed on its cover a photograph of Nguyen Kim Thanh, a young woman who worked in Saigon as a secretary and a travel agent. She wore an *ao dai* for the photo shoot, and inside the magazine, a photo layout entitled "Women of Vietnam" depicted two Vietnamese actresses clad in *ao dais*.[103] In 1969 and 1970, the Vietnam Council on Foreign Relations published two editions of an English-language pamphlet titled "An Introduction to Vietnam," both of which featured on their covers Vietnamese women wearing the *ao dai*. A *Vietnam Observer* article maintained that "the *ao dai* is considered by Westerners to be one of the most elegant and feminine national costumes in the world." According

---

98 Bernard Weintraub, "Americans' impact on Vietnam is profound," *New York Times*, July 6, 1968, 1.

99 "Beyond the Blue Horizon," *Time*, October 17, 1969, http://www.time.com/time/magazine/article/0,9171,840229,00.html.

100 "Saigon Under Siege," *Time*, March 8, 1968, http://www.time.com/time/magazine/article/0,9171,899971,00.html.

101 *Area Handbook for South Vietnam*, 100. See also, "Saigon: Where to Go, What to See," *Life in Vietnam*, September 24, 1966, 36. Glenn Helm Collection, Folder 03, Box 01, The Vietnam Archive, Texas Tech University; *Vietnam Magazine*, Vol. IV, 1971, Anonymous Collection (#5), Folder 01, Box 01, The Vietnam Archive, Texas Tech University; "The Ao Dai: World's Loveliest Garment," *Vietnam Observer*, October and November 1968, 37, John Cheney Collection, Folder 01, Box 01.

102 "Saigon: Where to Go, What to See."

103 *Vietnam Magazine*, Vol. IV, 1971.

FIGURE 3. A group of Vietnamese women, dressed in the traditional *ao dai*, stand in front of the 62nd Engineer Battalion Headquarters. Elwin C. Vanderland Collection, The Vietnam Archive, Texas Tech University.

to the article, Vietnamese women who traveled overseas often wore the *ao dai*, which was recognized throughout the world.[104] Another *Vietnam Observer* story, highlighting educational and professional opportunities for women in Saigon, featured a photograph of *ao dai*-clad young Vietnamese women working with new computer technology. Embracing the technological side of modernization, South Vietnam's urban intellectual class – the journalists, politicians, and academics who published *Vietnam Observer* and *Vietnam Magazine* – used the *ao dai* to show that South Vietnam retained its cultural independence even while accepting U.S.-funded economic change.[105]

Americans may have brought the miniskirt to South Vietnam's cities, but images in U.S. military and government publications reveal that they, too, had an affinity for *ao dai*-clad Vietnamese women (Figure 3). For Americans, the ao dai was not about cultural independence as it was for Vietnamese critics of U.S. depravity. When depicted in American publications, the ao dai represented a pliant South Vietnam that would

[104] "The Ao Dai: World's Loveliest Garment," 37.
[105] "Computers in Vietnam," *Vietnam Magazine*, Vol. IV, 1971, 23–26.

not resist the hand of U.S.-led modernization efforts. A 1967 issue of the U.S. military publication *Stars and Stripes* featured a photograph of women wearing *ao dais*, with a caption reading, "Vietnamese women make a pleasing sight in their native dress."[106] The U.S. Foreign Service Institute's training manual on Vietnamese women noted that "among Vietnam's loveliest sights are the thousands of high school girls all in white *ao dais* sailing down the street on bicycles, long hair floating in the breeze."[107] In September 1966, *Life in Vietnam*, a magazine published in Saigon and distributed to U.S. military installations throughout South Vietnam, featured on its cover an Air Vietnam stewardess named Nghiem Ngoc Thuy dressed in an *ao dai*.[108] The cover of the Defense Department's *Pocket Guide to Vietnam*, published periodically throughout the 1960s, featured an illustration of a Vietnamese woman wearing an *ao dai* and riding a bicycle (Figure 4). The images idealized an innocent femininity in line with American domesticity and thus worthy of protection. In reality, however, the U.S. presence more frequently pushed Vietnamese women into positions of sexual depravity rather than middle-class respectability. Despite attempts to portray benevolent modernization as represented by the *ao dai*, the war's domination of Vietnamese women's lives manifested itself through the miniskirt. Carrying different meanings for South Vietnamese intellectuals and U.S. government and military personnel, the *ao dai* was a powerful symbol of the tension between independence and nation building.

The deployment of the *ao dai* as a symbol of a modern Vietnam contradicted the reality for most Vietnamese women in Saigon. Bill Davis, an Air Force flight mechanic stationed in Vietnam in 1968, bought a postcard of two Vietnamese women walking down a street in Saigon, both wearing the *ao dai*. A drawing of a woman in an *ao dai* graced the cover of his Vietnamese phrasebook. He observed, however, that most of the Vietnamese women he encountered in Saigon were peasant refugees, often in revealing Western clothing. The woman in the *ao dai* was "the idealized version of the Vietnamese woman," not the reality. "Seeing women walking around like that was gone by the time I got there," he said. "It [the *ao dai*] was traditional, but traditions change when the military moves in."[109]

---

[106] *Stars and Stripes*, March 17, 1967.
[107] "Women in Vietnam," 10.
[108] *Life in Vietnam*, September 24, 1966.
[109] Author's interview with Bill Davis.

"Be nice, Cuthburt! Where
could I be hiding
grenades?"

FIGURE 4. Images such as this one, from the back cover of *Be Nice!*, an obscure collection of GI humor, cartoons, and limericks related to the Vietnam experience and published by an author whose pseudonym was "Ken Melvin," were common in GI culture and reflected an incarnation of the dragon lady whose sexual allure was dangerous.

Some wealthy Vietnamese recognized the difficult reality poor women faced in the midst of war. When asked about bar girls, a young Vietnamese woman named Hong Khac Kim Mai, a well-to-do student at the University of Saigon, replied that she thought "they deserved pity more than reproach. The war has hurled them from the countryside into the city. What can they do when the cost of living is so expensive? It's no wonder they've got to choose that job." She qualified her statement by adding that "there are ... certain girls who want to live in luxury."[110] Whatever the motivations, the lived realities of South Vietnamese women

---

[110] *Mekong Features*, November 12, 1967, Douglas Pike Collection: Unit 06 – Democratic Republic of Vietnam, Folder 24, Box 17, The Vietnam Archive, Texas Tech University.

subverted the attempts of both the Vietnamese authorities and American politicians to present a positive image of modernization and development. Focusing on gender in an analysis of the Vietnam War, the Cold War ideology of fighting to protect an idealized version of femininity and masculinity comes unraveled.

The problems of gendered morality were clear to some U.S. policy-makers. In 1966, Senator J. William Fulbright, the Arkansas Democrat, unleashed a lengthy criticism of the situation in Saigon in gendered terms, speaking specifically about how the U.S. presence in the city affected some Vietnamese women. He argued that "both literally and figuratively, Saigon has become an American brothel." Fulbright criticized the stress that the U.S. presence placed on the Vietnamese family structure, which had an especially destructive effect on rural and poor families. The growth of the service and sex industries that catered to American men in Saigon and other cities disrupted the Vietnamese family because it created an economy in which young women could make more money than their fathers. Fulbright castigated Americans for creating a situation in which Vietnamese men had to "put their wives or daughters to work as bar girls or to peddle them to American soldiers as mistresses."

He went on to note that it was "not unusual to hear a report that a Vietnamese soldier has committed suicide out of shame because his wife has been working as a bar girl." Also at issue was the effect Americans had on class earning power. Fulbright stated that "as a result of the American influx, bar girls, prostitutes, pimps, bar owners, and taxi drivers have risen to the higher levels of the economic period."[111] By contrast, some middle-class Vietnamese families could no longer afford to rent homes in Saigon, and some "Vietnamese civil servants, junior Army officers, and enlisted men are unable to support their families because of the inflation generated by American spending and the purchasing power of the GIs."[112]

In James Gibson's work on the war's impact on Vietnamese society, he quoted an American GI who viewed the situation this way: "Women had to fuck in order for whole families to survive."[113] A 1966 study conducted by Ted Britton, a RAND Corporation consultant who created the Vietnam Summer Youth Program for the U.S. Operations Mission to

---

[111] E. W. Kenworthy, "Fulbright issues a warning to U.S.," *New York Times*, May 6, 1966, 2.

[112] Ibid.

[113] James Gibson, *The Perfect War: The War We Couldn't Lose and How We Did* (New York: Vintage, 1986), 262.

Vietnam (USOM) to try to gain the support of young Vietnamese, stressed the concerns of Vietnamese students regarding the increase in prostitution that corresponded with the deployment of additional U.S. troops. The rise in both prostitution and mixed-race children alarmed the students with whom Britton worked; they suggested that USOM establish supervised brothels on the outskirts of towns and provide contraceptives for customers. Noting the negative impact of prostitution and out-of-wedlock pregnancies on Vietnamese family life, the students argued that regulating the sex trade could staunch growing anti-Americanism.[114] Troops were not the only American men who enjoyed the services of bar girls (Figure 5). U.S. diplomats angered the wives of their Vietnamese hosts – women considered to be "that single group in the South tougher than the Viet Cong," a harkening back to the days of Madame Nhu – by bringing bar girls as their dates to parties.[115]

Attempts to change the situation in Saigon did not remove the underlying dynamic between American men and Vietnamese women. In 1966, a group of Vietnamese women who were teachers, writers, and social workers formed the Committee for the Defense of the Vietnamese Woman's Human Dignity and Rights to address the problem of prostitution in Saigon. Committee members blamed the war, and in particular, U.S. involvement. "The miserable conditions of war have forced our people to sell everything – their wives, children, relatives, and friends – for the American dollar," one member told an Associated Press reporter.[116] An organization called the Committee of Women's Action for the Right to Life was formed in July 1970 to protest the presence of U.S. military forces in Vietnam, blaming them for the prostitution problem in the cities. A month later, representatives from women's groups met in the Cholon district of Saigon to draw attention to the impact of American troops on Vietnamese women. Signs at the conference featured slogans such as "Prostitution represents U.S. civilization in Vietnam" and "Prostitution has resulted from the presence of one-half million U.S. and satellite troops."[117]

[114] "Notes of Dr. Ted Britton," no date. John Donnell Collection, Folder 16, Box 06, The Vietnam Archive, Texas Tech University.

[115] A. J. Langguth, "Our policy-making men in Saigon, *New York Times*, April 28, 1968, SM22.

[116] Susan Brownmiller, *Against Our Will: Men, Women, and Rape* (New York: Bantam Books, 1976), 95.

[117] "New Saigon Women's Movement Asks U.S. Troop Withdrawal," Liberation Press Agency, Oct. 26, 1970. Douglas Pike Collection: Unit 05 – National Liberation Front,

FIGURE 5. Two men seek the services of Vietnamese prostitutes on Tu Do Street in Saigon. Donald F. Harrison Collection, The Vietnam Archive, Texas Tech University.

President Nguyen Van Thieu attempted to address the situation more than once. In 1967, he issued a plan to close bars in Saigon; Nguyen Phuc Que, South Vietnam's minister of social welfare at the time, suggested creating an entertainment district on the outskirts of Saigon where the

Folder 06, Box 04, The Vietnam Archive, Texas Tech University; "Representatives of Women's Associations Hold Seminar," Liberation Radio, Aug. 3, 1970. Douglas Pike Collection: Unit 05, Folder 06, Box 04.

government would license and regulate all establishments and employees. Patrons would pay an entry fee that would go to government coffers. The discussions prompted a protest march through downtown Saigon of about two hundred Vietnamese women representing the bar girls and "taxi dancers" who made their living serving American GIs.[118] They argued that closing the taverns would encourage an increase in prostitution because the women who had worked in the bars would be put out of work.[119] Again, in 1971, Thieu attempted to shut down all of Saigon's bars and nightclubs, but very few complied with the order. Establishments that advertised and were licensed as restaurants operated as bars, employing bar girls who cuddled with their customers in the dimly lit dining room.[120]

"Miniskirts Thinner than Memories Denied"

By 1970, GI traffic in Saigon had begun to wane as U.S. forces withdrew from South Vietnam. Reporting on the changes occurring in the city, *New York Times* reporter A. J. Langguth described the effects of America's gradual departure on bar girls, who worried about their uncertain futures. One woman, who appeared to be about thirty – an age at which her marriage prospects were limited – planned to move to a village where no one knew her, hoping that "the size of her dowry would compensate for her past and her silicone breasts," which she presumably had had implanted for the enjoyment of American men.[121] Yusef Komunyakaa, an American Vietnam veteran and Pulitzer Prize-winning poet, told a story about bar girls at the close of the war in a poem called "Saigon Bar Girls, 1975." Their customers had all departed back to their lives in America, so the women wrapped up their work, "washing off makeup," throwing away "their lists of Mikes, / Bills, Joes, & Johns" and taking off their "miniskirts / thinner than memories / denied." Some of the former bar girls looked back on the war, sad, through "plaintive windows," perhaps wondering what happened to a man who had purchased Saigon tea, missing loved ones who had been killed in combat, or pondering

[118] "Cleaning Up Saigon."
[119] Saigon plan to close clubs is protested by bar girls," *New York Times*, November 21, 1967, 9.
[120] Gloria Emerson, "Saigon is closing sleazy bars for GI's," *New York Times*, December 7, 1971, 10.
[121] A. J. Langguth, "1964: Exhilaration 1968: Frustration 1970: Hopelessness," *New York Times*, Oct. 4, 1970, 220.

what they would do for income now that the wartime economy was gone. Perhaps there had been a spark behind a kiss that a girl had charged a few dollars for but had cost so much more. Other bar girls Komunyakaa described returned "to home villages / as sleepwalkers, leaving / sloe gin glasses / kissed with lipstick."[122] In vacant bars in Saigon, the women left reminders that they, too, had been at war.

Chicago Tribune reporter Ron Yates covered Saigon during the final days of the war. One person he interviewed, identified as a "longtime resident" of Saigon, told him that "Saigon is a dying place, but she is dying like a whore who is desperately trying to turn her last trick."[123] Whether the speaker was Vietnamese, American, French, or some other nationality, the description conjures images of bar girls and prostitutes caught in an economy that served the emotional and sexual needs of American men. The frantic attempt to "turn her last trick" says more about the human consequences of the war than about the morality of the women who worked in the sex industry. The militarization of these women's lives pushed them out of their rural environs and into jobs that the American presence in Vietnam created.

In the minds of Americans in Southeast Asia and on the home front, Vietnamese women, in image and in reality, played several important roles in shaping and justifying U.S. policies toward and Americans' actions in Vietnam. When photographs or drawings of them appeared on the covers of U.S. government handbooks and other official publications about Vietnam, Vietnamese women – for a time represented by Madame Nhu – symbolized the nation that the United States hoped to save from communism through modernization. As more and more ground troops set up camp in South Vietnam, the image of the dragon lady and the reality of the exploited sex worker moved to the center of the stage. Underlying American GIs' thoughts about and interactions with Vietnamese women were expectations about heterosexual masculinity that informed policymaking during the Kennedy and Johnson administrations and were part of the boot camp lexicon.

Americans did not create the economy that employed Vietnamese women to sell their sexual appeal and their bodies. It had existed at least since the era of French colonialism, and probably before. The U.S.

---

[122] Yusef Komunyakaa, "Saigon Bar Girls, 1975," *Dien Cai Dau* (Hanover, NH: Wesleyan University Press, 1988), 54–55.

[123] Ron Yates, "Saigon's Elite Still Enjoying 'the Good Life,'" *Chicago Tribune*, April 21, 1975.

presence increased the numbers of women working as bar girls and prostitutes, who became part of both the wartime landscape and American soldier mythology. GI legends sometimes cast prostitutes and other
Vietnamese women who worked closely with Americans as dangerous
spies – dragon ladies – out to harm unsuspecting troops, and such stories
were wrapped into justifications for violence against Vietnamese women.
Images of American women played an equally crucial part in establishing
the importance of gender roles as means for conveying why U.S. troops
fought. The "girl next door" – the antithesis of the dragon lady – was a
powerful symbol of the Cold War America that communism threatened,
and the women who signed up for a Red Cross program designed to boost
troop morale were to embody that girl as a reminder to servicemen of
who and what waited for them back home.

2

"She Could Be the Girl Next Door"

The Red Cross SRAO in Vietnam

One night in the spring of 1968, Dorothy Patterson and a couple of her fellow Red Cross volunteers convinced some GIs who had access to a jeep to drive them to Sin City. Located in An Khe, about a mile from where Patterson's Red Cross unit was stationed, Sin City was "a place where prostitutes and bar girls prospered" on the dollars and desires of U.S. soldiers. In polite terms, Sin City was a cluster of rinky-dink establishments where GIs could go to enjoy live music and dancing, drink beer, and sample local cuisine. In reality, many went to spend time with Vietnamese women in the privacy of a "boom-boom parlor," local parlance for a room in a brothel. Sin City was surrounded by a barbed-wire fence and guarded by U.S. military police. Division commanders cooperated with local Vietnamese pimps to ensure that brothels provided the desired services to U.S. troops.[1] Military medics, hoping to prevent the spread of venereal disease among the troops, subjected the Vietnamese women who worked there to regular examinations.[2]

There was no written rule that forbade American women from visiting Sin City, but when U.S. servicemen saw Patterson and her friends at a café there, they flashed looks that made the women feel as though they were not welcome. "These GIs walk by on their way to the back room, and they were really almost indignant that we were there, wanted to know what we were doing there," Patterson recalled. "They didn't want us to see them messing around with the Vietnamese women. I just got

---

[1] Susan Brownmiller, *Against Our Will: Men, Women, and Rape* (New York: Bantam Books, 1976), 98.
[2] Author's telephone interview with Dorothy Patterson, June 2006, Madison, WI.

the feeling that they were embarrassed to think that we might see them." Sin City, she noted, was "a place for GIs to go to be with a female" – a Vietnamese female.

If, in the culture of the Vietnam War, Vietnamese women were cast as dragon ladies – sexually alluring, yet also dangerous – the role assigned to American women who volunteered for the Red Cross Supplemental Recreational Activities Overseas (SRAO) program was to remind soldiers of the "girl next door." As Nancy Warner, who went to Vietnam with the Red Cross in 1969, remembers her experience, SRAO volunteers represented "all that was wholesome and good about girls, women, moms, sisters, wives" waiting for U.S. servicemen back home.[3] SRAO volunteers – called "donut dollies" in a nod to the history of Red Cross women serving coffee and donuts to U.S. troops overseas – symbolized the American way of life that soldiers were fighting to protect. Drawing on a white, suburban, domestic ideal – which was, in fact, being challenged on the home front – SRAO intentionally constructed an image of American women as wholesome, girlish, and chaste, the antithesis of the mysterious dragon lady. The meticulous construction and regulation of their image by the Red Cross and the Defense Department illustrates in potent ways the thoroughly gendered nature of Cold War conceptions of national security and the "American way of life," as well as the values supposedly at stake in Vietnam. However, a look at donut dollies' experiences in Vietnam reveals another aspect of the contradictions embedded in those values.

The Red Cross initiated SRAO in 1953 when it sent teams of women to South Korea to work with U.S. troops fighting in the Korean War. From 1965 through 1972, the program sent approximately 700 women to sites throughout Vietnam to boost the morale of U.S. troops. Some staffed recreation centers on large posts; others journeyed to remote troop encampments whose missions required them to move far from a larger permanent base. Defense officials also requested that donut dollies work at recreation centers established by the Army's Special Services division and the USO.[4] Traveling by jeep, truck, and helicopter, the women, whose teams were known as "clubmobile" units, took games, music, cold drinks, and their smiling faces to the troops in hopes of providing a pleasant diversion from the monotony of waiting for combat.

[3] Author's e-mail correspondence with Nancy Warner, July 2007, Madison, WI.
[4] "Department of Defense Request for SRAO in Vietnam," June 4, 1965, National Archives, Record Group 200 – Records of the American National Red Cross, 1965–1979 [hereafter NARA RG 200], Box 75.

FIGURE 6. February 1971, LZ San Juan Hill, Central Highlands. Two Red Cross "donut dollies" and a GI look over the side of the hill at a group of GIs working. Don Kilgore Collection (Americal Division Veterans Association), The Vietnam Archive, Texas Tech University.

The program was open only to female college graduates between the ages of 21 and 24, so the women tended to be a few years older than the average U.S. GI in Vietnam. Parents had to give written permission for their daughters to go to Vietnam.[5] It was a stark contrast to the draft, which could send any man 18 or older to Vietnam without parental approval. Defense Department authorities noted that U.S. troops might be in Vietnam for a "long duration" with infrequent combat moments and thus considerable idle time. Boredom coupled with isolation could make it "difficult to maintain the morale of trained, combat ready troops."[6] From 1967 to 1968, the program's peak year in Vietnam, an average of 280,500 servicemen participated in SRAO activities monthly at twenty major bases. Clubmobile units traversed an average of more than 27,000 miles each month to fire support bases – encampments for infantry operating far from a permanent post (Figure 6). The Red Cross estimated that

[5] "Department of Defense Request for SRAO in Vietnam," June 4, 1965, NARA RG 200, Box 75.
[6] "Department of Defense Request for SRAO in Vietnam," June 4, 1965, NARA RG 200, Box 75.

clubmobile teams traveled more than two million miles during the seven years the SRAO program operated in the Vietnam War.[7]

From the beginning, SRAO aimed to be a reminder of the "America" U.S. troops defended throughout the world. Dorris Heaston, who served with SRAO in Vietnam in 1969, believed that the purpose of the donut dollies was to remind soldiers why they were fighting communism. The notion of fighting for the Vietnamese inspired few young American men, but the sight of a young American woman might provide a sense of urgency and validate what the troops were doing. It was part of the idea that donut dollies were to bring a "touch of home" to the battlefront.[8] According to an Army pamphlet for personnel stationed in Vietnam, donut dollies went to the war to support troop morale by providing "a bit of America in Vietnam."[9] The Red Cross noted that SRAO workers might bring an "air of stability that is not found in the present situation" for soldiers stationed in Vietnam.[10] J. Holley Watts, a former donut dolly, believed that her duty was to provide the "illusion of calm in Vietnam."[11]

From their powder-blue A-line dresses to their duties as soldiers' emotional caretakers, donut dollies participated in the Vietnam War effort without openly disrupting the masculine character of combat or challenging the gender roles that Cold War-era popular culture had prescribed for them. Because the donut dolly image was based on the suburban domestic ideal, embodied in the "girl next door," the SRAO program enforced the gender stereotypes that formed the basis for both Cold War domesticity and foreign policy.[12] Whereas the toughness of U.S. troops symbolized American strength, the motherly concern of donut dollies symbolized the nation's virtue, with motherhood grounded in the ideology that women and men operate in different spheres of society (Figure 7). The notion of "republican motherhood" indicated that even though the public sphere was open to men only, women had significant power because they were

---

[7] "Red Cross Clubmobile Girls Coming Home from Vietnam," American Red Cross News Service, May 26, 1972, Jeanne Christie Collection, University of Denver Penrose Library, Special Collections, Denver, CO, Box 1.

[8] Author's telephone interview with Dorris Heaston, October 2009, Hattiesburg, MS.

[9] Headquarters, Department of the Army, "Helpful Hints for Personnel Ordered to Vietnam," pamphlet no. 608–16 (Washington, DC: U.S. Government Printing Office, 1968), 30.

[10] "Red Cross Report on establishing SRAO in Vietnam," NARA RG 200, Box 75.

[11] Author's telephone interview with J. Holley Watts, June 2006, Madison, WI.

[12] Elaine Tyler May, *Homeward Bound: American Families in the Cold War Era* (New York: Basic Books, 1999).

FIGURE 7. Donut dollies at Dong Ba Thin, December 23, 1968. Jennifer Young Collection, The Vietnam Archive, Texas Tech University.

responsible for shaping their sons' and husbands' character. This ideology found new expression in the donut dolly image. The actual experiences of donut dollies in Vietnam, however, illustrate the breakdown of those stereotypes, revealing how Cold War gender ideology had begun to collapse.

The image of the girl next door embodied ideas about middle-class domesticity and contained sexuality, two hallmarks of American Cold War culture regarded as essential if the United States were to triumph over Soviet communism.[13] To enforce SRAO's innocent image, sexual activity was specifically discouraged. Warner said Red Cross officials believed that sexual expression by SRAO workers "was totally destructive to the mission" of the program in Vietnam. If the girl next door gave up her purity, sinking to the level of a Vietnamese whore, then what was America fighting for? In the shape of the dragon lady, Vietnamese women had come to symbolize both an unreliable ally and the elusive Viet Cong.

[13] Ibid., 85.

American women, in contrast, should remind troops of Cold War social order, which would modernize South Vietnam and stop communist infiltration. However, just as Vietnamese women got caught in the contradiction between benevolent nation-building and the desire for domination, American women experienced the tensions between the image of domesticity and the reality of changing social norms on the home front. SRAO women were supposed to embody the domestic ideal, but many of them signed up to escape, or at least postpone, the constraints of domesticity. Exacerbating the contradiction, although the Defense Department and the Red Cross attempted to export traditional gender and sexual ideals to Vietnam, some donut dollies discovered that such beliefs were not well suited to the realities of the war zone. Donut dollies were meant to represent a chaste femininity, but they became objects of illicit male desire and sexual frustration, and, at an extreme, victims of violence.

Red Cross women were also intended to be emissaries of a united, patriotic, democratic America. SRAO remained overwhelmingly white, however, reproducing the open racial conflicts that were spreading from the South to the cities of the North and West. In addition, returning the United States to "normalcy" after World War II provided the justification for protecting the "American way of life" from the communist threat, but that way of life subordinated, and was being challenged by, African Americans, women, and gay Americans. By the late 1960s and into the early 1970s, disillusionment with the war affected the morale of both troops and Red Cross women and further contributed to a rejection of the values assigned to Americans, Vietnamese, and the war itself.

Domesticity on the Battlefront

Donut dollies grew up in a world in which women's domestic role was a main part of Cold War national ideology. Stable nuclear families, anchored by strong heterosexual couplings, would serve as bulwarks against communist infiltration, it was thought. In this model of domesticity, sexuality ostensibly was appropriate in marriage but taboo outside it. By extension, some sociologists, psychologists, and government officials saw sexual deviance as a threat to national security, as it threatened the integrity of the hetero-normative American home.[14] Sexuality had been implicated in the McCarthyist paranoia that swept the United States

[14] Ibid.

in the early 1950s, and the hunt for homosexuals in public and private institutions, coupled with rigid definitions of men's and women's social roles, created an intensely repressive atmosphere. The movement of middle-class women into the workforce during World War II, and their continued presence in wage-earning jobs outside the home after the war, fueled concerns about sexuality. The most hysterical concerns about lesbians were rooted in the fear that women's refusal of the roles of wife and mother – and, hence, their failure to reproduce – might lead to "the destruction of the human race, albeit a white, middle-class race."[15] Social critics and policymakers indeed reasoned that containing sexuality within the home and encouraging women to sustain sexually satisfying marriages would protect "the American way of life."[16]

Much of this was wishful thinking. Despite the sometimes frenzied defense of the gendered normality, the norms themselves had begun to change in the years leading up to Vietnam. Some organizations had begun to push for the creation of women's roles outside the home in national defense as early as the Korean War. The National Manpower Council (NMC), founded in 1950 at Columbia University, called for a mobilization of "womanpower" as well as manpower and advocated the employment of women in government and the private sector to advance national security in the Cold War world. Although it acknowledged that employment "must not detract from the importance of their roles as wives and mothers," the NMC argued that women could help "to expand our industry to new heights, to assist our allies, and to maintain a military force strong enough to deter aggression."[17] In 1961, President Kennedy created the President's Council on the Status of Women, a committee given the task of determining how U.S. policymakers could "strengthen family life and at the same time encourage women to make their full contribution as citizens." Although the rhetoric of Kennedy and the council gave primacy to familial and domestic roles for women, it implicitly acknowledged that the changing economic system required women to work outside the home.[18]

[15] Donna Penn, "The Meanings of Lesbianism in Postwar America," in *Gender and American History Since 1890*, ed. Barbara Melosh (London: Routledge, 1993), 106–24.

[16] May, 80–118.

[17] Susan Hartmann, "Women's Employment and the Domestic Ideal in the Early Cold War Years," in *Not June Cleaver: Women and Gender in Postwar America, 1945–1960*, ed. Joanne Meyerowitz (Philadelphia: Temple University Press, 1994), 84–100.

[18] Ruth Feldstein, *Motherhood in Black and White: Race and Sex in American Liberalism, 1930–1965* (Ithaca, NY: Cornell University Press, 2000), 155.

The increasing presence of women – especially white, middle-class, married women – in the paid workforce revealed the contradictions in the ideology of domestic containment. Alice Echols has noted that "the contradiction between the feminine mystique and the emancipatory possibilities of the fifties (higher education, more democratic marriages, paid work, and better sex) created 'dry tinder' for the spark of women's liberation."[19] Ruth Rosen writes of a double generation gap faced by the "daughters of the fifties." In addition to the divide between parents and children, the image of the "ordinary housewife" – a woman devoted to childrearing and housekeeping – loomed over baby boomer girls.[20] In fact, most of them would inhabit a quite different world. By 1960, more than 30 percent of married women worked for wages, pushed out of the home by consumption patterns that required two incomes.[21] By the middle of the decade, many young suburban Americans sought a way out of the world their parents had built, and for some white, middle-class women, the path eventually led them to a movement for women's equality and freedom.[22]

Many SRAO volunteers participated in the program specifically to avoid the constraints of the ideal they were supposed to represent. Some donut dollies had not yet begun careers when they joined SRAO, but they sought to escape the pressure to marry and start a family, even if temporarily. Nancy Warner served her tour of duty in Vietnam beginning in July 1969, but it was not the war itself that motivated her to volunteer. She wanted to travel the world, and she sought adventure that graduate school at Old Dominion University in Norfolk, Virginia, did not provide. For Warner, it was a perfect solution to post-college restlessness. Her father had served in World War II, and, surrounded by fellow military brats in a relatively conservative part of the United States, she had not given much thought to questioning the war.[23] Jeanne Christie headed to Vietnam with the Red Cross in January 1967 to flee Wisconsin winters and the watchful eyes of her parents. It seemed a good way to "break away from home" after she graduated from the University of Wisconsin. Mary Robeck did not want to "do the married after high school thing,"

[19] Alice Echols, *Shaky Ground: The Sixties and Its Aftershocks* (New York: Columbia University Press, 2002), 78.
[20] Ruth Rosen, *The World Split Open: How the Modern Women's Movement Changed America* (New York: Penguin Books, 2000), 39.
[21] Echols, 78.
[22] Echols, 59.
[23] Author's telephone interview with Nancy Warner, June 2006, Madison, WI.

so she joined the Red Cross in 1971 after graduating from the University of Southern Mississippi with a master's degree in sociology. Although Susan McLean's family expected her to "have a big wedding and stay home and make babies" after she graduated from Longwood University in Virginia, she was not ready for that life.[24] J. Holley Watts joined the Red Cross to go to Vietnam because she "was affected by JFK's inaugural speech," in which he called on Americans to help spread the ideals of freedom and democracy throughout the world. She also wanted to travel, and when she graduated with a psychology degree from Rosemont College in Pennsylvania, she was interested in neither graduate school nor marriage.[25] The irony of these women as symbols of the life they were fleeing is inescapable.

Even though some donut dollies were not motivated to go to Vietnam specifically in response to domestic expectations, their decisions to join SRAO indicate that they sought options outside traditional middle-class women's roles. Jennifer Young left her home in suburban St. Louis in 1968 after graduating from college and joined the Red Cross because she wanted to help the young men sent off to war. She believed it was unfair that women got a "free ticket" out of service in Vietnam. "I just felt so bad for what some of them were having to experience because of the draft," she said.[26] When Linda Wilson graduated from the University of Mississippi in 1968, she found few job options for using her degree in sociology, and serving in Vietnam was on her mind because she had many friends in the Reserve Officers Training Corps (ROTC) at Ole Miss. Going to Vietnam was a way she could show her support for them, and she served with SRAO in Vietnam from September 1968 until October 1969.[27] Marj Dutilly was raised in a family in which both her mother and her father were Red Cross volunteers. She served throughout high school and college and knew she wanted to continue her service after graduation. Wanting to honor her fiancé, Dave, who was killed seven weeks into his tour of duty on an Army long-range reconnaissance patrol in An Khe, Joyce Denke joined the SRAO program and went to Vietnam in 1970.[28]

[24] Author's telephone interviews with donut dollies over a period of approximately three years, summer 2006 through fall 2009, including Jeanne Christie, June 2006, Madison, WI; Mary Robeck and Susan McLean, October–November 2009, Hattiesburg, MS.
[25] Author's telephone interview with J. Holley Watts.
[26] Author's telephone interview with Jennifer Young, June 2006, Madison, WI.
[27] Author's telephone interview with Linda Wilson, October 2009, Hattiesburg, MS.
[28] Author's telephone interview with Marj Dutilly, October 2009, Hattiesburg, MS.

Because the program required that all participants have a college degree, many donut dollies had begun to make career plans before joining the Red Cross and viewed service with the Red Cross as career development.[29] Patty Wooldridge, a graduate of the University of Tennessee, worked as a nutritionist before she went to Vietnam. Employed by the Social Security Administration in Chicago after graduating from DePaul University, Kathleen Huckabay, who was planning to go to law school eventually, intended to save some money while serving with the Red Cross in Vietnam for a year. Nancy Calcese used her social work degree from Florida State University to get a job as a social worker at Scott Air Force Base in Illinois.

Other donut dollies went to Vietnam specifically to help resolve their questions about the war. Rene Johnson's father was in the military and had spent time in Vietnam in the early 1960s. He returned home believing that the United States was "getting ready to make the biggest mistake that it's ever made. He said he would fight to the death to defend his country, but that's not what we were doing." At the time, the Johnson family lived at Fort Benning, Georgia, and Rene was in college in Tallahassee at Florida State University, so she heard both sides of the Vietnam debate. The soldiers she knew at Fort Benning argued that the United States was bringing freedom and independence to the Vietnamese, but on campus at Florida State, students expressed the belief that the war was unjust and immoral. "As the years went on and I was losing friends, I just ended up deciding I needed to go over and see for myself what was going on," Johnson said.[30] Eileen O'Neill signed up for SRAO because she was curious about the war and had dated a man who had served a tour of duty in Vietnam in 1968. Ultimately, though, "it was as much for the travel and adventure as anything else," she said. She suspected that the war "had to be more complicated than either side of the demonstrators were arguing. We'd still hark back to Kennedy's inaugural address of going places and doing things for the rest of the world, and a lot of idealism and the sense of, this couldn't be really as bad as it appears."[31]

Newspapers and magazines for troops in Vietnam featured articles about donut dollies, which illustrated women's reasons for joining the program. Lieutenant Tom Sileo, a reporter for *The Hurricane*, the

---

[29] Author's interviews with Patty Wooldridge, Kathleen Huckabay, Nancy Calcese, and other donut dollies, October–November 2009, Hattiesburg, MS.
[30] Author's telephone interview with Rene Johnson, June 2006, Madison, WI.
[31] Author's telephone interview with Eileen O'Neill, June 2006, Madison, WI.

magazine of II Field Force in Vietnam, profiled an SRAO team for the magazine's June 1969 issue. A number of women he interviewed told him about their jobs, why they joined the Red Cross, how GIs reacted to them and their programs, and what they thought their purpose in Vietnam was. By and large, their motives were not political, Sileo discovered to his surprise. The women he spoke with said they came "to help the troops, not to debate the war." Doreen "Smiley" Miley, the unit director of the SRAO team at Long Binh, joined because she saw it as "a chance to be patriotic, to gain some self-confidence, and to mature." She told Sileo that she loved "to travel, and this is a golden opportunity to see things and meet people."

The antiwar movement inspired Karen Melgaard, unit director for the donut dollies at Cu Chi, to go to Vietnam, but not because she agreed with the protesters. She was living in Berkeley at the time, teaching sixth grade. The war began to bother her, but so did those who stayed home and rallied against it. "I began thinking, 'What are the people at home doing for the troops here?'" Melgaard said. "I thought that the presence of women could help, so here I am." Miley believed that the presence of the Red Cross women *did* help. "Just seeing a living, breathing American female makes it a little nicer for the guys out there digging foxholes," she explained.[32] As the various reasons for joining SRAO indicate, the program provided an uneasy combination of old beliefs and new opportunities, asserting Cold War domesticity even as it allowed its mostly white, middle-class members to enter into traditionally masculine spaces.

Living conditions for SRAO workers varied depending on where they were stationed. Some lived on bases; others lived in small houses or apartments in communities adjacent to U.S. military installations. On-base billets ranged from Quonset or wood huts with detached bathrooms and showers to air-conditioned trailers with indoor plumbing. The women stationed at Phu Bai, Cam Ranh Bay, Phan Rang, Long Binh, Binh Thuy, and Chu Lai lived in air-conditioned trailers. Each trailer slept up to four women and included a lounge and a kitchen with a stove and a refrigerator. At Da Nang, some SRAO workers lived in single rooms on the upper floor of an Army barracks and shared a lounge with Special Services and USO women. Others stayed in a five-bedroom, two-bathroom house surrounded by a wall. A twelve-bedroom Quonset hut with an air-conditioned lounge and kitchen housed the women at Bien Hoa.

[32] Lt. Tom Sileo, "She Could Be the Girl Next Door," *The Hurricane*, June 1969, No. 20, Jeanne Christie Collection, Box 1.

The luckiest women were those stationed in Qhu Nhon, a seaside village, who lived in an old French hotel that had ocean views.[33] Some billets hired Vietnamese women to clean and do laundry, but in other locations, donut dollies did their own housekeeping.[34] Housing arrangements intentionally kept donut dollies' living quarters separate from men's billets.

Dorothy Patterson and her fellow donut dollies lived in "really nice" two- and three-bedroom air-conditioned trailers. A fence surrounded the compound, and military guards stood watch outside. Off-duty, life was good. "We had everything we needed," Patterson said. "We could get steaks right and left. We had marshmallow roasts because my mom sent marshmallows and things along to make s'mores." Out at the firebases, however, accommodations were primitive, and being a woman seemed to upset the flow of daily life. "One night two of us got stranded at one of the support bases because the weather got really bad and the helicopter couldn't get back in to get us," Patterson said. "So we had to stay there all night. That just threw [the Army unit] in a tizzy because they had to empty a whole barracks for the two of us to stay in because they didn't have sleeping facilities for females. They didn't have bathrooms for women, a lot of the bases did not have bathrooms for women, they would just kind of clear the area if we were there and needed to use a bathroom, and stand guard while we went in and used it."[35] Deeply ingrained beliefs about who belonged in a war zone made ordinary functions challenging.

Girl Next Door Gone to War

Jeanne Christie poured orange soda into a cup and handed it to an exhausted soldier. He still had dirt caked on his hands, and a wash of sweat, tears, and grime streaked his face. His unit had just come in from an especially tough battle; a large number of the men had been killed. The games she and the other Red Cross women had planned for the day seemed inappropriate now, so she ladled the orange soda – it was warm by then because ice was no match for Vietnam's heat – into a few more cups and headed over to a pile of sandbags where a group of soldiers sat. They invited her to join them. Some wanted to talk about their buddies; others needed to cry. Some were unable to speak, still shocked by what

---

[33] "How the SRAO Staff Live in Vietnam," NARA RG 200, Box 65.

[34] "Information for Vietnam-Bound SRAO Personnel," January 1969, Jeanne Christie Collection, Box 1.

[35] Author's telephone interview with Dorothy Patterson.

FIGURE 8. Donut dollies play a game with GIs at Camp Holloway in Pleiku, July 23, 1970. William Bruce Bartow Collection, The Vietnam Archive, Texas Tech University.

they had seen and done. Christie sat down and sipped her soda, offered her ear and her shoulder, and tried to figure out how to give the guys some comfort. It was her job, one that that required emotional strength and quick thinking, and it was tough.[36] Moments such as this revealed how messy and emotionally draining the work of domesticity could be.

Although donut dollies were expected to maintain a sunny disposition for the sake of troop morale, their jobs were both emotionally and physically exhausting. At recreation centers and on mobile runs out to firebases, donut dollies usually worked ten-hour shifts. They organized quiz shows, group participation games (Figure 8), fashion shows, talent shows, birthday parties, and parties for children from nearby orphanages. They served coffee and cold drinks, and talked with soldiers. "In our centers we sat down and played cards with them, we had Kool-Aid and coffee and shot pool, played ping-pong, whatever we happened to have in our center. Just sat and visited, gave them an ear to listen to if they wanted," explained Dorothy Patterson. Regarding the games Red Cross women set up for soldiers, Jeanne Christie noted that "games like

---

[36] Author's telephone interview with Jeanne Christie.

concentration and match games were very good because you had to deal with enlisted personnel – who were barely high school graduates in some cases – to the officers, so you had to have a range of abilities, you had to be able to carry it off. They had to be quick, down and dirty. And you could set them up and move them very easily."[37]

Games and activities varied by location, but in general, SRAO members polled troops in their area to determine interests and needs. Programs usually lasted for about one hour at a time, with various programs scheduled throughout the day depending on the location. Some teams emphasized educational value, whereas others tried to encourage group interaction or provide relaxation. If there were enough budding thespians in a platoon, SRAO teams worked with them to stage plays and musicals.[38] Sometimes the women gave presentations on topics such as the "Roaring '20s," Vietnam, U.S. presidents, England, France, psychology, and science. If areas were unsafe or the troops stationed there did not have much free time, donut dollies made mobile runs to drop off magazines and puzzle books. For the soldiers who simply wanted to sit down and write a letter, SRAO staff kept supplies of pens and paper on hand.[39] The attitudes of the donut dollies were just as important to the functioning of the recreation centers and clubmobiles as were the games and activities. "Our job was to be upbeat and light," Christie said. "The smiling, airhead façade covered the serious nature of what was going on."[40] A donut dolly named Cathy Monaghan told reporter Tom Gable of the Army magazine *Uptight* that SRAO offered "a diversion for the men from war." She added that she wanted the GIs "to live, to laugh, to forget about time." Sara McKay saw her job as trying to make GIs forget about the war. "I really feel as though I've accomplished something when I see the guys laughing and smiling," she told Gable.[41] Reflecting on her work in Vietnam, Nancy Smoyer, who went to the war with SRAO in 1967, recognized that there was only so much that donut dollies could understand about servicemen's experiences. "We were so naïve that a lot of times we just couldn't grasp what they had been through."[42]

---

37 Ibid.
38 Author's telephone Interview with J. Holley Watts.
39 Various SRAO Vietnam Quarterly Reports, NARA RG 200, Box 65.
40 Author's telephone interview with Jeanne Christie.
41 SP5 Tom P. Gable, "To Live, to Laugh, to Help Forget." *Uptight*, United States Army, Fall 1969, Jeanne Christie Collection, Box 1.
42 Christian G. Appy, *Patriots: The Vietnam War Remembered from All Sides* (New York: Viking, 2003), 188–90.

Quarterly SRAO reports from Vietnam provide glimpses of donut
dollies' daily life. A typical week at a base with a Red Cross team might
have gone something like this. Donut dollies might have eased the troops
into a Sunday morning with a laid-back game of "Playboy," a quiz on
men's fashions, etiquette, and popular resort areas in the United States.
As the days went by, soldiers may have joined in a game of "Political
Pretensions," a mock presidential campaign and election culminating in
a "Mad-Lib" acceptance speech. A group of GIs could have checked out
guitars from the recreation center and stolen away to practice their cover
of "Purple Haze" for the talent show the donut dollies had planned for
Friday night. They were sure they would win, but little did they know that
another band of soldiers determined to win the competition had recruited
one of the donut dollies, who sang a mean "Chain of Fools." "Fashion
Fantasy" gave GIs a chance to prove that men could be both soldiers
and fashion designers. They could be models, too. The activity required
soldiers to channel their inner Mary Quant, designer of the miniskirt, to
create their own women's fashions using materials found on base. Fellow
soldiers modeled the new lines in a runway extravaganza. A quiz game
tested soldiers' knowledge of famous women, songs containing women's
names, and women's products. All the while, the cast and crew of the
base's production of *Barefoot in the Park* rehearsed for their Saturday
performance. Not all troops on base participated in SRAO activities, but
for some soldiers, the chance to sit down in the recreation center and read
a magazine or work on a puzzle helped ease the restlessness of waiting
for combat.[43]

Women who volunteered for SRAO learned immediately that their job
was to be morale boosters for the troops, reassuring symbols of home.
J. Holley Watts, who arrived in Vietnam to begin her Red Cross tour in
1966, understood that her function was to provide the soldiers "the face
of the girl next door, their connection to family, community, home."[44]
SRAO volunteers were supposed to be what Cynthia Enloe has called
"warm fuzzies," reminders of hearth, home, and all that was good in
the meaning of "America."[45] Representing these archetypes required a
specific look. The Red Cross instructed donut dollies that, when packing
civilian clothes for Vietnam, "practicality should not be carried to the

---

[43] Various SRAO Vietnam Quarterly Reports, NARA RG 200, Box 65.
[44] Author's telephone interview with J. Holley Watts.
[45] Cynthia Enloe, *Does Khaki Become You? The Militarization of Women's Lives* (London:
      Pandora Press, 1988), 109.

extent that femininity is lost." Mandates included skirts at knee length, hair styled neatly above the collar in keeping with the rule regarding military women's hair, and no platinum blond locks. Women were not to wear shorts or pants in public unless they were participating in sports or spending time at the beach. Even then, Red Cross rules stressed that clothing should be "conservative in style."[46] SRAO volunteer Penni Evans noted, "We were to be non-sexual symbols of purity and goodness."[47]

Both the donut dollies and articles in military publications summed up the SRAO in-country persona as "the girl next door," an image that is difficult to describe but that is charged with meaning. Patty Wooldridge, an SRAO unit director in Vietnam from 1965 to 1966, described the girl next door as the symbol of ideal American womanhood – wholesome, a pal rather than a paramour, a mother or a sister rather than a pin-up girl. She considered the girl-next-door image to be part of the "psychological warfare" of Vietnam. American troops fighting on foreign soil, without a clear reason for being in Vietnam or a definite distinction between ally and enemy, could look to the donut dollies for reminders of what they had to look forward to back home, and what they were fighting for.[48]

Race and sexuality complicated the image. The vast majority of women who served in SRAO were white, suggesting that whiteness was a characteristic of wholesome American womanhood and, by extension, the American values worth protecting against communism. Although the image of the girl next door implied chaste, platonic relationships with the men who loved her, dropping a handful of young women into a male-dominated war zone and keeping them at arm's length sometimes demoralized and angered servicemen. Linda Wilson noticed that some troops completely shut down emotionally when the donut dollies arrived. It was how they had learned to deal with the war, and "to have two American females drop out of the sky in a helicopter and play these silly games" was too much for the servicemen to handle.[49] A few servicemen told Eileen O'Neill that she did not belong in Vietnam, and that her presence simply frustrated the men because she was a woman they could see but not date or touch.[50]

---

[46] "Information for Vietnam-Bound SRAO Personnel," January 1969, Jeanne Christie Collection, Box 1.
[47] American Civilian Women in Vietnam." Lily Adams Collection, University of Denver Penrose Library, Special Collections, Denver, CO, Box 1.
[48] Author's telephone interview with Patty Wooldridge.
[49] Author's telephone interview with Linda Wilson.
[50] Author's telephone interview with Eileen O'Neill.

Donut dollies were to lift servicemen's spirits by symbolizing a place far from the war zone and helping create a home front at the battlefront. They were, in short, at the war but not part of it. "When a tired GI saw an American girl, me, wearing a skirt, it was more than he expected, especially in a combat zone," one donut dolly told journalist Ron Steinman. Reflecting on the GI's response, Steinman noted that "seeing a Donut Dolly, often close to the action, changed his life, if only for a moment. She was as far from home as he was and it made a world of difference to him. His increasingly violent world of war seemed distant when that typical American girl just happened to drop by on a helicopter."[51] Joyce Denke, who served in the SRAO program for a year beginning in 1970, believed that the donut dollies' light blue uniforms also gave the troops a visual break from the olive drab of war. Misty Lettieri described for *Hurricane* reporter Lieutenant Sileo a Christmas she spent with the troops of the 199th Light Infantry Brigade at Long Binh. "We sang Christmas carols near a bunker and around a dead, brown Christmas tree decorated with grenade pins, paper scraps, and beer and soda can fliptops," she said. It was among her favorite memories of her time in Vietnam.[52] The women and men all were far from home, but out of the litter that surrounded them – pieces of hand grenades jarringly juxtaposed against the holiday scene – they created something familiar.

Many of the donut dollies' activities took place at specific locations set aside from the soldiers' normal routines. The time spent in combat was short for most GIs, and idle moments held the potential for soldiers to seek the company of a Vietnamese prostitute, a stiff drink, or a joint. Ever mindful of the dangers of boredom to troop morale and vigor, military authorities asked the Red Cross to "maintain and staff a recreation center for the guys to come to as an alternative to their going to the EM Club or NCO club to just drink themselves, or if there's entertainment there, you know the Korean strippers, as an alternative. Kind of wholesome recreation, pool, ping pong, games, cards, whatever," said donut dolly Jennifer Young.[53] The Red Cross rec center at An Khe was typical – the windowless building boasted air conditioning and had telephone equipment available to soldiers who wanted to make calls to the United States. It featured a lounge, a kitchen, a ping-pong table, a bookshelf, and tables

[51] Ron Steinman, *Women in Vietnam: The Oral History* (New York: TV Books, 2000), 24–25.
[52] Ibid.
[53] Author's telephone interview with Jennifer Young.

for playing board games. Metal folding chairs sat open throughout the center for anyone looking to sit down, and posters sent from the national SRAO headquarters adorned the walls. A stage awaited performers; military personnel could borrow musical instruments, including guitars, at the center. For other music options, center staff spun records on a small record player.[54]

Throughout the course of the Vietnam War, the Red Cross received numerous requests for SRAO teams. They came mostly from platoon commanders whose men were encamped far from large bases or population centers. Their letters pleaded the cases of their units, describing loneliness, monotony, and boredom and explaining why a "Red Cross girl" would make the situation more bearable. Some offered to create special accommodations on their bases for SRAO women, and others promised to devote men to securing the women's safety. The requests offer a glimpse of the mental and emotional states of the troops in the most remote reaches of the war, and their leaders' hopes that a "girl next door" would provide some solace. By 1968, the peak year of the program in Vietnam, the demand for donut dollies had outstripped the supply, and in an effort to meet military needs, the Red Cross launched special recruitment efforts aimed at college women in their junior and senior years.[55]

The number of soldiers stationed at each firebase varied, but some included several thousand military personnel, such as the 7,000 encamped at Phu Bai, a village outside Hue, the former imperial city located in the northern part of South Vietnam. Although the Phu Bai installation was near Hue, city authorities generally limited the number of U.S. military personnel in the city to seventy at a time, and they could visit the city during daylight hours only. For a period of time in the spring of 1966, Hue was placed entirely off limits. Even when it was open to U.S. military personnel, the seventy-person restriction meant that an individual soldier could go to Hue only once every hundred days. Therefore, "aside from regular movies and beer drinking there are practically no other opportunities for recreation," explained Lieutenant Colonel Richard McMahon of the Eighth Radio Research unit at Phu Bai. He described the "tedium and tensions of the daily routine" and emphasized that an SRAO team

---

[54] Memo from Jessica Hunter, Director of SRAO Vietnam, to Mary Louise Dowling, National Director of SRAO, August 9, 1966, NARA RG 200, Box 66.

[55] Memo from Mary Louise Dowling to Quinn Smith and Sue Behrens, "Assistance in Recruitment," Oct. 3, 1968, NARA RG 200, Box 66.

would "significantly contribute to the morale of several thousand American military men in the Phu Bai area." The men of the unit would gladly provide comfortable, private, secure accommodations for Red Cross women.[56]

In 1966, U.S. military personnel at Tan Son Nhut Airbase, a major processing center located about three miles north of Saigon, sought an SRAO unit to provide activities for troops processing into and out of Vietnam. Anywhere from 1,500 to 3,000 soldiers were at the "processing mill" for periods of one to four days. Personnel could not leave the processing depot, so they could not take advantage of entertainment on the base or in nearby Saigon. The area commander was "quite concerned" about troops with "much time on their hands with nothing to do and nowhere to go." There were neither room nor facilities to house women at Tan Son Nhut, so the commander suggested that SRAO workers live in Saigon. He had heard about the program in Korea, and he wanted to bring it to his men in Vietnam.[57]

Lieutenant Colonel James Hilmar and his men of the 3rd Brigade, 4th Infantry Division were stationed in a tiny village called Dau Tieng. In the winter of 1967 a tropical form of cabin fever descended on his men. The firebase was so far from the nearest U.S. military installation that it was difficult for the SRAO teams stationed there to make regular trips out to Dau Tieng. The women tried to visit about once a week, but arranging transportation was a recurring challenge, so Hilmar wrote to the Red Cross asking whether it would station an SRAO unit permanently at Dau Tieng for his soldiers. The brigade had already begun to prepare accommodations for the women, restoring an old French colonial house that featured "excellent facilities including a shower." Hilmar added that they would provide "all other personal conveniences required to support the girls."[58]

Some captains, colonels, and other military leaders sent letters to the Red Cross in praise of the SRAO workers they received. Colonel Charles Hayward of the 1st Brigade, 25th Infantry Division, thanked the Red Cross for "the outstanding support that the American Red Cross has provided" to his men. "An immeasurable morale booster for the soldiers in the field and those in the rear areas is the ever-presence of the

---

[56] Letter from Lieutenant Colonel Richard McMahon to Enrique Canas, Field Director, American Red Cross, April 6, 1966, NARA RG 200, Box 66.

[57] Memo from Quinn Smith to George Hand, "Request for SRAO, Tan Son Nhut, Army," March 16, 1966, NARA RG 200, Box 66.

[58] Letter from Lieutenant Colonel James Hilmar to Jessica Hunter, SRAO Director, Southeast Asia Headquarters, January 19, 1967, NARA RG 200, Box 66.

Red Cross girls from Cu Chi," Hayward wrote. "The 'Donut Dollies,' as they are often referred to, have spent many hours visiting the units of the 1st Brigade to provide entertainment and a relaxing diversion from a routine day. These girls are American in the true spirit. Their endless devotion to serving the soldier and pride in their accomplishments are in keeping with the highest traditions of the American Red Cross."[59]

Captain Jesse Pearce of the 4th Battalion, 9th Infantry, wrote to the Red Cross to acknowledge that "the frequent visits by the Red Cross girls has [*sic*] played a matchless role in raising the morale of our men."[60] Captain Gren Fleming of the 4th Battalion, 23rd Infantry, offered "sincere appreciation" on behalf of his men, "for services the Red Cross have performed for this unit." Fleming explained that the SRAO workers were "a great morale factor to the troops who are stationed in the base camp area and to the ones who are temporarily recuperating from combat operations. These girls give the men a chance to relax, enjoy themselves, and even smile in a place where these things are a rarity."[61]

The Defense Department and military leaders must have gauged the response to SRAO to be positive because officials approached the Red Cross about sending teams of donut dollies to Cambodia, where U.S. troops were deployed in an unpopular – and for a long time, secret – expansion of the Vietnam War. The request came on May 18, 1970, just two weeks after National Guard troops gunned down students on the campus of Kent State University who were protesting the U.S. invasion of Cambodia. Joseph Carniglia, Red Cross director of operations at the time, replied that the agreement between the Red Cross and the Defense Department approved SRAO teams in South Vietnam only. He also remarked that he was concerned about "the possible public relations and political implications of Red Cross girls being associated with this operation."[62] A visit from a team of donut dollies might have been nice for the troops involved in the Cambodia mission. Donut dolly Jeanne Christie believed that, for the most part, American soldiers appreciated the Red Cross women, sometimes just for their presence during tough moments.

[59] Letter from Colonel Charles Hayward to John F. Higgins, Director of Operations, American Red Cross, Apr. 17, 1969, NARA RG 200, Box 66.

[60] Letter from Captain Jesse Pearce to Commanding Officer, 1st Brigade, 25th Infantry Division, Apr. 15, 1969, NARA RG 200, Box 66.

[61] Letter from Captain Glen Fleming to Commanding Officer, 1st Brigade, Apr. 17, 1969, NARA RG 200, Box 66.

[62] Memo from Joseph Carniglia, Red Cross Director of Operations, to Robert Lewis, Red Cross Vice President, May 18, 1970, NARA RG 200, Box 66.

For many GIs, donut dollies had the intended effect. The image of the smiling, perky, young donut dolly recurs throughout military press coverage of SRAO programs and the women who ran them. Words such as "perky," "zesty," "affable," and "pretty" painted pictures of lovable, if slightly ditzy, young women who fit the description of a buddy better than that of a love interest. The articles generally expressed an appreciation for the SRAO workers. A squad leader told a reporter for the Army magazine *Uptight* that "I was at this grubby fire base waiting to go out again and the next thing I know, there were two girls standing there talking to me. You can imagine how good perfume smells in the boonies. I mean, you know, an American girl, it kind of makes the place a little more sane, if that makes any sense."[63]

SRAO workers discovered that ordinary acts of primping were some of the strongest reminders of home for GIs. Former donut dolly Rene Johnson happened to apply lipstick in view of some GIs, and they told her later that "they loved it because it was like being back home and seeing their mother or their girlfriend or their sister do it. It wasn't bright red, but that was the kind of thing I discovered they liked. Not lusted after, liked."[64] Other women defied the rule that hair could not touch their collar, and wore long hair down to the joy of men on base.[65] Still other donut dollies unleashed the power of perfume. When Eileen O'Neill and a few of her Red Cross colleagues tried to slip quietly into a movie theater in Da Nang, the scent of their perfume distracted the all-male audience. O'Neill also remarked that "they appreciated our looking like women. There were women military and of course they were stuck with the camouflage."[66] The article in *Uptight* described the donut dollies in their "perfume and lipstick, smiles, red crosses, and blue cotton dresses" who arrived to work with the 9th Infantry Division. Soldiers told the reporter for *Uptight* that "all the men enjoy the programs and look forward to a break from combat or work when two young girls walk in."

Journalistic exaggeration aside, not all GIs welcomed the feminine presence. The tensions associated with women in Vietnam revealed the gap between SRAO's goals and the ways in which soldiers perceived and experienced the presence of the donut dollies. Lieutenant Sileo described the feelings of some of his fellow GIs on the arrival of donut dollies at

---

[63] SP5 Tom P. Gable, "To Live, to Laugh, to Help Forget." *Uptight*, United States Army, Fall 1969, Jeanne Christie Collection, Box 1.

[64] Author's telephone interview with Rene Johnson.

[65] Author's telephone interview with Jeanne Christie.

[66] Author's telephone interview with Eileen O'Neill.

their bases. Some servicemen enjoyed the donut dollies' attempts "to add a zesty spark to life in the foxhole,"[67] and their "come-get-me energy, coy and flirtatious." As long as they remained "perky and fresh-faced, like a cheerleader," women were "good for morale."[68]

To other GIs, the props, the games, and the presence of women seemed out of place in the mess hall, recreation center, or dusty outdoor gathering place. Susan McLean found that the troops she worked with either loved or hated donut dollies. Those who loved them were protective of the women and had fun with the SRAO programs even if they seemed silly. For other servicemen, though, the presence of donut dollies did more harm than good for troop morale. They thought "we were teasing them, or we reminded them of home and they didn't want to think of home, or they would say that we were just there for the officers," McLean remembered.[69] Sometimes, the troops just did not know what to do when donut dollies arrived, Nancy Smoyer recalled. "Sometimes they were just stunned into silence by seeing us unexpectedly, or they'd try to flirt with us but they were so out of practice they could barely do it, or else their rough language would get in the way and they'd embarrass themselves."[70]

Dorris Heaston and other donut dollies who went to Vietnam after the Tet offensive noticed a much lower morale than those who went earlier; even though donut dollies were meant to be reminders of what the troops were fighting for, as the war dragged on, protecting the girl next door was no longer a sufficient justification. GIs stationed in the rear areas seemed to suffer from lower morale than did combat troops, Mary Robeck observed, as a result of boredom and a sense of uselessness in a war that had no purpose.[71] The steep decline in morale eventually affected the very women who were charged with lifting the spirits of the troops. Sent to Vietnam in 1971 as an SRAO assistant director, Nancy Calcese encountered donut dollies breaking rules regarding uniforms, makeup, and hair; she viewed the insolence as part of a larger rejection of authority that was occurring among the troops as well. Having been stationed in South Korea before going to Vietnam, Calcese had a point of comparison between the SRAO workers in her first tour, who were respectful and loyal to their managers, and Vietnam donut dollies, who

---

[67] Sileo, "She Could Be the Girl Next Door."
[68] Tim O'Brien, "Sweetheart of the Song Tra Bong," in *The Things They Carried* (New York: Penguin Books, 1990), 106.
[69] Author's telephone interview with Susan McLean.
[70] Appy, *Patriots*, 188.
[71] Author's telephone interview with Mary Robeck.

seemed to identify more with the troops than with the Red Cross.[72] Similar to the representations of Vietnamese women, the girl-next-door image masked underlying tensions that emerged from a closer look at the reality of life on the ground in Vietnam. The ideology might have posited an asexual femininity, but both the donut dollies and the soldiers were living in a world in which that fantasy no longer mirrored reality – if it ever had.

Just as tension existed between American women and men serving together in Vietnam, some SRAO volunteers sensed hostility from military women. Warner believed that nurses considered donut dollies and the work they did frivolous. Nurses viewed SRAO women as "sunshine girls, whereas nurses were doing painful work," Warner said.[73] Jennifer Young remarked on the differences between the work of nurses and that of the donut dollies. "They were mainly having to deal with the casualties and the wounded, whereas our work was mainly with the able-bodied," she noted. "So you couldn't have a more different take on what was going on. We were kind of like the girls next door, whereas they were, you know, they had a tough job."[74]

J. Holley Watts remembers a poem a military nurse wrote to express her feelings about Red Cross workers: "'Twitty, overage cheerleader in a baby-blue uniform that shouts shoot me. What the fuck are you doing in a war zone, sugar? If you can't start an IV, get out of my way. This was no shake and bake where little girls can help. We need nurses, they send Barbie dolls.'"[75] Jeanne Christie added, "they thought we were total airheads because they were so serious dealing with the wounded." When Christie was stationed in Nha Trang, the Red Cross moved donut dollies from billets in the base hospital to rooms in town. They were assigned to a neighborhood where many prostitutes lived, "which only reinforced the stereotype" of donut dollies as camp followers and contributed to resentment from military women, Christie said. Young believed military women liked them "if they got to know us as individuals," but "from a distance, personally, I think they thought we were ridiculous."[76] Having gotten to know some nurses, Rene Johnson noted "that nurses weren't all hard-nosed and they discovered that we weren't all silly little girls."

[72] Author's telephone interview with Nancy Calcese.
[73] Author's telephone interview with Susan McLean.
[74] Author's telephone interview with Jennifer Young.
[75] Author's telephone interview with J. Holley Watts.
[76] Author's telephone interview with Jennifer Young.

Johnson said the "silly little girls" comments always surprised her, considering that the Red Cross required SRAO members to have college degrees.[77]

Some nurses and WACs resented donut dollies because they got to have fun with the troops – playing games, singing songs, organizing parties – while nurses faced the wounded and the dead. Looking back at her time in Vietnam, Judy Davis, who worked at the 67th Evacuation Hospital in 1971, remembered that nurses were jealous of donut dollies. "They came in there all clean and looking good, and we were like all being hard worked and exhausted," she said. "We were vying for the attention. In that environment, that's what I think it was." Marj Graves recognized that donut dollies performed a needed service for U.S. troops even though she did not acknowledge their importance in 1971 when she was a nurse at the 24th Evacuation Hospital. "I think we had a tendency to look down a little bit," Graves said. "Here we thought we were the superheroes. [But] they had time to do some of the things we did not have time to do with the patients, and it was really unfortunate on our part to treat them with any less respect than what they deserved because they helped pass the time for a lot of our soldiers. Everybody had their role." Lola McGourty, also stationed at the 67th Evac, wondered why the Red Cross never created any programs to boost the morale of nurses. Rumors about donut dollies' sexuality circulated among military personnel, challenging the image of the chaste girl next door. Air Force flight nurse Linda Pugsley heard gossip that donut dollies were prostitutes, although she was never able to verify it beyond hearsay.[78]

Despite their cheery exteriors, SRAO workers had an emotionally draining and challenging job. "The smiling, airhead façade covered the serious nature of what was going on," Christie said.[79] "There were days that we lost friends, too," Christie said. "And you just learned that there was no room for [grieving] in your job," she continued. "Your job was '24–7.'"[80] Nancy Warner learned to shut part of herself down to cope with sorrow and maintain the demeanor her job required. A soldier she had befriended lost his legs and his hearing in battle, and she was "totally undone by it. I mean, I kept it together in the unit visiting him and all

---

[77] Author's telephone interview with Rene Johnson.
[78] Author's telephone interviews with Judy Davis, Marj Graves, Lola McGourty, and Linda Pugsley, October–November 2009, Hattiesburg, MS.
[79] Author's telephone interview with Jeanne Christie.
[80] Author's telephone interview Nancy Warner, June 2006, Madison, WI.

that stuff and walked out of there and burst into tears," she said. "The chaplain happened to be out there and found me, and I was a wreck." She considered quitting her job and returning home, fearing she would not be able to handle seeing more friends get wounded, or even die. She stayed, but she kept her guard up from then on, smiled and nodded, but did not get close to soldiers after that.[81]

Emily Strange stopped learning the names of the soldiers she met in Vietnam after her good friend, Michael, died in a helicopter accident. He had been one of her first friends in Vietnam, and they had bonded playing guitar on base together. Mourning was not in her job description. She was there to cheer up the troops with games and smiles, and that's what she did. "I didn't want to know names," Strange said. "That way, if somebody said 'Joe so-and-so got killed,' I had no face to put to it. I still do not remember names. There's guys on the Wall [Vietnam War Memorial]; I know them, but I don't have names to put to them."[82]

Lieutenant Sileo's article in *The Hurricane* told the story of Ann Spillane, an SRAO worker stationed at Lai Khe who offered to help a GI who wanted to send a doll to his daughter back home for her birthday. She went out in search of a doll, found one, and put it in the mail. When she went to find the GI to assure him that the doll would arrive in time for his daughter's birthday, she learned that he had been killed in action that day.[83] Sometimes, no matter how much donut dollies believed in their duty as morale boosters, the trauma of war overshadowed the intentions of the SRAO program. The symbolism of domestic sanctuary broke down in the wake of the donut dollies' experiences, which illustrated that "home" was not a sure place of escape.

Additionally, the jobs of a donut dolly were dangerous at times, and SRAO women worked in areas off limits to military women. The clubmobile runs went directly into battle zones to reach combat troops. By contrast, members of the Women's Army Corps were confined to Saigon or major military installations. "No one, not even the other women in Vietnam, realized what we were up to and where we went," Warner said. "In some areas, all we did was go out to the field, to the firebases and forward areas where the men were fighting. We felt tremendous loyalty and duty to get out there at every opportunity." The women believed that

[81] Ibid.
[82] Author's interview with Emily Strange, May 2002, Johnson Creek, WI.
[83] Ibid.

if combat soldiers had to deal with the mud, heat, and humidity, then they could handle it, too, Warner said.[84]

Often SRAO teams got caught in the middle of rocket and mortar attacks, although no donut dolly died in a combat-related incident. Patterson said she was surrounded by danger but never felt threatened, even though there were times her SRAO team narrowly escaped attack. "We were right out in the thick of things many times," she said. "The areas we visited were supposed to be secure areas according to the military brass, but I can remember one fire support base that we had visited one afternoon, and that night they were almost all killed in a mortar attack," she said. "Again, I guess we really didn't think about the possible dangers that we could be in."[85] Nancy Smoyer pointed out the visible contradiction between the donut dolly uniform and the troops' protective gear. "We wore baby blue seersucker dresses. The guys all around us had flak jackets, helmets, and weapons, and we were in our little blue dresses. The incongruity was amazing."[86] Unarmed because they were civilian women, yet deployed to combat zones to do the women's work of boosting troop morale, donut dollies were put in harm's way even though they were supposed to be protected. Donut dollies may have reported for duty with rosy cheeks and red lipstick, but the thick, wet heat of Vietnam was like a washcloth, and the rotors of helicopters kicked up tornadoes of dust that settled where blush had been.

Aware of the contradictions in their own positions in Vietnam, some donut dollies sympathized with Vietnamese women and the role they played in the war's culture. For Nancy Warner, serving in Vietnam opened her eyes to what the war did to the Vietnamese. "We made whores out of their women and emasculated their men and made beggars out of their children. That was how I felt about what this war had done for the Vietnamese people. Nothing good."[87] Kathleen Huckabay also doubted that the U.S. presence did any tangible good for the Vietnamese, and she pitied the Vietnamese women who were rumored to have had plastic surgery and breast implants in hopes of making themselves more appealing to American men.[88] Seeing the impact of the war on the Vietnamese, Mary Robeck joined an outreach program run by Baptist missionaries.

---

[84] Author's telephone interview with Nancy Warner.
[85] Author's telephone interview with Dorothy Patterson.
[86] Appy, *Patriots*, 188.
[87] Author's telephone interview with Nancy Warner.
[88] Author's telephone interview with Kathleen Huckabay.

She formed a choir for local children and visited an orphanage on Sundays, hoping that her actions would help the GIs with whom she worked to see the Vietnamese as people. Eileen O'Neill believed the Vietnamese women who did the laundry for her SRAO team liked working for them because "they didn't have to put up with any harassment from the GIs."[89] Jennifer Young remarked that "I think those poor women were constantly having to tell the GIs no, I'm not a boom-boom girl."[90]

"Nonsexual Symbols of Purity and Goodness"

The image of purity that donut dollies were supposed to embody conflicted with the realities of sexual behavior in Vietnam; it also contradicted changing realities on the home front, where women, and some men, had begun to challenge Cold War notions of domesticity. In theory, donut dollies were the opposite of Vietnamese prostitutes who, according to myth, mixed sex and violence by spreading disease and maiming U.S. GIs who bought their services. According to this line of thinking, whereas the destructive sexuality of the Vietnamese female could literally castrate American power, the virtuous, chaste femininity of the donut dollies reinforced American masculine strength. SRAO was not enough of a distraction to prevent servicemen seeking out prostitutes, however, and donut dollies knew about places such as Sin City near U.S. military installations. Some recognized a rule, both written and unwritten, ordering them to exhibit an alternative, "wholesome" femininity to distract U.S. servicemen from the Vietnamese women who worked at places such as Sin City.[91]

In Ann Laura Stoler's words, American women were to "conserve the fitness" of U.S. servicemen by preventing them from falling under the degenerative spell of Vietnamese women. However, moral regulations were not well enforced. As far as Dorothy Patterson could tell, any soldier who could arrange transportation and a pass to leave the base could go there without disciplinary consequences. She heard Sin City called "Dodge City" as well, a reference to the Kansas town on the old Santa Fe Trail whose dance halls and saloons were popular among buffalo hunters, railroad workers, and soldiers from nearby Fort Dodge.

---

[89] Author's telephone interviews with Eileen O'Neill and Mary Robeck.
[90] Author's telephone interview with Jennifer Young.
[91] Based on author's interviews with donut dollies, including Dorothy Patterson and Nancy Warner.

Like Patterson, Dorris Heaston experienced the anger of U.S. service-men when she and another donut dolly arrived at a bar in Sin City, the entertainment district in An Khe. The saloon reminded Heaston of a scene out of the Old West, its parlor featuring scantily clad Vietnamese women beckoning to potential customers. "You knew there were back rooms, and you knew what was going on," Heaston said. "We basically were told 'get the hell out of here' by American troops with rank."[92] The girl next door was not meant to see an American soldier slumming with a Vietnamese prostitute, but sex with local women has been a regular part of wartime culture throughout history. It became a problem, though, in the context of the images and ideas that shaped American intervention in Vietnam.

Joining the SRAO team at An Khe in October 1969, Nancy Warner soon learned about Sin City. "Much like *M*A*S*H*, every base had its vice zones outside," she said, adding that while the U.S. military did not approve of them officially, "the goings-on were often ignored." In addition to Sin City, Warner heard about bars and brothels "enticing GIs to spend their money" along the roads Army truck convoys traveled. She also heard tales of "Coke" girls – Vietnamese women who took coolers of soda to areas where U.S. troops were on patrol and offered to sell the soda. They offered "other things as well," Warner said. Troops often suspected the women of packing their coolers with hand grenades in addition to cans of Coca-Cola, so they usually forced the women to leave.[93]

J. Holley Watts, who also served at An Khe, believed that the military simply chose not to acknowledge its connection to Sin City, by pretending it was not "really" there; the Vietnamese women who worked there were not "officially" under the care of Army doctors. But she maintains that U.S. military doctors performed examinations and treated venereal disease among Vietnamese women who worked in Sin City. She described Sin City as a collection of "tin roofed shacks – not attractive, but the women were beautiful." Watts also was stationed in Da Nang; she said there was a place called "Dog Patch" there that was similar to Sin City. She said she never went to either place because of the Red Cross's "strict orders against impropriety." If it appeared that a donut dolly had placed herself into a sexually compromising position, the Red Cross would send her home, Watts said.[94]

---

[92] Author's telephone interview with Dorris Heaston, Oct. 2009, Hattiesburg, MS.
[93] Author's e-mail correspondence with Nancy Warner.
[94] Author's telephone interview with J. Holley Watts, July 2007, Madison, WI.

For six months, Patterson was stationed at Cam Ranh Bay, which had a place similar to Sin City. Once a week, U.S. military authorities closed the complex "so that the Vietnamese girls could have medical exams and make sure that they were 'clean,'" she said. She knew that U.S. military doctors performed the exams on the women at Cam Ranh, and she suspected they also did so at An Khe. Although she could not say that the military brass approved of complexes like Sin City per se, she guessed that they considered them places of "relaxation and enjoyment for the troops." Stationed at Cam Ranh Bay three years after Patterson, Marj Dutilly knew of a place called "Meat Market," which, as she remembered it, the Army regulated to ensure that the prostitutes available to servicemen were free of venereal diseases. It seemed that the Army took a "boys will be boys" attitude toward sex in Vietnam, Dutilly said. "If the military wanted their troops to be battle-ready, and they didn't want them all in the clinic with VD and stuff, then they were going to police that," she added. "That sent a message right there that well, you know, this is going to be happening so just look out."[95]

In contrast to military regulation of areas such as Sin City and Meat Market, donut dollies were instructed not to touch the soldiers with whom they worked; dating enlisted men was frowned on, even though an unspoken assumption among some GIs and officers was that SRAO women were sexually available to officers.[96] Jeanne Christie noted that touching a GI "could start a riot. They'd kill each other. We went in pairs, we were two girls and all these guys."[97] Despite Red Cross efforts to maintain the girl-next-door image, some military men considered donut dollies to be camp followers, available to turn tricks like Vietnamese prostitutes and distract enlisted men from their combat duties.

In his article on SRAO in *The Hurricane*, Lieutenant Tom Sileo wrote that some GIs frowned on donut dollies as "man-hunting" in a place where women did not belong.[98] Jeanne Christie described the situation from a donut dolly's perspective. "You're just a sex object, for one thing. You're over there to tease the boys or to service them. Service them or distract them," she said. "It was not uncommon to have a GI come up and ask you how much you charge. Because they had been told that that's what we did." A few times during programs Linda Wilson facilitated for

[95] Author's e-mail correspondence with Dorothy Patterson, July 2007; author's telephone interview with Marj Dutilly.

[96] J. Holley Watts, *Who Knew? Reflections on Vietnam*, published by J. Holley Watts, 2004, 14, 35.

[97] Author's telephone interview with Jeanne Christie.

[98] Sileo, "She Could Be the Girl Next Door."

troops, men yelled out "sixty-five dollars," referring to the gossip that donut dollies charged sixty-five dollars for sex. According to Wilson, hazardous duty pay was sixty-five dollars per month, which possibly suggested GI concerns about contracting venereal disease from women they considered to be loose. Other donut dollies have corroborated this rumor. "The rumor was that for sixty-five dollars combat pay you could bed a donut," Nancy Warner said. "It became a rumor that fostered some thoughts that we might be there making lots of money selling sexual favors."

Some officers tried to interfere with donut dollies' programs, telling them that the GIs were working out in the field or otherwise unavailable, whereas others refused to allow the Red Cross women to set up their activities.[99] These officers saw in donut dollies not nonsexual caretakers, but rather sparks that could ignite the explosive sexual tension that was thick in the air. Warner mused that "if the Red Cross had sent camp followers, the guys might've been a lot happier than playing games with two girls they weren't gonna have any chance of getting close to. Maybe a thousand camp followers would've done a better morale building job."[100] Veteran Jim Mifflin remarked that, even though he longed for "round-eye women" – the nickname GIs gave American women, denoting the shape of their eyes compared with those of Vietnamese women – it never occurred to him to make a pass at an SRAO volunteer or any other American woman he saw in Vietnam. "They were around, but to me they were kind of like off limits," he said. "Maybe I didn't think I could get to first base with those women. Too much competition, I don't know. It was easier, and it was less threatening, just to go with the hookers, to be honest with you."[101] The donut dollies' lives were much more complex than the images assigned to them suggested, and the gap between image and reality reflects the fundamental instability of the gendered ideology intended to buttress the U.S. war effort.

Servicemen's assumptions about donut dollies' reasons for being in Vietnam spoke to the notion that American women did not belong in the war zones of Southeast Asia. Nancy Warner met soldiers who were shocked that she had chosen to come to the war. "I would say ninety-nine percent of them were stunned that we were there, overwhelmed by the fact that we had volunteered to be there," Warner said. "They thought

---

99   Author's telephone interview with Jeanne Christie.
100 Author's telephone interview with Nancy Warner.
101 Author's telephone interview with Jim Mifflin.

that was the craziest thing they'd ever heard. When we told them that we had a curfew and if we broke the curfew that they'd send us home, they'd say, 'you ain't broken the curfew yet?' In their minds, it's like, 'what are you waiting for?'" Warner also met a few soldiers who thought she should be back home protesting against the war. "I had one guy... that became a dear friend who said to me, 'what the fuck are you doing here? Why aren't you back home in the states marching and getting us the hell out of here?' Like his feeling was, our support was support for the war effort and in his opinion no one should in any way, however great or small, do that."[102]

Although some military leaders supported the work of SRAO, Nancy Warner suspected that they viewed donut dollies as "very incidental to the war effort." The brass "would've been happy to just have us hang around and go to general's mess on Saturday night all dressed up," Warner said. Even those who tried to prevent the women from doing their jobs would "make us show up for these stupid dinner parties and stuff that they would have just so they could have some girl on their arm, you know, the female company thing and perfume in the room. That kind of stuff used to make me mad. I hated going to general's mess."[103] Jennifer Young, a donut dolly who served in Vietnam in the late 1960s, noticed a paradox in military attitudes toward Red Cross women:

I think they appreciated the femininity because they would say, "Oh you guys are like a breath of fresh air," "Ooh you smell good, you look nice." And that was our job... we wanted that, and yet at the same time there were probably some who thought we were teasers. Like, "What are they doing? We're at war here and they're coming out smelling like Tabu [perfume].... But the paradox was, as much as the guys... were very chivalrous, very nice, some of them I'm sure would say to this day that we were there to be call girls for the officers particularly. And that even though we worked in the centers and even though we flew in the aircraft and went out, at night we were making a lot of money and were setting our retirement plans, our retirement nest eggs up. Which blew me away... it was the last thing I expected because it wasn't true.[104]

Rene Johnson heard that "there were a lot of American soldiers that all knew somebody who knew somebody who knew somebody who knew somebody who screwed a donut dolly. You never knew a guy who'd actually done it, but the talk went around." In light of these perceptions,

[102] Author's telephone interview with Nancy Warner.
[103] Ibid.
[104] Author's telephone interview with Jennifer Young.

Marj Dutilly saw her job as a contradiction. "We were there to help the troops, and instead we were perceived by a whole lot of them as there to provide a [sexual] service," she said.[105]

Rumors about donut dollies' motives combined with the sexually charged atmosphere in Vietnam to create a strange brew that left some SRAO volunteers concerned about their safety, which sometimes seemed to be doubly threatened. Although they were noncombatants, they risked being caught in the crossfire of combat simply by being in Vietnam. In addition, they stood at a dangerous intersection of gender, sex, and violence, at which assumptions about appropriate gender roles and sexual behavior disintegrated in a heated war zone that had its own conventions dictating women's purposes and acceptable sexual expression. Donut dollies went to Vietnam to represent the girl next door, a wholesome symbol of Americana, but in the minds of some troops, the presence of women made sense only in sexual terms. When it became clear that the women were to be seen but not touched, sexual tension sometimes transformed into aggression. Dorris Heaston noted that terms such as "date rape" were not part of the American lexicon in the 1960s, so even if threats of sexual assault loomed in Vietnam, donut dollies did not have the words to articulate what it was that they feared.[106]

On rare occasions, that tension led to violence. Such was the case in the murder of donut dolly Virginia Kirsch, a twenty-one-year-old Ohio native, in August 1970. Early in the morning on August 17, 1970, screams awakened the donut dollies stationed at Cu Chi with the 25th Infantry Division. Witnesses saw a man run from Kirsch's bedroom; when they looked in on her, they found her stabbed to death in her bed. She had been in Vietnam only about two weeks when she was murdered. The killer later was identified as Gregory Kozlowski, a nineteen-year-old Milwaukee resident who was stationed in Vietnam with the 25th Infantry's artillery battalion.[107] Susan McLean arrived at her post in An Khe three days before Kirsch was murdered, and although it was shocking to learn that Kirsch had been killed by a fellow American, McLean did not process the incident at the time. "We were so busy and so out of our element, and it was such a shock just to be there that this was just piling onto the other shocks, and nothing was really being talked about," McLean said.

---

[105] Author's telephone interviews with Rene Johnson and Marj Dutilly.
[106] Author's telephone interview with Dorris Heaston.
[107] "Man admits slaying in Vietnam," *Milwaukee Sentinel*, Sept. 27, 1972.

She later came to believe that internalizing death and projecting the upbeat donut dolly persona were the ways she and other SRAO workers handled the daily loss of life around them in Vietnam.[108]

After Kirsch's death, the Red Cross temporarily closed its operations at Cu Chi and transferred the donut dollies to other locations. The incident raised concerns among Red Cross staff about safety in Vietnam and opened discussions about how to best protect donut dollies stationed throughout the country. A month after the killing, the Red Cross launched an investigation into security at donut dollies' living quarters, replacing or adding locks to windows and doors throughout the billets.[109] Some military personnel refused to cooperate with Red Cross efforts, believing the security concerns to be overblown. In January 1971, Mary Louise Dowling, national director of SRAO, wrote a letter to Robert Lewis at the Red Cross national headquarters regarding security at the Red Cross compound in Da Nang, stating that "the concerns of our staff regarding their security did not seem paramount" to the military's various issues. Despite the lack of support, Dowling called on the Red Cross to continue its examination of SRAO billet security and take measures to enhance safety.[110]

Although Kirsch was the only donut dolly murdered in Vietnam, her story illustrates the risk involved. When Marj Dutilly arrived in Da Nang in August 1971 for her tour of duty with SRAO, she noticed the new locks on all the doors in the Red Cross living quarters. She soon learned of the murder of Virginia Kirsch, and it set the tone for her entire tour. "It made me realize what the military really thought of us. We're just a bother to the command. If I'm gonna be safe, it's gonna be up to me to keep myself safe, even though we'd been told we'd be protected," Dutilly said. She believed that both GIs and the brass assumed that American women who chose to go to Vietnam were asking for trouble because they were invading a man's world and thus deserved what they got. At Ben Hoa, another place where she was stationed, the Quonset huts where the donut dollies lived were surrounded by barbed wire because, she was told, a serviceman had broken in and assaulted a donut dolly.[111]

---

[108] Author's telephone interview with Susan McLean.
[109] Memorandum to Harry L. McCullohs, Jr., Director of Operations, Southeast Asia, September 30, 1970. SRAO Quarterly Report, July, August, September 1970. NARA RG 200, Box 76.
[110] Memo from Mary Louis Dowling to Robert C. Lewis, January 5, 1971. NARA RG 200, Box 76.
[111] Author's telephone interview with Marj Dutilly.

Dorris Heaston and Linda Wilson heard rumors of donut dollies being raped by U.S. servicemen, and Wilson said that one of the main reasons donut dollies always traveled at least in pairs was that they were more vulnerable when alone. Mary Robeck and her fellow donut dollies obeyed the Red Cross curfew to protect their reputations and deflect the accusations that the only reason an American woman would come to the war zone in Vietnam was for sex, a belief that could justify sexual harassment or assault. As their time in the country progressed, Dutilly and other SRAO workers found servicemen they could trust and relied on them for security. For the most part, donut dollies found that GIs were not dangerous; in fact, they tended to be protective and respectful of SRAO women. Dutilly rarely heard an enlisted man so much as swear in the presence of donut dollies. "They were so careful that these were American girls and 'we're going to treat them nice,' and that's how the average grunt treated us," she said.[112] Rumors and assumptions were more the norm than real assaults, but they bred fears that challenged the purpose of SRAO.

Race and SRAO

Just as the SRAO presence in Vietnam reflected the contradictions in America's attitudes toward gender, racial tensions growing out of the civil rights and Black Power movements affected donut dollies' experiences and shaped their symbolic meaning. The vast majority of American women who joined the SRAO program were white. As Rene Johnson remarked, "We were about as WASP-y as you can get."[113] It was not until 1967 that the Red Cross sent an African American donut dolly to Vietnam. Barbara Lynn, a graduate of Bennett College in Greensboro, North Carolina, and a former Peace Corps volunteer, arrived at Cam Ranh Bay in July 1967. "As soon as I had arrived, the word spread like wild fire that there was a 'soul sister' at the Red Cross Recreation Center," Lynn told a reporter from *Ebony*, in language echoing the ideology of the girl next door. "Many fellows told me that it made them feel good to know that they had someone there to remind them of home. The white girls at the center were nice, they said, but seeing a 'sister' when you came back from the rice paddies was something else."[114]

[112] Author's telephone interviews with Marj Dutilly, Dorris Heaston, Mary Robeck, and Linda Wilson.
[113] Author's telephone interview with Rene Johnson.
[114] Barbara Lynn, "Good Samaritan in Vietnam," *Ebony*, Oct. 1968, 179.

A fellow Peace Corps volunteer had told Lynn about SRAO, and to her
it sounded like a chance to travel, serve her country, and learn firsthand
about the Vietnam War. Lynn's father had served in World War II, and
he supported her desire to join SRAO. Her grandmother also encouraged
her, viewing it as an opportunity that had not been available to African
American women when she was young. In Vietnam, Lynn was a unit
director, managing about eight donut dollies and acting as the liaison
between the Red Cross and the platoons her unit served. Black GIs she
met in Vietnam told her that they "thought they had been forgotten, that
the women back home didn't care for them or maybe were not being
invited to come over" to Vietnam. Although donut dollies worked with
all GIs regardless of race, African American soldiers sought Lynn out for
companionship.[115]

Some officers were aware of the disjunction between the overwhelmingly white SRAO and the composition of their troops. In August 1968,
Major General Charles Stone, commander of the 4th Infantry Division
stationed in the Central Highlands, wrote a letter to Quinn Smith, director
of the SRAO program in Vietnam, asking for an African American donut
dolly. Stone told Smith that African American troops made up nearly 14
percent of his division, and he thought those men would be more likely
to participate in SRAO programs if African American women were there.
Stone assured Smith that the white donut dollies did not discriminate
against black soldiers, but he noticed that the black servicemen often
seemed reluctant to participate in the SRAO activities. He thought that
black women would make them feel more comfortable taking part in the
games and entertainment.[116]

The experiences of white donut dollies with black servicemen varied
from friendship to hostility. J. Holley Watts experienced strong camaraderie with the Elegant Lads, an a cappella ensemble of African American Air Force servicemen that performed at every variety show her
SRAO team organized.[117] Skin color did not prevent one black GI from
approaching Dorris Heaston, who had short, dark hair, and telling her
that she reminded him of his aunt. It made Heaston feel like she truly was
a "touch of home" to all servicemen regardless of race. Some donut dollies
got caught in racial animosities that developed among troops or because

---

[115] Lynn, 182.
[116] Letter from Major General Charles Stone, Commander of the 4th Infantry Division to
Quinn Smith, SRAO director in Vietnam, Aug. 7, 1968. NARA RG 200, Box 66.
[117] Author's telephone Interview with J. Holley Watts.

of unofficial policies enacted by authorities. At the Red Cross recreation center in An Khe, Dorothy Patterson recalled black GIs, dismissive of the music donut dollies played at the center, coming in with their own tape players "playing really, really loud music, drowning out our music, and then the white guys were starting to complain." On at least one occasion, she said, military police had to break up fights between black and white troops. In Qui Nhon in the late 1960s, Kathleen Huckabay met white servicemen who got angry if the donut dollies, all of whom were white during her time there, sat down to eat with black troops. Because of that racial tension, Huckabay did not believe that she represented a touch of home to the black GIs. After Marj Dutilly began jogging with some African American servicemen, her Red Cross field director told her to stop because it was inappropriate for her to be seen with black men outside her official SRAO work. Age-old taboos about sexual contact between black men and white women found new expression in Vietnam, highlighting the limits of the girl next door as morale booster image.[118]

Nancy Warner saw a difference in race relations between troops in the field and GIs working various jobs in the rear. Combat troops looked out for each other, and the survival and protective instincts trumped racial differences, she said. But hostilities simmered in the rear, "where the guys had way too much time on their hands." Soldiers in the rear worked in supply and support units, and at times boredom turned to irritation on the part of white GIs who were wary of black servicemen wearing their hair in Afros and exchanging a handshake known as the dap. The recreation center at which Warner's SRAO team at Da Nang worked featured a beer garden because it also served as an in-country R&R spot, and she added that alcohol likely fueled tensions. Out at the firebases, troops were focused primarily on the fighting at hand.[119]

While stationed at Camp Baxter from September 1970 through July 1971, Rene Johnson noticed that racial tensions were more complex than black–white troubles. She observed conflict between African American and Chicano servicemen in the transportation corps at the rear. She believed that many of them had come into the military as part of Project 100,000, a Defense Department program established in 1966 that lowered admissions standards for draftees and enlistees in to increase manpower in the armed services. During a race riot on base, someone threw a hand grenade into the recreation center, and as a result of repeated racial

---

[118] Author's telephone interview with Dorothy Patterson.
[119] Author's telephone interview with Nancy Warner.

strife among GIs, donut dollies were confined to their living quarters after dark.[120] Sent to Vietnam to be morale boosters for troops, donut dollies observed racial tensions among U.S. servicemen that SRAO games and activities could not quell.

Red Cross officials, working to address these racial issues, encountered problems tied to the changing conditions on the home front, especially after the assassination of Martin Luther King, Jr., on April 4, 1968, which sparked a sharp increase in racial tensions among troops. In the summer of 1968, Lieutenant General James Lampert, the deputy assistant of the Manpower Reserve Affairs division of the Defense Department, visited U.S. military installations in Vietnam to get a sense for the morale and welfare of the troops. When he met with John Gordon, the director of operations for the Red Cross Southeast Asia division, he asked how many African American women worked in the SRAO program. One, Gordon told Lampert, emphasizing that the Red Cross had launched recruitment campaigns aimed at attracting more black women to sign up for tours in Vietnam. When Barbara Lynn returned home from her tour of duty, the Red Cross made her a recruiting specialist focused on African American women and pitched stories to various media outlets, especially African American publications such as *Ebony*.[121]

Red Cross recruiters contacted black colleges, the National Council of Negro Women, the Urban League, and African American employment agencies. The Red Cross also allowed SRAO units to exceed their quotas of women stationed in Vietnam if an African American applicant needed a placement.[122] Despite these efforts, by August 1968 only 1 of the 113 SRAO women stationed in Vietnam was African American.[123] "We are very concerned about the lack of Negro staff in this particular Red Cross program," Smith wrote to Stone. "Unfortunately, there have always been difficulties in recruiting young Negro women for service in the SRAO program, and these difficulties have been unusually severe in recruitment for Vietnam. Even the most concerted efforts to attract the qualified

[120] Author's telephone interview with Rene Johnson.
[121] Letter from John Gordon, Director of Operations, Southeast Asia Area Headquarters, American Red Cross, to Robert Lewis, Vice President, American Red Cross, July 3, 1968, NARA RG 200, Box 66.
[122] Memo from Robert C. Lewis of John F. Higgins, July 31, 1968, NARA RG 200, Box 66.
[123] Letter from Quinn Smith, SRAO Director in Vietnam, to Major General Charles Stone, Commander of the 4th Infantry Division, Aug. 15, 1968. NARA RG 200, Box 66.

young Negro woman have met with only minimal success."[124] By the end of December, the situation was not much better.[125] Pondering the difficulty recruiting black women for SRAO, Robert C. Lewis, a Red Cross vice president, observed that "it is interesting to note that SRAO has had an integrated staff from its very beginnings, but it has been far more difficult to obtain recruits from young Negro college graduates in the last five years because there are so many other opportunities now being made known to them."[126]

Although the Red Cross justified its recruitment difficulties as a byproduct of the civil rights movement's success, increasing black opposition to the Vietnam War probably was a more important factor. As Gerald Gill has demonstrated, black women had criticized U.S. intervention in Vietnam as early as 1964. Some, including Coretta Scott King and veteran civil rights activist Diane Nash, appealed to a maternal instinct to protect children from combat and to resist foreign policy maneuvers that caused wars.[127] Nash, who traveled to Hanoi along with three other American women and met with members of the North Vietnamese government, including Ho Chi Minh, in December 1966, explained that a photograph of a Vietnamese woman holding a wounded or dead child inspired her to go to Vietnam. "I saw myself in this mother's place, and the more I thought about it, the more determined I was to find out, once and for all, if such pictures are only propaganda," said Nash, herself a mother. "The death and destruction I witnessed was [sic] far worse than any picture could communicate."[128]

Writing an account of her trip for the magazine *Freedomways*, Nash recounted her meetings with Vietnamese mothers who had lost children due to American bombing raids on Hanoi. She told the story of a woman, eight months pregnant, whose child was blown out of her body during a bombing. Her body and that of her unborn baby were "recovered some

---

[124] Letter from Quinn Smith, SRAO Director in Vietnam, to Major General Charles Stone, Commander of the 4th Infantry Division, Box 66.

[125] Letter from Mary Louise Dowling, National Director of SRAO, to Quinn Smith, SRAO Director in Vietnam, December 31, 1968, NARA RG 200, Box 66.

[126] Memo from Robert C. Lewis of John F. Higgins, July 31, 1968, NARA RG 200, Box 66.

[127] Gerald Gill, "From Maternal Pacifism to Revolutionary Solidarity: African-American Women's Opposition to the Vietnam War," in *Sights on the Sixties*, ed. Barbara L. Tischler (New Brunswick, NJ: Rutgers University Press, 1992), 177–78.

[128] "1st Negro Woman to Visit Ho in Hanoi Tells Why America Cannot Win in Asia," *Muhammad Speaks*, February 10, 1967, 7–9.

distance apart from each other.[129] In an article in the Nation of Islam newspaper, *Muhammad Speaks*, Nash described seeing the remains of houses, churches, and schools that had been destroyed by U.S. bombs. Calling on African Americans to oppose the war, Nash stated that "the people of Vietnam identify and sympathize with the struggle of black people in America," and that it was time for African Americans to "realize that the powerful U.S. military machine is murdering friends of black people. And it is time Negro youths decide whether or not they want to help murder other non-white people."[130] Some African American women denounced the war as a waste of black men's lives, and others considered it an imperialistic act of aggression by white America against people of color.[131] It seems likely that the opposition of prominent black women to the war influenced younger black women who might otherwise have considered joining SRAO.

In January 1971, in hopes of boosting recruitment for the year, the Red Cross enacted a quota setting aside four positions in the summer recruiting drive for black women.[132] Red Cross public relations also continued its press campaign, preparing articles profiling African American SRAO workers such as Vivian Hayes, a graduate of North Carolina A&T University. When she arrived at Camp Eagle, where the 101st Airborne division was stationed, Hayes made it a point to work with African American GIs. "I think it's only natural," she said. "I'm going to say hello and visit with them especially because I think they often feel sort of left out." The only black member of SRAO in Vietnam at the time, Hayes believed the program would be limited in its usefulness to black soldiers until it sent more black women to Vietnam. "The men want to see more black girls over here," Hayes said. "If I were talking to a Sister, trying to persuade her to come over here, I would say, 'You've got Brothers over here who need your help. They need to know we care.'"[133] Still, during the year that Nancy Calcese served as an SRAO assistant director in

[129] Diane Nash, "Journey to North Vietnam," *Freedomways*, Second Quarter, 1967, 118–28.
[130] "1st Negro Woman to Visit Ho in Hanoi Tells Why America Cannot Win in Asia," *Muhammad Speaks*, February 10, 1967, 7–9.
[131] Gill, 178.
[132] Memo from Mary Louise Dowling to George Hand, "SRAO Recruitment for 1971," January 25, 1971, NARA RG 200, Box 66.
[133] "Vivian Hayes is a Red Cross Clubmobile Girl in Vietnam," Red Cross Press Release, January 1971, NARA RG 200, Box 66.

Vietnam, beginning in May 1971, only three of the sixty-five donut dollies she oversaw were black.[134]

Because so few African American donut dollies served in Vietnam, those who did sometimes found that the attention from black GIs could be overwhelming. Shirley Hines, who had been serving with the Red Cross in South Korea, was transferred to Vietnam in 1971 as part of the effort to address the shortage of black donut dollies there. The youngest of thirteen children and the only girl, Hines grew up in Fort Pierce, Florida, in a military family. Similar to many other donut dollies, Hines saw the SRAO program as an opportunity to travel; at the time, she was more concerned with helping the servicemen in Vietnam than with the politics of the war. She went to Vietnam when she was twenty-two and was stationed in Chu Lai, Cam Ranh Bay, and Ben Hoa.

Although she was brought in on behalf of black servicemen, she found herself remaining emotionally distant to manage the attention. Black GIs treated her very well and were protective, but they constantly wanted a piece of her time, her listening ear, or a date. There were so few African American donut dollies in Vietnam that a GI once told Hines that he knew of another "sister" in-country. He showed her a picture of the donut dolly, but it was a picture of Hines. As time went on, Hines discovered that bonding with troops was not always just about race. Fellow Floridians, white as well as black, enjoyed talking with her about home. Hines connected with older servicemen, regardless of race, because they reminded her of her brothers. African American GIs confided in her about racial tensions and discrimination, but Hines did not experience any hostilities personally. She kept her guard up, though. "When you go into a place where you are the only black person, you never know whether people are going to be nice to you or what," Hines said. "You never know what is in store for you."[135]

Failed efforts by the Red Cross to recruit African American women point to the contradiction between the donut dolly's theoretical symbolic function as representative of a unified America – that which must be protected – and the reality that that image was under increasing stress at home. Vivian Hayes' statement that she would encourage other black women to join SRAO because black servicemen needed them reveals a sense of responsibility regardless of her opinion of the Vietnam War.

---

[134] Author's telephone interview with Nancy Calcese, October 2009, Hattiesburg, MS.
[135] Author's telephone interview with Shirley Hines, November 2009, Hattiesburg, MS.

The United States went to Vietnam in the name of freedom and democracy, but on the home front, African Americans and other minorities, barred from the American dream, increasingly agitated for greater political, economic, and social power. The SRAO program reflected the realities of a divided America, and through it, the tensions and problems of "home" were exported to Vietnam. In a context in which a young woman embodied "a bit of America in Vietnam," the absence of black donut dollies in Vietnam enforced the stereotype of white suburbia as the embodiment of the American Dream. The "girl next door" was a symbol of that fantasy. As Black Power, youth movements, and women's liberation assailed American normalcy, the Defense Department continued to view the donut dollies as symbols of a home that no longer existed.

"Round eyes" and Pretty Smiles in the Combat Zone

As the U.S. armed forces phased out their troop presence in Vietnam, the Red Cross began to send its SRAO teams home, with the last donut dollies leaving in May 1972. For some of the soldiers, the women had been integral parts of the war. By doing their jobs, the donut dollies provided some comfort, a respite from the terrifying bursts of combat and the droning stretches in between. Donut dollies symbolized one of the ways in which Americans sought to enforce gender stereotypes, made all the more pronounced under the pressure of the sexual tension that marked the war zone in Vietnam. The tensions, contradictions, and instabilities in that ideal, however, were exported to Vietnam along with SRAO women. On the battlefront where U.S. troops fought to defend an American way of life symbolized by the Cold War domestic ideal, the experiences of donut dollies and the soldiers they encountered demonstrated the failure of the ideal.

3

"We Weren't Called Soldiers, We Were Called Ladies"

WACs and Nurses in Vietnam

During her tour of duty as an Air Force flight nurse, Linda Pugsley saw the carnage of war up close. Death was not always the worst part of it – sometimes a severely wounded soldier drove home hard the reality of what the war did to those who fought in it. On one of her runs, she treated a young serviceman who had suffered a massive abdominal injury and had lost his testicles, a leg, an arm, and his sight. As she prepared patients to be evacuated from Vietnam, he called her over and asked her whether she thought his girlfriend would still love him. She took his remaining hand and said reassuringly, "Oh sure, honey. You're gonna go home a hero." It might have been a lie, but in that moment, it was what he needed to hear. "To the wounded, we were like angels," Pugsley said.[1] Having a female nurse to talk to allowed servicemen to be emotional in ways they could not be with their comrades. "They have to be strong for their buddies. You don't show a lot of emotion around your buddies," said Paula Quindlen, an Army nurse who served at the 27th Surgical Hospital in Chu Lai, adding that many wounded men, especially amputees, sought a woman's reassurance as they wondered whether their girlfriends would reject them because of their injuries.[2] Seen as confidantes, nurses bore the weight of wounded soldiers' emotions, revealing once again the emotionally exhausting nature of women's work as defined by the ideology of domesticity.

Lynda Van Devanter, the Army nurse whose memoir *Home Before Morning* was one of the first works to bring attention to American

---

[1] Author's telephone interview with Linda Pugsley, November 2009, Hattiesburg, MS.
[2] Author's telephone interview with Paula Quindlen, November 2009, Hattiesburg, MS.

women's Vietnam experiences, explained in a 1980 interview that whereas men of her generation were taught stoicism, women were taught to be emotionally expressive. In Vietnam, however, "women were forced to negate these emotions in order to attend to the higher priority tasks at hand." Although nurses were expected to present an image of womanhood reflecting Cold War domesticity, "staying feminine became an impossible task," Van Devanter said. "There's a toughness you take on. It's thought of as a masculine, macho characteristic. It's not masculine, but an attitude of strength and trying to survive."[3]

In the wounds of the soldiers they cared for, nurses were exposed to combat every day. Depending on where they were stationed and what was going on in the war, some nurses saw the most gruesome consequences of battle on a regular basis throughout their tours of duty. Even infantry troops did not engage in combat or confront its costs continuously the way nurses did. Female nurses in Vietnam straddled a line between the girl next door, providing an image of home to wounded men, and a combat soldier, who came face to face with the fear and death that accompanied the war. The higher survival rate among soldiers with severe wounds, made possible by rapid evacuation and improved medical technology, made their situation even more challenging than it had been for nurses in previous wars. It did not, however, exempt them from the tensions and contradictions experienced by the donut dollies. Their attempts to balance the two personas were further complicated by the gender tensions on the home front, where demands for women's equality were chipping away at traditional roles for men and women.

Similarly to the donut dollies, military women such as nurses and Women's Army Corps personnel sometimes became stand-ins for the wives, girlfriends, mothers, and sisters of servicemen. It was the way in which troops made sense of American women being in places that were exclusively male, according to the popular culture they had grown up with, modern equivalents of the "Indian country" where John Wayne and other cowboys protected their women and homesteads from savages.[4]

---

[3] Diane Elvenstar, "Mary Comes Marching Home," *California Living, Los Angeles Herald Examiner*, December 14, 1980.

[4] Tom Engelhardt, *The End of Victory Culture: Cold War America and the Disillusioning of a Generation* (New York: Basic Books, 1995); Richard Slotkin, *Gunfighter Nation: The Myth of the Frontier in Twentieth-Century America* (Norman, OK: University of Oklahoma Press, 1992); Loren Baritz, *Backfire: A History of How American Culture Led Us Into Vietnam and Made Us Fight the Way We Did* (New York: William Morrow and Co., 1985).

In reality, women also served a military function, however, and their presence in Vietnam was a pivot point in the broader transformation of American culture. Despite women's circumscribed place in the war's gender ideology, they were armed forces personnel who often worked alongside their male counterparts, experiencing combat even though they did not slog through the jungle. Incorporating military women into the Vietnam War story complicates the notion of what it meant to experience combat and challenges the dominant image in American popular culture of the combat moment as the defining image of the Vietnam War.

By looking at the American women who were in Vietnam, we get a much more representative sense of the war experience, for men as well as women. Although women did not serve in infantry units, the consequences of combat shaped their lives – from nurses who cared for wounded soldiers to Women's Army Corps personnel who processed killed-in-action reports. Female nurses were crucial in those early hours and days in which wounded servicemen processed the impact of the fighting on their bodies and their lives. Even though American women did not technically participate in combat maneuvers, they – especially nurses – dealt with warfare in ways that profoundly affected them and the men they served.

As Van Devanter and countless other military women learned, maintaining the persona of a smiling, comforting reminder of home was difficult, if not impossible, under the pressure of war. Hospitals were targets for enemy fire, which meant that all personnel working or being treated in them were in combat. Medics and nurses had to protect not only themselves but also their patients during an attack; doing so required the intense physical labor of moving wounded patients, and the equipment needed to keep them alive, to safety. This reality alone destroyed the notion of nurses as dainty young ladies in need of protection. The physical work of medical care in a combat zone was intensified by the emotional strain of dealing with human suffering every day. For nurses such as Van Devanter, coping meant shutting down her "feminine" side that was supposed to be emotional, taking on what she called a "macho characteristic" of steeling herself in to survive. Van Devanter wore ribbons in her hair and perfume to try and maintain the image expected of her, "but in the mirror you see an exhausted, half-dead person with grimy hair pulled back, in drab fatigues," she said.[5] Although she was

---

[5] Elvenstar, "Mary Comes Marching Home."

describing herself, the picture she painted could have been anyone, regardless of gender, whom the war had beaten down.

"Share the Army Adventure"

Although American women served in all branches of the U.S. armed forces in Vietnam, the largest group after nurses came from the Women's Army Corps (WAC). Throughout the course of the war, about 700 WACs worked in Vietnam as stenographers, typists, clerks, air traffic controllers, cartographers, reporters, and photographers. Some women worked in communications and military intelligence; others processed casualty reports and paperwork related to troop movements. The WAC detachment was stationed at Tan Son Nhut Air Base until the end of 1968, when it moved to new barracks at Long Binh. In general, WACs worked in offices, but some found themselves dodging bullets and shrapnel, escaping grenades and bombs, and diving into barracks alongside men.

The Army established the WAC in 1943 as a means to organize womanpower efficiently for the war effort. Despite the popular sentiment in support of full mobilization of all Americans doing their part for freedom, the WAC faced resistance from those who did not think women belonged in the military. Historian Leisa Meyer explains that the opposition reflected social and cultural anxieties about women's sexuality and the strength of traditional gender roles. To assuage critics, WAC leaders deliberately created a "feminine" image of WACs to establish a place in the Army for women without disrupting the conventional wisdom about the military as a masculine institution.[6] That image remained into the Vietnam era, a period in which similar anxieties about gender and sexuality were challenged by the social movements of the 1960s. In his request for military women to come to Saigon, Brigadier General Ben Sternberg, personnel officer for U.S. forces in Vietnam, asked for a captain or major who was well versed in WAC policies, and who was "extremely intelligent, an extrovert and beautiful."[7] Colonel Emily Gorman, WAC

---

[6] For an in-depth study of the creation of the Women's Army Corps, see Leisa D. Meyer, *Creating GI Jane: Sexuality and Power in the Women's Army Corps During World War II* (New York: Columbia University Press, 1996). See also Jeanne Holm, *Women in the Military: An Unfinished Revolution* (Novato, CA: Presidio Press, 1992); Bettie J. Morden, *The Women's Army Corps, 1945–1978* (Washington, DC: U.S. Government Printing Office, 1990).

[7] Letter from Brigadier General Ben Sternberg to Colonel Emily Gorman, November 17, 1964, National Archives Record Group 319 – Records of the Army Staff, Women's Army Corps, 1945–1978 [hereafter NARA RG 319], Box 50.

director, responded to Sternberg with a letter in which she wrote: "the combination of brains and beauty is of course common in the WAC."[8] Men did not just impose those norms – some women of the corps embraced them, whether personally or by necessity of their military position.

In January 1965, WACs went to South Vietnam to help ARVN mobilize women for military service and develop a training center for the Women's Armed Forces Corps (WAFC).[9] After Duong Van Minh's coup overthrew the Diem government in 1963, Minh disbanded Madame Nhu's Women's Paramilitary Corps, but his successor, Nguyen Khanh, reinstated a women's military auxiliary. Major Kathleen I. Wilkes and Sergeant 1st Class Betty L. Adams went to Saigon and worked with Major Tran Cam Huong, director of the WAFC. To be eligible for officer training, WAFC recruits had to pass a test demonstrating that they had the equivalent of a U.S. eleventh grade education. All other recruits needed the equivalent of a U.S. junior high school degree.

Most WAFCs came from middle-class backgrounds, for a Military Assistance Command Vietnam (MACV) memo about the Vietnamese women's corps observed that "most report for duty in the flowing Vietnamese *ao dai*,"[10] typical middle-class attire.[11] By the end of 1967, membership in WAFC had risen to about 2,700; by 1969, the number had jumped to 4,000. At the WAFC school, which was completed in March 1965, recruits took an eight-week basic training course, in which they participated in physical training, first aid, sanitation, and the use of weapons. An officer training program was created in October 1966, which required officer candidates to take an additional twenty-week course after completing the eight-week basic training. In addition to the skills learned in basic training, officer candidates studied military tactics, public speaking, leadership, and military justice.[12] As part of the officer training program, fifty-one Vietnamese women officers completed advanced training with

---

[8] Letter from Colonel Emily Gorman to Brigadier General Ben Sternberg, November 23, 1964, NARA RG 319, Box 50.

[9] A precedent for WAC service in Asia was set during World War II, when WACs served in India, China, Burma, and Ceylon. However, the Army did not deploy WACs to the Korean War. See Holm, 207–09.

[10] Phung Thi Hanh, "South Vietnam's Women in Uniform" (Saigon: Vietnam Council on Foreign Relations, 1970), Douglas Pike Collection: Unit 11 – Monographs, Folder 21, Box 05, The Vietnam Archive, Texas Tech University, Lubbock, TX.

[11] Harvey H. Smith, et al., *Area Handbook for South Vietnam* (Washington, DC: U.S. Government Printing Office, 1967), 138.

[12] Phung Thi Hanh, "South Vietnam's Women in Uniform."

the Women's Army Corps at the WAC headquarters at Fort McClellan, Alabama.[13]

Similar to the WACs, WAFC officers and enlisted personnel provided a wide variety of support services for their male counterparts. WAFC personnel worked primarily in secretarial roles to assist ARVN in its various clerical needs.[14] Some WAFCs also worked as nurses and in "welfare service," taking care of dependents who traveled with ARVN soldiers, while others operated schools for ARVN dependents. WAFCs were not trained in combat, but those employed in the welfare service stayed near combat zones with troops, thus performing "the most dangerous assignments in the corps."[15] Lieutenant Ha Thi Tuoi joined the military to be a social worker because she wanted to work with children. Tuoi lived with her parents in Saigon; four days a week, she worked at a camp for ARVN dependents at Tan Son Nhut Air Base. In her job caring for the wives and children of soldiers gone to war, Tuoi traveled "from house to house and ask the people if they need anything, see if they are well, and try to cheer them up a little." When she worked at Tan Son Nhut, about one thousand families lived impoverished in shanties; they relied on WAFCs to bring items such as food, medicine, soap, and blankets that humanitarian agencies and the government donated. Although officially Tuoi and other WAFCs were Vietnamese counterparts to the U.S. WAC, they also performed the work of donut dollies, traveling to visit troops and boost their morale. Traveling by jeep or helicopter, Tuoi was a messenger bringing news to troops from their families, and she helped soldiers write letters home.[16]

Also similar to American women's experiences in Vietnam, some WAFCs faced resistance from ARVN troops. A WAFC officer noted that "some military men still do not accept the idea of a woman in uniform. They expect the WAFCs to do their cleaning and wait on them hand and foot. That is not what we have been trained to do!"[17] Despite all that Tuoi had accomplished in WAFC, she intended to leave the military once she had children, agreeing to the demand of her fiancé, an architecture student in Saigon. Some military women agreed with the notion that they could be used best in service roles, however. Mrs. Nguyen

[13] Morden, 217.
[14] Marguerite Higgins, *Our Vietnam Nightmare* (New York: Harper & Row, 1965), 64.
[15] Memo, "Women's Armed Forces Corps," Office of Information, U.S. Military Assistance Command Vietnam, November 12, 1966, NARA RG 319, Box 100.
[16] Phung Thi Hanh, "South Vietnam's Women in Uniform."
[17] Ibid.

Hong Nguyen, a commissioner with the People's Self-Defense Force in Saigon, believed that "there is no need for women to be combat troops now. With men on the front lines, the women's job is to provide support and encouragement."[18] As support staff and morale boosters, WAFCs exhibited a type of femininity that mirrored American gender ideals and provided a link in values between the United States and South Vietnam.

Once the WAC presence in South Vietnam was established through its work with the WAFC, the Army continued sending WACs to fill office positions at major bases so male troops were free to serve in combat positions and other jobs not open to women.[19] Recruitment materials, along with articles in newspapers and magazines, propagated the image of women as sex objects in need of protection. Often, the face of the Women's Army Corps in recruitment brochures was an attractive, young, white woman with perfectly coiffed blonde hair. The typical tour of duty, as presented in the brochures, sent women to "romantic" destinations abroad, where attractive, young, white servicemen waited for them. The recruitment pamphlet for officer candidates explained that members of the Women's Army Corps "have a busier social life than ever before! That's because you'll have the opportunity to meet and work side-by-side with the young men in the Army." It went on to encourage WACs to marry, highlighting the matchmaking potential of military life. Women officers, the brochure asserted, "will continue to meet and get to know people of your own background and interests. So it's likely, then, that you may meet your future husband at some point in your Army career – as so many WAC officers do."[20] One brochure touted "the facilities of today's Army posts," including "service clubs, libraries, movies, swimming, bowling, and golf."[21] Another brochure listed "glamour" as one of the perks of joining the military.[22] Few recruitment materials mentioned the Vietnam War. They focused instead on the "fun, travel, and adventure" to be had by signing up.

Some recruitment materials did tout the career opportunities available to military women in fields such as communications, technology, finance, and intelligence. In that way, recruitment of WACs illustrated the gradual

[18] Ibid.
[19] Holm, 209.
[20] Ibid.
[21] "Opportunity Awaits You in the Women's Army Corps" (Washington, DC: U.S. Government Printing Office, 1963), NARA RG 319, Box 93.
[22] "For You: An Officer's Career in the Armed Forces." (Washington, DC: U.S. Government Printing Office, no date), NARA RG 319, Box 93.

reassessment of gender roles that never really stopped occurring after World War II. However, changes in military opportunities for women were not meant to challenge the acceptable gender roles of the time. In a frequently-asked-questions section in the officer candidate brochure, one of the questions was: "Is military life compatible with femininity?" The answer to the question maintains that although "the WAC officer does important work and shares equal status with male officers of the same rank," her military service "in no way interferes with the fact that she's a woman – albeit a woman doing a special job, like the woman executive, woman doctor, or woman diplomat. Far from losing femininity, WAC officers gain the poise, self-assurance, and dignity that comes from holding a responsible job and holding a position of respect."[23]

Clothing played a significant role in ensuring that WACs in Vietnam did not disrupt conventional gender roles. Marilyn Roth, who joined the Women's Army Corps in 1964, remembers that military women out of uniform had to wear a dress, nylon stockings, and high heels in Vietnam. Women could wear pants if attending or participating in a sporting event, but otherwise dresses and skirts were the rule. "It was the military's way of saying, 'You're in the Army, you're not boys, you're not men. We want you to dress like ladies.' That's what we were called – ladies. We weren't called soldiers, we were called ladies and we were treated as ladies. You had to wear nail polish, you had to wear makeup, you had to wear lipstick, you had to be just perfect," Roth said.[24]

Concerns about WACs' appearance in Vietnam reached all the way to Washington. In January 1969, an issue of the MACV *Observer* landed on the desk of Colonel Elizabeth Hoisington, WAC director. The paper featured a tribute to American military women serving in Vietnam, and the photographs accompanying the article showed corps members in "the unflattering women's field uniforms" – fatigues and combat boots – rather than the Army Green Cord, a polyester and cotton skirt and top. Even worse, in Hoisington's mind, was that the paper had published the photos alongside pictures of nurses in white dresses, members of the Women's Air Force in "skirted summer uniforms," and a civilian female employee in a sundress. In response, Hoisington wrote a letter to Major Gloria Olson of the WAC Public Information Division in Vietnam expressing her dismay at the photographs and the image she feared they portrayed of WAC troops. She worried that parents, whose permission

---

[23] "For You: An Officer's Career in the Armed Forces."
[24] Ron Steinman, *Women in Vietnam* (New York: TV Books, 2000), 228–29.

was required for high school graduates to enlist, would get the wrong idea about women's service in Vietnam. "They do not like to envision their daughter in terms of the rough, tough environment conveyed by the field uniform," Hoisington wrote. In her opinion, pictures of "WACs in these trousered uniforms" would hurt recruitment efforts. Only nurses, she wrote, could be photographed in work uniforms without harming recruiting because the public understood the role of the nurse in a war zone.[25]

The controversy over the *Observer* photos was not the first time Hoisington had taken issue with the appearance of WACs stationed in Vietnam. In early 1967, she exchanged letters with Major Shirley Heinze of the WAC Career Branch regarding efforts to ensure that WACs maintained a "feminine appearance at all times." At that time, the particular problem was combat boots. Hoisington argued that WACs should wear service shoes – low-heeled black pumps. Heinze explained that "boots are highly desirable for field wear since they offer maximum protection from snakes, mosquitoes, and undesirable terrain and conditions which prevail here."[26] Hoisington was not easily swayed, and it was not until 1969, after the Tet offensive, that combat boots became an official part of the WAC uniform.[27]

As discussions of how WACs should look continued, Captain Joanne Murphy, commanding officer of the WACs in Vietnam, sent a memo to the WAC brass regarding the uniform issue. It listed some facts of life in Vietnam that made the Green Cord uniform impractical. The post exchange at Long Binh, home of the WAC detachment, carried scant supplies of girdles, garter belts, hosiery, and slips – all required because the women's uniform included a skirt rather than slacks, and women had to wear nylon stockings. Pumps, particularly the heels on them, did not hold up well on gravel roads and sank into muddy spots, but there were no shoe repair shops on or near the base. The memo also noted that washers and dryers at the base often broke down, and several were completely unusable. It blamed Vietnamese maids for ruining uniforms when they ironed them using the wrong setting. Finally, the memo reminded readers that attacks sometimes occur during on-duty hours, meaning that WACs

[25] Letter from Col. Elizabeth Hoisington to Maj. Gloria Olson, January 1, 1969, NARA RG 319, Box 101.
[26] Letter from Maj. Shirley Heinze to Col. Elizabeth Hoisington, March 4, 1967, NARA RG 319, Box 101.
[27] Morden, plate 34.

could have to "hit the dirt" – gravel, concrete, actual dirt, depending on where they were – in their dress uniform.[28]

The lengthy memo revealed the absurdity of requiring military women to wear pumps, skirts, and hose in an environment where the temperature often exceeded 100 degrees and featured oppressive humidity, where helicopters regularly created gusts of dirt and dust during takeoff and landing, and where heavy rains made mud the rule rather than the exception. Appealing to the femininity issue, the memo argued that sweaty blouses and skirts stained reddish-brown from dust would create "an unkempt and unsightly appearance." Furthermore, "the women will present an unladylike appearance when getting into/out of jeeps and scouts in their fairly form fitting skirts." Last, women walking to the mess hall or other places on base often were "splashed with mud by passing vehicles during the rainy season."[29] Murphy knew that, in Vietnam, mud and sweat wiped away the kind of femininity that Colonel Hoisington wanted WACs to exhibit.

Embedded in the desire for the Green Cord uniform was the attitude that WACs should be morale boosters for male troops. Murphy's memo stated that there was "a substantial number of individuals" who believed that the Army Green Cord would "improve the image of the WAC" and "improve the morale of the men." In a survey of WACs stationed at Long Binh, one woman responded by writing, "What about our morale? We'd like to see men in khakis [instead of fatigues]." Another woman responded, "I came to help out. If I had known I was coming to improve the morale of men, I wouldn't have come." One woman wrote, "Being feminine doesn't mean wearing a dress." On the subject of femininity, a respondent stated: "there is hardly any doubt that the WACs here are aware that a small part of their femininity has been sacrificed. But then, are we here to satisfy the desires of the male ego which prefers women in dresses, or are we here to do a job?" Another continued, "Now I'm sure the Army didn't send the WACs over here for the mere purpose of 'prettying' up an office or for the morale of the men!" Another WAC wrote: "I work in an office that is unbearable with the window closed and almost cloudy with dust when it's open. Just sit in front of the detachment and watch the dust fly in from the road. Our fatigues, while not particularly attractive or stylish, are serviceable, reasonably

---

[28] Memo: "Wearing Class A Uniform – WAC Personnel," June 26, 1968, NARA RG 319, Box 92.

[29] Memo: "Wearing Class A Uniform – WAC Personnel."

comfortable, and suitable for this area." One woman wrote, "I think we look just as feminine with our fatigues on as we do with our Class A. If they can't see that we are ladies, then they need glasses."[30] In 1968, in light of the Tet offensive and the subsequent increase in fighting in Saigon as well as the countryside, the Army approved a new women's uniform consisting of lightweight fatigues, a baseball-style cap, and black boots.[31]

The regulations policing WACs' appearance highlighted a cultural conflict between conservatives and the women's movement. Bettie J. Morden, a WAC historian, has written that if any group of American women was going to reject the changes brought by the women's movement, it was "the conservative, tradition-minded WAC leadership. To them, changes that appeared to make women more like men meant a decline, not an improvement, in the status of women."[32] The debate over military women's clothing was symbolic of the cultural tug-of-war that accompanied the Vietnam War. The gendered ideas that shaped the ways in which military leaders imagined the roles for men and women in the war effort often diverged sharply from the lived experiences of personnel on the ground.

As if to counter any doubts about the femininity of WACs, military newspapers and magazines published in Vietnam foregrounded their "womanly" qualities. The June 1969 issue of *Army Digest* featured an article about the Women's Army Corps and included a sidebar about efforts to incorporate a course called "Personal Standards and Social Concepts" into the WAC curriculum. According to the report, the class was "a charm course – how to feel, be, and look your best; how to be feminine and a soldier, too." The sidebar quoted Major Ruth G. Kuhl, the "attractive redhead" who spearheaded the effort to add the course to the curriculum, saying that "we're soldiers to be sure, but we're women, too. We should take more advantage of our advantage." The piece noted that the class included "instruction in personal hygiene, basic etiquette, personal conduct, spending money, makeup, how to sit and walk, fashion basics" – in short, all the things necessary to insure that the girls are watched when the music is played. The accompanying photo featured a woman in an Army uniform applying eye shadow.[33] In August 1970, *Pacific Stars and Stripes* published an article entitled "The Sarge Wears

---

[30] "Individual responses to uniform survey," NARA RG 319, Box 101.
[31] Morden, 244, 472.
[32] Morden, 233.
[33] "Women on the Go," *Army Digest*, June 1969, 43, NARA RG 319, Box 94.

Eye Shadow," which opened with a description of a sergeant at the WAC headquarters in Fort McClellan, Alabama. "The glassy shine on the black pumps reflects the hem of the pale blue skirt, starched as stiff as an open umbrella," the story read. "The little cap is angled jauntily on hair teased into puffy wings. The blue eye shadow and pink iridescent lipstick are on just so."[34]

The photograph of a smiling young white woman named Lynn Kussman graced an article in a 1971 issue of *Pacific Stars and Stripes* entitled "Long Binh WACs Provide a Study in Women's Lib" (Figure 9). Praising the WACs, a male major told the newspaper that "the young woman who works in my office does twice as much work as the guys. Besides that, she's a lot better looking." As for GIs who reported to women officers, one told *Stars and Stripes*, "If you're low man on the totem pole, you're going to have to work for somebody, right? So why not have somebody who's pretty to look at while she is chewing you out?" The article described Captain Marjorie Johnson as "the pretty detachment commander," and the caption under Kussman's photo read that Kussman's "big smile... helps brighten up her office." Describing her encounters with men on arrival at Long Binh, Priscilla Moseby told the paper that "the guys sure make you feel wanted. The first day that I arrived at the detachment, I walked to the PX, about two blocks away, and before I got there I had received four ride offers, requests for nine dates, and three proposals of marriage."[35]

Lynn Kussman also made the pages of *Army Times* as its "WAC of the Week," a featured modeled on home front news features introducing a "girl of the week." The first thing the article did was describe her appearance. Calling her "the best thing to ever happen to a set of jungle fatigues," the report's opening paragraph contended that "petite Lynn Kussman would brighten any office anywhere, and at the Military Personnel Directorate, Long Binh, where she performs as a clerk, she is particularly illuminating." The story went on to explain that, "although only four-feet, eleven-inches tall, our bright-eyed gal of the week performs a man-sized job." The statement implies that Kussman was able to execute her military duties *despite* her gender, as though any wartime military job, even one behind a desk, was naturally a man's job. At first

34 "The Sarge Wears Eye Shadow," *Pacific Stars and Stripes*, August 23, 1970, NARA RG 319, Box 103.
35 "Long Binh WACs Provide a Study in Women's Lib," *Pacific Stars and Stripes*, November 5, 1971, NARA RG 319, Box 100.

Pacific Stars & Stripes   5 Nov 71

Long Binh Wacs Provide A Study in Women's Lib

By S. SGT.
FRANK MADISON

LONG BINH, Vietnam (Special) — Pallas Athene has gone to war, and like everything else she does, she is doing it with class and style.

Pallas Athene is the patron goddess of women soldiers, and is depicted on the brass of the Women's Army Corps.

"Pallas Athene is also the goddess of victory," one WAC captain quipped. "Maybe if we had gotten here sooner. . . ."

The WAC is represented in Vietnam by an approximately 70 women at Long Binh. They fill mostly clerical and administrative slots at various commands around the post, an arrangement that seems to suit everybody just fine.

Most units fortunate enough to have a WAC working for them feel that the WACs are worth their weight in mink stoles. "The young woman who works in my office does twice as much work as the guys," a major said. "Besides that, she's a lot better looking."

The women who come to Vietnam are screened for ability, attitude and stability. And they are all volunteers. Most have at least a year's service prior to Vietnam, and all must be at least specialist 4. Add to that the fact that a lot of them extend, sometimes as much as two full tours. The additional job training makes for improvement.

Most of the women here are at least specialist 5, and there is a liberal sprinkling of noncommissioned officers. Which means women are actually the bosses in quite a few offices.

Strangely enough, except for a few chauvinists who quickly find new jobs, most men don't object at all. "I'm the supervisor of

A big smile from Spec. 5 Lynn Kussman helps brighten up her office. (USA)

five men," Spec. 5 Brenda Burk said, "and I only had trouble once. He was kind of new, so the other guys took him outside and had a long talk with him. I don't know what they said to him, but I never had any more trouble."

A GI working at the hospital explained it this way, "If you're low man on the totem pole, you're going to have to work for somebody, right? So why not have somebody who's pretty to look at while she is chewing you out?"

Capt. Majorie Johnson, the pretty detachment commander,

feels there is not a stabler, more mature group of women anywhere in the world. "Maybe it is because of our common bond, but all of the girls get along great. And disciplinary problems are almost non-existent."

What's it like to be a WAC in Vietnam?

"Well, one thing for sure," Spec. 4 Priscilla Moseby said, "the guys sure make you feel wanted. The first day that I arrived at the detachment, I walked to the PX, about two blocks away, and before I got there I had received four ride offers, requests for nine dates, and three proposals of marriage."

"Our living conditions have to be among the best in Vietnam," Spec. 6 Joyce Oakes said. That was a common feeling among the women soldiers. Their area looks more like a summer resort than a billeting area in a combat zone. There are trees and well manicured lawns, air-conditioned barracks and a reception area where the women may receive guests.

Most of the detachment has never seen a shot fired in anger, but a few of the veterans were here during the 1968 Tet offensive.

S. Sgt. Rose Jackson was one of those. "The worst part was having to wear a helmet all of the time. Oh, there were a few rocket attacks, and the bus that I was riding once got hit by machine gun fire, but those helmets were heavy."

Even though many of the women do extend, most are glad when their tour is over. S. Sgt. Audrey Bergstresser expressed the sentiments of most of the girls when she said, "I wouldn't trade the experience that I have had for a million dollars. This has been one of the most interesting years of my life, but I am glad to be going home."

FIGURE 9. "Long Binh Wacs Provide a Study in Women's Lib," *Pacific Stars and Stripes*, November 5, 1971. National Archives Record Group 319. Records of the Army Staff, Women's Army Corps, 1945–1978.

glance, the article seems complimentary of Kussman's abilities and work in Vietnam. But as was typical of the 1960s, by presenting her stature as something she had to overcome in to do her job, the article assumes that, in an ideal situation, a man would occupy her position.[36]

When *Army Times* featured Susie Carter as its "WAC of the Week," it went so far as to include her "measurements" – the size of her chest, waist, and hips – in the profile. Adding the details of her height and weight, it judged her "good-figured." The story offered a brief character sketch of Carter, an African American woman, describing her as "our happy-go-lucky dazzler," "personable and attractive," "young lovely," "young personality miss," and "vivacious." Although the piece mentioned Carter's job as a clerk at Long Binh and the volunteer work she did at a hospital and an orphanage in Vietnam, it read like a cross between a personals ad and a beauty pageant biography. She enjoyed horseback riding, swimming, acting, dancing, and modeling, the article reported. The author also expressed surprise at the revelation that Carter once had been a "tomboy" who enjoyed baseball, basketball, and football.[37] To judge by the tone of the article, Carter's credibility stemmed from her potential for attracting men, not from her educational or employment credentials. It painted a picture of the ideal military woman as one whose pretty face and perky demeanor gave purpose to her presence in the war zone of Vietnam.

Features like "WAC of the Week" reflected the sexism of contemporary civilian workplaces, where verbal harassment and physical come-ons were acceptable parts of the culture. In her work on "second wave" feminism and the women's movement, Ruth Rosen describes the overt sexual advances some women faced on the job. She interviewed women who reported being groped by their bosses and propositioned by male coworkers, who saw nothing wrong with their behavior. The term "sexual harassment" did not exist in the 1960s, but when women refused advances, the angry rebuffed men labeled their female colleagues tramps and whores. Clothing enforced sexual and gender stereotypes and divisions, with skirts and dresses signaling acceptable femininity as more women entered the workforce.[38] Popular culture further buttressed the stereotypes and attitudes about appropriate relations between men and

[36] "One of 85 in 'Nam," *Army Times*, November 10, 1971, NARA RG 319, Box 100.
[37] "Model Vietnam Vet," *Army Times*, September 30, 1970, NARA RG 319, Box 100.
[38] Ruth Rosen, *The World Split Open: How the Modern Women's Movement Changed America* (New York: Penguin Books, 2000), 23–24, 163.

women, with Hugh Hefner's bachelor fantasy making its way into American consciousness via *Playboy*.[39] The "WAC of the Week" features were not unlike the "Co-ed of the Month" column Hefner introduced in the University of Illinois humor magazine *Shaft* when he was a student there in the 1940s. By no means unique to the Army, the gender and sexual stereotypes deployed in "WAC of the Week" reflected the dominant attitudes about relations between men and women on the home front. As on the home front, those attitudes were under increasing duress.

"Women of strength were always my heroes"

An assortment of factors motivated American women to join the Women's Army Corps in the post–World War II era. Despite policies clearly intended to enforce conventional femininity, few of the women who enlisted in the WAC did so because they aspired to those gender norms. Some recruits saw the Army as an escape from the gender roles they were expected to fill on the home front. Some joined because they needed employment, whereas others enlisted because they wanted to help the war effort. Rank and attitude toward military service shaped the ways in which individual WACs experienced Vietnam. Intentionally or not, their experiences both enforced and challenged gender norms that were increasingly under fire at home.

One afternoon during her senior year of high school, Linda McClenahan rode the bus home, as she always did. It was 1968, and she lived in Berkeley, California. On that particular day, the bus she rode was rerouted because of an antiwar demonstration that had erupted into a riot. Through the bus window, she saw a police car on fire, and at that moment, she knew she had to go to Vietnam to learn the truth about the American war effort. Accompanied by her reluctant father, she went to the Army recruiting office in Berkeley to sign up for the Women's Army Corps and a tour of duty in Vietnam. Serving at the U.S. Army Vietnam (USARV) Communications Center at Long Binh from November 1969 through November 1970, McClenahan and one other WAC were the only women in her office, and they worked with forty to fifty men on each shift.[40]

Similar to the boys of her generation who grew up watching Westerns and aspiring to be gunfighters in the image of John Wayne,

---

[39] Rosen, 47.
[40] Author's interview with Linda McClenahan, December 2005, Racine, WI.

McClenahan admired Annie Oakley and other strong-willed, independent female characters featured in Westerns. "Women of strength were
always my heroes. I mean, Miss Kitty on *Gunsmoke*, this woman was an
independent businesswoman, very successful, and a tough lady. Calamity
Jane, Annie Oakley. I had an Annie Oakley air rifle," McClenahan said.
She loved Patricia Neal in the 1965 film *In Harm's Way*, in which she
played a nurse, and John Wayne's girlfriend, on the day the Japanese
attacked Pearl Harbor. As a young girl, McClenahan saw the character
as a strong woman who had no regrets about the life she lived. "There
was something about her that was so worldly and so wise," McClenahan
said. However, she added, "you only see the glory in those movies. You
don't see the gory, only the glory."[41]

Like McClenahan, Karen Offut needed her reluctant parents' permission to join the Women's Army Corps at age nineteen. The way she saw
it, it was unfair that young men had to fight while she stayed home. "I
just didn't see any differentiation between the men and the women as
opposed to why should someone be putting their life on the line and not
me just because I happened to be female," said Offut, who worked as a
stenographer in Long Binh and Saigon. "I didn't know anything about
women's lib. I just knew that it didn't seem right for me not to go."[42] To
Marilyn Roth, Vietnam sounded like an adventure. She said she was not
like the other Jewish girls with whom she grew up in Brooklyn. "Jewish
women don't join the Army. [But] I couldn't afford to go to college or
marry a doctor or a lawyer, so I decided to join the army," Roth said.
"I felt I'd get to travel, I'd get an education, and get experience, which
my friends back in New York have never experienced." As were most
other WACs, Roth was stationed at Long Binh, where she worked in
intelligence, writing encoded messages for helicopter pilots.[43]

Growing up in Grand Tower, Illinois, a town on the Illinois–Missouri
border that had a population of about 1,200 at the time, Susan Franklin
saw the Army as her only way out of a place that had nothing for her.
She had quit high school before she turned eighteen, and many of her
peers already had children. Franklin got her GED and enlisted in the
WAC in November 1964 with her family's blessing. "They knew there
was nothing in that town," she said. Her father had served in the Army in

[41] Ibid.
[42] Ron Steinman, *Women in Vietnam: The Oral History* (New York: TV Books, 2000),
256.
[43] Ibid., 224.

World War II, and her brother was in the Navy, so military service was a family tradition, and it did not make much difference to her parents that she was a woman. In 1969, Franklin, then twenty-one, volunteered to go to Vietnam and was stationed at Long Binh until 1970. She had friends there, including several cousins, and she wanted to be with them. In Vietnam, Franklin was the only woman in the office in which she worked, but considered her purpose simply to do a job. She wore a peace sign around her neck throughout her tour of duty.[44]

For Nancy Jurgevich, serving in Vietnam as the WAC detachment commander was the high point of her career. She arrived at Long Binh in October 1968 and managed about one hundred women who worked in communications, engineering, intelligence, and logistics. She noted that most of the women stationed there were in their early twenties, and they were dedicated both to their jobs and the U.S. mission in Vietnam "at a time when many Americans were turning their back on the United States." Jurgevich viewed ensuring the health and safety of the WACs she oversaw as her primary responsibility in Vietnam, and she admired their professionalism and strength. During her tour of duty, Jurgevich had the opportunity to take a unit of WACs to visit the training center of the WAFC, South Vietnam's counterpart to the WAC. There she experienced a strong sense of camaraderie between the American and Vietnamese women.[45]

The desire to advance her military career encouraged Lieutenant Colonel Janie Miller to volunteer for Vietnam. She had been in the WAC for nineteen years, having enlisted in 1950 during the Korean War, and she had decided to make a career out of the military. "Many of my male counterparts had served in Vietnam more than one tour of duty, and I considered myself a career Army officer, so as such I needed this assignment for career advancement," Miller said. She served in Vietnam from 1969 to 1970, assigning incoming officers to units that needed their particular skills. As part of her job, Miller monitored the personnel needs of the mortuary in Saigon. "We rotated the personnel there every three months because of the stress related to the assignment," Miller said. "I happened to be there once when choppers were bringing in KIAs [soldiers killed in action] following a firefight. The processing of the bodies was very efficient from the initial identification to the final placement into a black body bag."[46]

---

[44] Author's telephone interview with Susan Franklin, October 2009, Hattiesburg, MS.
[45] Steinman, 233–38.
[46] Author's e-mail correspondence with Janie Miller, October 2009, Hattiesburg, MS.

The violence of combat was often a regular part of the WAC experience. Linda McClenahan was intensely aware of the toll of combat. Working in the USARV Communications Center, she processed reports from units in the field, including killed-in-action reports. "A lot of classified information went out of our offices," she said. "Troop movements, surveillance reports, and every casualty report from Vietnam went out through our office. I often would tell the combat troops that I knew more about the battles they were in than they did because we were getting pieces from all over the place."[47]

Pinkie Houser, an Alabamian who enlisted in the WAC in 1964 after graduating from high school and volunteered for Vietnam in 1968, lost the general she worked for when the helicopter he was riding in was shot down over Pleiku. Houser, who had a classified position with the U.S. Army Engineer Corps, had gotten to know the general well and liked him, and one of her most difficult tasks in Vietnam was processing his records and personal effects to send back to his family. "I cried a lot, I really did, because by that being such a small command, the general personally would come in and talk to me, you know. So I knew him quite well."[48] It could have been Houser on that helicopter, for sometimes she went out with officers to inspect bridges and other infrastructure. When she did, even though she was working as a secretary taking notes on the inspections, she wore a bulletproof vest and carried a .45.[49] The contrast between the illusion of women as noncombatants and the real danger they faced in a guerrilla war theater was stark.

First housed at Tan Son Nhut Air Base, in 1968 the women moved to a new WAC detachment at Long Binh, headquarters of the USARV.[50] The WAC detachment hired Vietnamese women to do laundry and provide other types of maid services. Most WACs worked in offices with servicemen and socialized with them when off duty. In addition to working with men in the USARV Communications Center, Linda McClenahan said she and other WACs had "constant" contact with male soldiers. "We worked, we rode on buses, walked in the street together, the few clubs that were there, we went together," she said. For the most part, they were good guys, especially the infantrymen. When they came in from the

---

[47] Author's interview with Linda McClenahan.
[48] Marshall, 43.
[49] Ibid., 39.
[50] Letter from Lieutenant Colonel Margaret Jebb to Major Carol Tilden, August 10, 1970, NARA RG 319, Box 92.

field, they always seemed happy "just to be able to sit down and talk to an American woman, to be able to dance a little bit with an American woman; they were great," McClenahan said. "We'd talk about music, we'd talk about getting home, we'd talk about what kind of car we're gonna get. We never talked about the war."[51]

For McClenahan, who grew up with two brothers, taking time to chat with combat soldiers was her way of supporting them. Joan Barco, a WAC who worked as an administrative officer at USARV headquarters at Long Binh in 1968, believed that the men with whom she worked looked out for both military and civilian women who worked for the Army. Servicemen often approached WAC Susan Franklin during her tour, but they usually just wanted to talk. She believed it was because she was a woman, and somehow talking with her was easier for a lonely soldier than talking with one of his comrades.[52]

"Sometimes you were the last one they saw"

Of the approximately 10,000 American women who served in Vietnam with the armed services, the majority were nurses in the Army Nurse Corps (ANC). As Kara Dixon Vuic has revealed in her in-depth study of the ANC in the Vietnam War, Army nurses were first deployed to Vietnam in 1956 to train Vietnamese nurses in Saigon. The number of ANC nurses in-country increased to a peak of 906 in June 1968 before declining as U.S. troops withdrew from Vietnam; in total, approximately 5,000 Army nurses served in the conflict between 1956 and 1973. Nurses served one-year tours, held various medical specializations, and worked in hospitals of all sizes, in Saigon and out in the field.[53] Vuic's work details how nurses in Vietnam experienced many of the same gender issues faced by members of the Women's Army Corps and donut dollies. Vuic's examination of ANC recruitment efforts, the in-country experiences of Army nurses, and representations of them after the war illustrate the impact of the Vietnam

---

[51] Author's interview with Linda McClenahan.
[52] Author's telephone interviews with Joan Barco and Susan Franklin, October 2009, Hattiesburg, MS.
[53] Kara Dixon Vuic, *Officer, Nurse, Woman: The Army Nurse Corps in the Vietnam War* (Baltimore: Johns Hopkins University Press, 2010), 2. See also Elizabeth Norman, *Women at War: The Story of Fifty Military Nurses Who Served in Vietnam* (Philadelphia: University of Pennsylvania Press, 1990); Lynda Van Devanter, *Home Before Morning: The Story of an Army Nurse in Vietnam* (Amherst, MA: University of Massachusetts Press, 2001); Winnie Smith, *American Daughter Gone to War* (New York: Pocket Books, 1994).

War experience on the social and cultural changes of the era, and vice versa. Vuic demonstrates that even though the Army attempted to attract more women to the ANC by responding to 1960s feminism, crafting an image of a military nurse as both an officer and a woman, changing the mindset of male military personnel and debunking a notion that was centuries old proved difficult.

Nurses had a variety of reasons for joining the corps, including the wish to avoid, at least temporarily, becoming wives and mothers. Even as they viewed the Army as an escape from the assumed social roles, nurses faced some servicemen who viewed them as angelic caregivers who were stand-ins for women back home, and others who resisted their authority and sexually harassed them, expressing either an unwillingness or an inability to accept female nurses as legitimate military personnel. Although male nurses served in the ANC, men composed fewer than 30 percent of the Army nurses in Vietnam, illustrating the staying power of the idea that nursing was women's work.[54]

Prior to the creation of the ANC in 1901, the wives, mothers, sisters, and widows of troops did the work of caring for wounded soldiers. Despite the obvious importance of their role and their constant exposure to the gore rather than the glory of combat, they faced resistance and hostility from male military leaders and hospital staff, for even though they recognized the need for nurses, they opposed the idea that women should have an official place in the Army.[55] Tensions regarding women's place in the military, as well as assumptions about the sexual licentiousness of female nurses, carried on into the Vietnam era. Although nursing eventually was professionalized and achieved the status of acceptable women's work, public attitudes toward nursing into the early twentieth century considered it the realm of poor women, who were viewed to be sexually available and willing to work as prostitutes, as opposed to chaste middle-class women. The image of the promiscuous nurse remained even after the establishment of the ANC; as historian Kimberly Jensen illustrates, during World War I, nursing professionals in the United States countered the association of nursing with prostitution by demanding that nurses adhere to middle-class standards of respectable femininity. This meant that nurses must project respectability while also taking care not to encroach on the Army's masculine character.

[54] Vuic, 2–12.
[55] Kimberly Jensen, *Mobilizing Minerva: American Women in the First World War* (Urbana, IL: University of Illinois Press, 2008), 116–41.

Although all Americans in Vietnam – military and civilian, whether stationed in Saigon or at fire support bases – were at risk of attack, nurses dealt most directly with the human consequences of the fighting. "You learn real soon that you can't fall apart over every nineteen-year-old you send home in a body bag," said Paula Quindlen. The work was intense – in hospitals, most shifts were twelve hours, and most nurses worked six days a week. Working in the intensive care units in Qhi Nhon and Saigon, Judy Davis treated patients who were "blown to hell." To cope, she lost herself in her work, using cigarettes and wine to medicate her own emotional pain. "You couldn't do enough but felt guilty because you wanted to do more," Davis said.

When she had downtime between flights, Linda Pugsley dealt with the pain by going to the officers' club, drinking, and dancing to the music of the Filipino cover bands that sometimes played concerts there. Among all the things the Air Force had trained her to do, it had not taught her how to deal with the emotions of war. Pugsley eventually decided that she would not learn the names of the men she treated, not wanting to see them as friends. Still, she said, "you couldn't help but just love these guys. They were so brave. They just kept doing what they were told to do and hoping for the best and just hoping they'd get home." Aware that Americans generally saw women as maternal, Pugsley was not surprised when she became a stand-in for a serviceman's mother or wife. "Sometimes when the young men would be crying, sometimes it was really kind of hard," she said. "They'd hold your hand and just cry for their mom or their girlfriend. Sometimes you were the last one they saw, and you didn't mind taking that place."

While working at the 12th Evacuation Hospital in Cu Chi, nurse Lily Lee Adams wore Chantilly perfume because she knew it brought her wounded patients a comforting connection to home. "I mean, I've got guys in shock, wide awake, telling me how good I smell. So I wrote home ... and said, 'Send me bottles and bottles of perfume.'" Other nurses wore ribbons in their hair and pigtails "because the guys loved it," Adams said. "They'd look you straight in the eye and say, 'You look so beautiful. You look so soft. You smell so good. You've got such nice eyes' – all this kind of stuff. Only it wasn't a come-on or a put-on. They were just so happy to see an American woman."[56]

Despite how difficult it was to handle the casualties, Lynda Alexander felt more useful in Vietnam than at any other point in her life. When

---

[56] Marshall, 220.

her tour ended, she did not want to go home. "This was the real thing," Alexander said. "You ever talk about having a feeling of satisfaction, such need? Somebody cared what you did. It was just the most down to the bone thing."[57] Sylvia Lutz Holland, a nurse who served at the 312th Evacuation Hospital in Chu Lai from 1968 to 1969, felt a high degree of professional fulfillment during her tour of duty. "It was the only time in my nursing career when I used every bit of knowledge I had and developed a sense of confidence in my judgment as a professional," Holland said.[58]

Money for college, a paycheck, a longing for adventure, and a desire to help U.S. troops motivated nurses to join the military. Marj Graves learned about the Army Nurse Corps when a recruiter came to Saints Mary and Elizabeth Hospital School of Nursing, where she was a student. When Graves told her parents about it, her father was surprised at first but saw it as a good career opportunity. He had gone to a trade school and was a tool and die maker, and Graves' mother did not have formal education beyond high school, so both parents wanted Graves and her two sisters to go to college and get into a profession. Living in Louisville, Kentucky, Graves was more aware of the race wars at home than the war in Vietnam, but in 1971, she volunteered for Vietnam service. She was a captain by then, and she had been the head nurse in the male orthopedic unit at Fort Hood, Texas, where most of the patients were Vietnam returnees.

Inspired by the men she treated at the Fort Hood hospital, Graves decided she wanted to care for wounded men in Vietnam. When she told her parents of this decision, they were a bit less supportive. Her father had been a minesweeper in the Navy during World War II, and he figured that with three daughters, he would never have to worry about any of them joining the military. Not only had one of his daughters joined the Army Nurse Corps, though, but she was also heading to a war zone. "I think it was a real fear about what I was going to experience, and I think the majority of Americans at that point had such a negative feeling about Vietnam, and certainly during that war, every night on the media the first thing you saw was how many soldiers were getting killed and injured," Graves said.[59] In Vietnam, Graves was stationed at the 24th Evacuation Hospital in Long Binh.

---

[57] Author's telephone interviews with Lynda Alexander, Judy Davis, Linda Pugsley, and Paula Quindlen, October–November 2009.

[58] Christian Appy, *Patriots: The Vietnam War Remembered from All Sides* (New York: Viking, 2003), 171.

[59] Author's telephone interview with Marj Graves, November 2009.

While attending the Spencer Hospital School of Nursing in Meadville, Pennsylvania, in the late 1960s, Judy Davis attended a presentation by recruiters from the Army Student Nurse Program. Davis was a junior, and she learned that the Army would pay for her last year of school in return for two years of service. The program appealed to her because her father, an ex-Marine, could no longer afford to support her financially. Davis wanted to travel, and she saw the Army as a way of seeing places she might not get to otherwise. Although she considered herself patriotic, she did not support the Vietnam War and did not want to go to Vietnam, a position she made clear to her recruiter, who promised Davis she would not have to go. The need for nurses trumped the recruiter's guarantee, though, and in 1971, at the age of twenty-one, Davis, a second lieutenant, found herself stationed in the intensive care unit at the 67th Evacuation Hospital in Qui Nhon. She worked there for three months before being transferred to the U.S. Army Hospital in Saigon.[60]

Lola McGourty also saw the Army Nurse Corps as a way to escape what she considered a boring life in Shreveport, Louisiana. She graduated from Northwestern State University and joined the Army in 1967 when she was twenty-one. Although she was "politically oblivious" and did not know much about the war, she knew U.S. troops were dying in Vietnam, and so she volunteered for a tour there to help. She completed officers' basic training at Fort Sam Houston in Texas and then deployed to Vietnam, where she was stationed at the 67th Evac. She worked in the tropical diseases unit, which doubled as a psychiatric ward, and then in the neurosurgical post-operation ward.[61]

Thinking about her life long-term, Sandra Pang joined the ANC in 1966 because she wanted a job that provided retirement benefits. She came from a military family – her father had served in the Navy in World War II, and she had uncles in the services – and she wanted to continue that tradition. Pang had graduated from the Jewish Hospital School of Nursing in Saint Louis, and she viewed the Army as a way to get out of her hometown. Pang's mother had different plans for her daughter: "She wanted me to stay home and get married and have lots of babies and live in my hometown," Pang said. "And that was definitely not my goal in life." After training to be a nurse anesthetist, Pang was sent to Vietnam, where she worked at the 24th Evac.[62]

60 Author's telephone interview with Judy Davis, October 2009.
61 Author's telephone interview with Lola McGourty, November 2009.
62 Author's telephone interview with Sandra Pang, October 2009.

The Vietnam War was not on Linda Pugsley's radar when she signed up for the Air Force Reserve in 1967. She was twenty-two and working as a registered nurse at Boston City Hospital, and a surgeon she knew encouraged her to join. Soon after she entered the reserves, she volunteered for Vietnam because she wanted to care for injured U.S. servicemen. In June 1968, she deployed with the 34th Aeromedical Evacuation Squadron, which airlifted wounded troops from Vietnam to hospitals in Japan and the Philippines. On each run, she spent several weeks in Vietnam stabilizing the injured for their flights. Pugsley, a second lieutenant, thought she had seen it all in her job in Boston, where one night shift might bring victims of gunshot wounds, stab wounds, and car wrecks. "I was a hot shot, I thought, 'hey, I can take this,'" Pugsley said. "But the numbers in Vietnam were staggering. In the fall of 1968, we were evacuating about 10,000 wounded a month."[63]

Another Air Force nurse, Lynda Alexander, volunteered for Vietnam in 1968 because she wanted to show U.S. troops that she cared about what they were going through. She had graduated from Temple University with a nursing degree and worked as a civilian nurse before joining the Air Force. She was following nurse friends who had already joined the military, as well as her brother, who also was in the Air Force. He had served in Vietnam from 1965 to 1966 as a flight surgeon during Operation Ranch Hand, a procedure that sprayed defoliants, especially Agent Orange, on South Vietnam. At the time she joined the Air Force, Alexander did not consider her service to be a political statement. "We never discussed and we never really thought about whether we should be there or not because we felt so ineffectual and so 'what difference does it make?', no one's going to hear our voice anyway," she said. Instead of thinking about the politics of the war, Alexander, who was stationed at Tan Son Nhut Air Base just outside Saigon, tried to focus her attention on doing what she could with what she had to take care of the wounded she encountered.[64]

The in-country experiences of nurses show how the gendered beliefs that informed the war collapsed under the realities of Vietnam. The injuries, often massive, that nurses treated and the death that they saw were consequences of the warrior ethos put into practice on the battlefields of Vietnam. It was not a Hollywood depiction of victorious American forces using their might to defeat an evil enemy. Rather, the realities

---

[63] Author's telephone interview with Linda Pugsley.
[64] Author's telephone interview with Lynda Alexander, October 2009.

behind the John Wayne myth were the broken bodies and lost lives of the servicemen who were implementing a foreign policy grounded in gendered beliefs about American power. Nurses, similar to WACs, also worked in the midst of combat; sometimes hospitals took direct hits, which destroyed the illusion that the maternal comforts of home could be recreated in a war zone. As Sandra Pang noted, nurses saw the "bloody consequences of war" up close, every day, in ways that others did not.[65]

As did the majority of male GIs, most nurses concentrated on the details of their duties rather than the politics of the war. For some, specific aspects of those duties raised their awareness of the tensions and contradictions of the American mission. One of those duties was taking care of wounded Vietnamese. According to Sylvia Lutz Holland, there was a hierarchy of priorities, with American GIs at the top, followed by ARVN troops, Vietnamese civilians, and Viet Cong. For part of her tour, Holland worked in the Vietnamese ward at the 312th Evacuation Hospital in Chu Lai, where she treated patients for a variety of injuries and illnesses, including children suffering napalm burns. She developed a profound sense of respect for the Vietnamese, who seemed to survive even as they lost their homes and their loved ones. "They took care of one another and would absorb people from other families who weren't even blood relatives," Holland said. "They were warm and caring. Family members were always in the hospital. They'd sleep under the beds or on the floor."[66]

For Sandra Pang and Lynda Alexander, treating wounded Vietnamese was simply part of the job. Lola McGourty pitied the Vietnamese patients she treated, but she was ambivalent about working with them because she felt that they did not want the Americans to be in Vietnam. She felt especially sorry for Vietnamese women, whose positions as sex objects for U.S. troops became clear as she treated troops' venereal diseases. "Some of them [Vietnamese women] were nurses, some of them were teachers, and the rest of them it seemed relied on prostitution to survive, and we made them prostitutes."[67] The hospital at which Paula Quinlen worked did not have a prisoner of war (POW) ward, but some POWs passed through her hospital, and she had to care for them in intensive care unit (ICU) recovery. "It was hard to treat them because they had blown up our guys," she said. Linda Pugsley differentiated between Vietnamese ally

[65] Author's telephone interview with Sandra Pang.
[66] Appy, 173.
[67] Author's telephone interview with Lola McGourty.

and enemy, considering the South Vietnamese to be "lovely people" but refusing to treat Viet Cong or North Vietnamese Army troops.[68] Nurses saw, and in some cases personally struggled with, the tension between the U.S. mission of protecting South Vietnam from communist insurgency and the bloody consequences of the war that accompanied that mission.

"There Is Always the Possibility of a Terrorist Attack"

Despite the ideology that assigned them the role of delicate creatures in need of protection, combat was a part of the daily lives of American women in Vietnam. Although recruiting brochures and news articles portrayed life as a WAC – even one stationed in Vietnam – as a distinctly "feminine" experience, different from that of men, WACs did the same things many male troops did. They managed the heat and the boredom, they worked in places that came under fire, they lost friends, and they resisted the rules of their elders. Incorporating their stories into the Vietnam War narrative changes our image of the typical Vietnam experience – most Americans were not slogging through the jungle. Estimated ratios of support troops to combat troops range from five-to-one to ten-to-one, indicating that a "typical" Vietnam War experience took place in the rear echelon, where service personnel worked as clerks, journalists, radio operators, and medics.[69]

American women in a war zone were potential casualties even though they were not members of combat units. During the Tet offensive in 1968, WACs were caught in the midst of combat.[70] Describing the WAC experience during the month-long campaign, Captain Joanne Murphy wrote to Colonel Hoisington to tell her of the "exciting evening" the WACs at Long Binh experienced in mid-February 1968. Rocket fire hit the base's ammo dump, causing "two spectacular explosions" that were "much more dramatic" than those from a prior attack. The rockets exploded in the middle of the night, about one o'clock in the morning, while most of the WACs slept. Sleeping through a rocket attack was unlikely, especially when the blast "bounced some women out of their beds." Although it was probably shocking the first few times, such wake-up calls became

[68] Author's telephone interviews with Sandra Pang, Lynda Alexander, Lola McGourty, Paula Quindlen, and Linda Pugsley.
[69] Christian G. Appy, *Working-Class War: American Combat Soldiers and Vietnam* (Chapel Hill, NC: University of North Carolina Press, 1993), 167.
[70] Holm, 230.

somewhat routine, Murphy wrote, and the women of Long Binh mastered the art of sleepwalking into fatigues and helmets in the middle of the night "quickly, quietly, and assuredly without hesitation or question."[71]

As the war waged and fighting intensified, WAC leaders worried that the images delivered to Americans through newspapers and networks would sway public opinion against stationing women in Vietnam. In February 1969, Lieutenant Colonel Lorraine Rossi, overseeing the WACs still stationed at Tan Son Nhut, tried to reassure Hoisington that the Army women generally were safe. "I imagine the news coverage at home once again has most of Vietnam in ruins from mortar and rocket attacks," Rossi wrote. "There has been activity in the last few days, but it has been scattered and relatively little damage has resulted." On her mind as she apprised Hoisington of the situation in Vietnam were the parents of the women serving there. "I know it is difficult to reassure parents, and you must get queries, but the quarters are all well-guarded, and the men are most protective of the women," she wrote. "Of course, there is always the possibility of a terrorist attack or a direct hit on a building, but the chances are slim, and as I write to my parents, I feel as safe (if not safer) here than I did in Washington DC."[72]

Those assurances did not always reflect the realities on the ground in Vietnam. Pinkie Houser experienced Viet Cong incoming fire on the ammo dump at Long Binh multiple times during her tour of duty. She remembered two attacks vividly. The first occurred on Christmas Eve 1969, early in the evening, while a group of GIs and WACs were opening presents and laughing at the gag gifts they had received. The first rounds of incoming hit close; that night, Houser heard shrapnel hitting her bunker. "Now I was scared and praying that night. I think that's the first time that I had really, really been scared."[73] During the second attack, incoming rockets hit an education center on base, and a sharp piece of iron from one of the rockets pinned a woman colonel to a wall, piercing her through her heart. After receiving the all-clear signal, Houser and some others went to inspect the remains of the education center, and the sight of the colonel shocked her. "I cried. I threw up because I had never seen that before. It was horrible. All my fear came back. My knees were knocking, you know,

[71] Letter from Captain Joanne Murphy to Colonel Elizabeth Hoisington, February 24, 1968, NARA RG 319, Box 101.
[72] Letter from Lieutenant Lorraine Rossi to Colonel Elizabeth Hoisington, February 25, 1969, NARA RG 319, Box 101.
[73] Kathryn Marshall, *In the Combat Zone: An Oral History of American Women in Vietnam* (Boston: Little, Brown and Co., 1987), 41–42.

because I had never seen nothing like that, and the education center just looked like a tornado had gone through it."[74] No promise of safety could withstand the reality of what Houser experienced in Vietnam.

Hospitals came under attack during the war, which meant that nurses often were in the line of fire. As Jeanne Holm as written, the dangers nurses faced "were generally greater than those experienced by the clerks, personnel specialists, intelligence officers, stenographers, and others, *male and female*" (emphasis Holm's) assigned to rear posts in Vietnam.[75] Nine Army nurses died in Vietnam, one of whom was Sharon Lane, killed during a mortar attack on the 312th Evacuation Hospital in Chu Lai in June 1968. Just as donut dollies and nurses struggled with the deaths of GIs they befriended and treated, servicemen were devastated by the loss of their women comrades. Sharon Lane's death had an overwhelming impact on Jay Maloney, a medic who worked with Lane at the 312th Evac. The rockets hit early on a Sunday morning, one landing directly on the Vietnamese ward where Lane worked. A piece of shrapnel hit her below her collarbone, cutting her aorta. The scene was a nightmare for Maloney. "Ward 4 was awash with smoke and screams," Maloney wrote years later. "But my strongest image from that morning is the ocean of bright red, rust-scented, still-warm blood that seconds earlier had filled her small body. Sharon Lane was a gentle, sweet-souled girl. And this one death, this one among the vast crowd, this one was so particularly purposeless, so cruel, that my light went out that morning. I was as empty as she was, extinguished and spent."[76]

Lane's death was equally traumatic for nurse Sylvia Lutz Holland, whom Lane replaced in the Vietnamese ward when it was time for Holland to move on to a rotation in the emergency room. A group of corpsmen rushed Lane into the emergency room after the attack, but Holland took one look at her and knew she was gone. "She had a big hole in her neck. She was pale and her pupils were fixed," Holland remembered. "The surgeon came in and tried to start an IV but there weren't any veins. Then he was gonna open her chest and massage her heart. I said there was no reason to do it, she's dead. He kept saying, 'No she isn't.' Then he started crying." It was as though nurses, the caregivers some wounded

[74] Marshall, 46–47.
[75] Holm, 207.
[76] Vuic, 2; http://krccnetwork.org/tbs/2010/05/31/for-them-a-memorial-day-tribute-by-jay-maloney-2/?utm_source=BenchmarkEmail&utm_campaign=For_Them_A_Memorial_Day_Tribute_by_Jay_Maloney&utm_medium=email

soldiers considered angels, should be immune to combat injuries and death, and when the realities of war pierced through that gendered ideal, it sometimes was more than a GI could handle. Holland struggled with survivor's guilt for a long time after Lane's death, knowing that she would have been the one in the line of fire had Lane not arrived in-country to replace her.[77]

Although not many nurses died as a result of combat, battles were part of their daily lives in Vietnam, not just in the treatment of wounded men but also in the need to be prepared for possible attacks on their hospitals. Despite official rhetoric about the safety of women and combat as the exclusive terrain of men, nurses had to endure the fighting just as noncombat servicemen did. For most of Lola McGourty's tour of duty at the 67th Evac in Qui Nhon, the base was under threat of attack, and service personnel were not allowed to leave the compound. The hospital was adjacent to the runway of a U.S. Air Force base, making it a target. Judy Davis began her tour of duty in Qui Nhon in 1971, but three months into her tour, the 67th Evac was overrun; she and the rest of the staff were evacuated, and eventually she was sent to the U.S. Army Hospital in Saigon. When word of a possible attack came down to the hospital at Tan Son Nhut Air Base, Lynda Alexander and other medical staff had to move all patients under their beds, which sometimes resulted in IV lines disconnecting, catheters being pulled out, and other sorts of mishaps nurses had to address while bracing for incoming fire.[78]

At the same time as they were at risk from enemy attack, women were aware of the dangers, real or potential, from some of their putative "protectors." Some women had either experienced or heard about sexual harassment and assaults perpetrated by U.S. troops. According to some nurses, there was a perception among male servicemen, especially officers, that American women in Vietnam were sexually available, and sexual promiscuity was the reason they were in Vietnam. Linda McClenahan saw that the majority of harassment came from the rear-echelon troops, those who often had desk jobs and generally did not participate in combat. "It was the guys who were in the, quote, 'safer areas,' they were a little bit of a problem sometimes," she said. WACs learned to endure rude comments and jokes, and some resigned themselves to accepting sexual harassment as part of the deal, she continued. "Women in the United

[77] Appy, 173.
[78] Author's telephone interview with Lynda Alexander, Judy Davis, and Lola McGourty.

States in business were facing the same kind of thing," McClenahan added. "But in the military, of course, the language was a little coarser."[79]

In Linda Pugsley's experience, male officers trying to grope women was common but rarely reported. The reality of how dangerous Vietnam could be for women hit Marj Graves shortly after she arrived in-country. She was sent to a replacement battalion while awaiting her assignment, and an MP was stationed outside the barracks where she and one other nurse stayed. The nurses were told to not leave the barracks area; Graves believes Army officials were concerned about possible assaults. She learned that although it could be exciting to be asked out on dates and have many suitors, the sexual tension could be dangerous, so she and other nurses stayed close to men they trusted for protection. "American women were really in the minority there," Graves said. "If you were attractive, you knew you were watched." Although Lola McGourty considered herself oblivious to any dangers during her tour, years later she heard stories of nurses who had been sexually assaulted walking to and from the hospital where they worked, of nurses who had been raped, and of abortions that had been performed to hide the evidence of rape. No one had warned her to be careful in Vietnam, and she believed that was because Army officials did not want to draw attention to the sexual danger.[80]

In her study of the Army Nurse Corps in Vietnam, Kara Dixon Vuic explains that some nurses reported that sexual harassment (suggestive remarks, groping), sexual assault, and rape were common threats in their daily lives. Incidents rarely were reported, Vuic found, but ANC reports and anecdotal evidence indicate that actual attacks, as well as an overall sense of fear, shaped nurses' Vietnam experiences. Patricia Murphy, chief nurse in Vietnam, wrote in her 1971 *End of Tour Report* that "I noted on prior trips to RVN [Republic of Vietnam, the official name of South Vietnam] and during this tour that very few female nurses worry or fear enemy attacks, rocket, sapper, or a real attack. The females are more fearful of assault by our own troops and with good reason from experience."[81] Murphy went on to write that some nurses had been victims of sexual assault and rape. In interviews about their Vietnam service, some nurses talked about fearing sexual attacks by U.S. troops more than any other wartime danger. A nurse named Wendy Weller kept a .38 pistol in her

[79] Author's telephone interview with Linda McClenahan.
[80] Author's telephone interviews with Marj Graves, Lola McGourty, and Linda Pugsley.
[81] Vuic, 144.

quarters "for the guys that were breaking in your hooch all the time."[82] Even though nurses served in a capacity that was considered acceptable for women, they were still subject to sexual harassment that sometimes turned violent. The rigidity of the gender ideology that shaped America's Vietnam War culture and the weight placed on heterosexuality in its construction of masculinity made all women targets of sexual aggression, even those who appeared to fill the appropriate woman's wartime role as caregiver.

Race and Military Women's Experiences in Vietnam

As was the case for donut dollies and male GIs in Vietnam, race complicated the experience in the WAC and Army Nurse Corps. Captain Lajoie Ricks, who worked at the Army's Third Surgical Hospital at Bien Hoa, mourned the deaths of African American soldiers in Vietnam. "God, how we need these young Negroes," she lamented.[83] Ricks's fellow captain, Marian Scott, who arrived in Vietnam in 1966, viewed her hospital role in gendered rather than racial terms: "These guys need the voice of a woman. They don't care what color she is, just so long as she is an American."[84] Ricks and Scott (both African Americans) viewed themselves as caregivers in the war, not necessarily as soldiers or counterparts of the men they treated.

Some African American nurses volunteered for Vietnam because they knew black men often found themselves in combat units. It was 1967 when Elizabeth Allen enlisted in the Army, and while men all over the country clung to college and graduate school to avoid the draft, Allen took her master's degree in nursing from Ohio State University, enlisted in the Army, and asked for an assignment to Vietnam. Her decision had nothing to do with love for her country, a belief in U.S. foreign policy, or a desire to see for herself what was happening in Southeast Asia. Allen, a captain with the ANC, was thinking about black soldiers when she volunteered to go to the war. "I knew African Americans were most likely to end up in battle units, in the death units, and I really wanted to do something. There are extremely few minority folks in health care. A lot of aides, but in terms of professional folks, very few. I needed to go. I made a quick decision on my own." Her hospital in Pleiku was the first

[82] Ibid..
[83] "The Angels of Saigon," *Ebony*, August 1966, 44–46.
[84] "The Angels of Saigon."

American hospital bombed during the Tet offensive.[85] Every night, the hospital got hit by incoming fire, but the nurses kept working. "Men's lives were dependent on me, and my being scared was not useful," Allen said. "You had these guys with massive wounds. . . . I had to protect him. I had to make sure he didn't bleed or choke to death. I had to make sure if a mortar hit, the shrapnel didn't hit him again."[86] In those moments, Allen experienced a gender role reversal in which she was the protector of the soldier.

Marie Rodgers' experience illustrates the prospects available to some black women in the military, but it also suggests the limits on African American advancement in the armed services. When she enlisted in the Army in 1952, she was hoping to escape the racism of Jim Crow Alabama. She worked her way up to the rank of colonel in the ANC and spent her first overseas tour of duty in Korea. In 1967, she volunteered for an assignment in Vietnam because she wanted to be closer to combat. Stationed at the 24th Evacuation Hospital at Long Binh, Rodgers managed the operating room; that year, the hospital received its first Meritorious Unit Citation. Rodgers later earned a Bronze Star, commending her management of her unit while under fire. She viewed the military as a place in which black women had opportunities not available to them in civilian life – "In other situations, as a black nurse, I wouldn't have gotten the kind of job I had." She noted, however, that she usually was the only black medical staff member in her unit. No black doctors or surgeons were ever assigned to her team.

The experience of Air Force Captain Juanita Forbes illustrates the ways in which black women in Vietnam challenged and at times overturned conventional roles. She was one of 350 Air Force nurses who rode with Military Airlift Command flights on medical evacuation missions. Forbes directed an Aeromedical Evacuation (Air Evac) team of two female nurses and three medical technicians who were white male sergeants.[87] With a black woman supervising white men, the team challenged gender and racial conventions of the time. In the 1960s, it would have been unheard of in parts of the United States for a black woman to command a group that included white men. Captain Olivia Theriot, another African American nurse who served with Forbes, stated that she fostered good relations between men and women by treating "the med techs like men, not like

---

[85] *We Were There*, 91–98.

[86] Ibid., 95.

[87] "Samaritans on Wings: Black Nurse in Vietnam," *Ebony*, May 1970, 60–66.

lower-ranking men."[88] An *Ebony* magazine profile of Forbes and her team, however, focused on women's roles as resourceful caretakers who remained calm under pressure and always were kind and sympathetic to their charges. It pointed out that one of the most remarkable traits Forbes and her fellow women nurses exhibited was "the ability to function efficiently, even cheerfully, in the face of indescribable human suffering and tragedy."[89] As on the home front, the change in roles met resistance. In the minds of the three men on Forbes' team, the image of women's leadership was a thin veneer. The sergeants said they did not mind that Forbes and other women nurse captains outranked them because they believed "actually, ninety percent of the time, they depend on us – and they know it." The men had a simple solution for dealing with women they considered to be difficult: "Every once in a while you run into an old hag who tries to push you around. Then you just ignore her."[90]

For the men and women who lived it, the intersection of race and gender marked a complicated and contended space, as the experience of Doris "Lucki" Allen bore out. Allen began her career in the Army seventeen years before going to Vietnam, inspired by her brother, a World War II veteran. She also had the support of her father, who encouraged her to "make the best of whatever I wanted to do in my life," she said. Allen went to college at the Tuskegee Institute, where she got to know some of the Tuskegee Airmen, members of African American combat units that included highly decorated World War II veterans. Her relationship with the men was one of "mutual respect," and it shaped her opinion of servicemen.[91] In 1967, Allen volunteered to go to Vietnam, hoping to discover the truth about what the United States was doing there. She served in the U.S. Army Intelligence Operations at Long Binh from October 1967 through March 1970, and then in Saigon from March 1970 through September 1970.[92] Early on, Allen learned that some of the men with whom she worked either distrusted or disregarded the information she gave them. One of her jobs involved processing intelligence reports, and in doing so, she was privy to knowledge of possible attacks on Americans. In one case, Allen warned a group of officers to cancel a convoy headed for the village of Song Be because she had evidence that an assault

---

[88] Ibid., 66.
[89] Ibid., 64.
[90] Ibid., 66.
[91] Keith Walker, *A Piece of My Heart: The Stories of Twenty-six American Women Who Served in Vietnam* (New York: Ballantine Books, 1985), 305–306.
[92] Ibid., 309.

was planned. The officers dismissed her information and went ahead with the trip. The platoon was ambushed, and five American GIs died in the maneuver. Another nineteen were wounded. "What they did made me feel ignored," Allen said. "Being black. Being a woman. Being a WAC. Being in intelligence. Black. Woman. Very tough. And at the time, I was a specialist. These prejudices, I know they're going around in my brain – black, woman, got no business here. WAC, you're not supposed to be in the Army. This is a man's job."[93]

On a day-to-day level, Allen believed that male troops generally accepted WACs. Initially, they were thrilled to see women with "round eyes," Allen said. "As soon as the reality set in that we were in Vietnam to do a job and certainly not there as the entertainment contingent, things went relatively well," she added. Rarely in Allen's experience did men do or say anything especially hurtful to the women. "I naturally heard some derogatory comments but the men were mainly trying to impress their comrades," she said. "I do not believe that men did not trust me as an individual." She blamed uncooperativeness on hormones – because of testosterone, some men refuse to ask for directions and have trouble taking orders from anyone, let alone a woman. Allen did note, though that it seemed to her some men did not "believe women should be doing 'a man's job,'" particularly a job in a war zone.

Although she grew up in segregated Alabama, Pinkie Houser did not experience any racial tension until she went to Vietnam. She had attended an all-black school, but her childhood neighbors in rural Autaugaville included a white family, and "we all grew up together, got along just like we were one family." Having white friends was normal to Houser, so it bothered her when black GIs and WACs criticized her for befriending whites in Vietnam. It seemed to her that the black men and women who had the most animosity toward whites were from Northern cities such as Chicago and New York, which likely speaks to the racial tensions that exploded in the urban North in the late 1960s.[94] Houser's experience was that of just one of many WACs who served in Vietnam, but it reflects the complexities of U.S. race relations during the Vietnam era and forms those issues took among American troops.

Race affected the experiences of white as well as black women in Vietnam. Marj Graves, a white woman, worked with a few black nurses

---

[93] Steinman, *Women in Vietnam*, 244.
[94] Marshall, 45–46.

and experienced no racial tension during her tour of duty.[95] When McClenahan served at Long Binh, she estimated the ratio of white women to black women to be about sixty–forty. "We had a softball team at the WAC detachment that was mixed," she said. "We all got along fine." But in 1970, McClenahan almost faced a race riot. She was the on-duty noncommissioned officer, and one of the other WACs called her out to a gathering area on the post. A group of white women stood on one side, and black WACs were on the other. "They're yelling and screaming and it's not looking good," McClenahan said. "I ran into the middle and said 'what's going on, can we calm down?'" The women dispersed, and, looking back, McClenahan credits Pat Paterson, an African American woman and the coach of the WAC softball team, for restoring the peace. When McClenahan came outside to assess the situation, Paterson stepped up and said, "Wait a minute, wait a minute, wait a minute. Mac's on duty. We don't want to do this to Mac, do we?" It was McClenahan's only encounter with serious racial tension.

When Colonel Hoisington toured the WAC detachment and other sites in Vietnam in December 1971, her report made note of racial tension among WACs in her report of the visit. She shared a story of some "militant" African American WACs who brought a "'black' puppy" to the base "as one additional means of separating the blacks and whites." Hoisington admitted it was a "minor" and "petty" action, but she went on to state that the "problem women" had almost completed their tours of duty and thus would be leaving soon. She argued that "the unit has been somewhat polarized because of the activism of a few of the black women. But the closeness of life at Long Binh (including a 2300 hours curfew after which the WAC compound was locked up), and the long seven-day work week puts everyone on edge." To handle racial conflict at the detachment, Hoisington suggested that the Women's Army Corps send "an outstanding young black officer to set an example and assist in dealing with race issues that may arise."[96] Nowhere in the report did Hoisington mention white WAC "activists" who might have instigated racial hostilities or tried to divide WACs along racial lines, nor did she suggest that a young white officer go to Vietnam to "set an example" for white enlisted women. As it was back in the United States, the WAC

---

[95] Author's telephone interview with Marj Graves.

[96] Colonel Elizabeth Hoisington, "Report of Visit to Vietnam, 18–26 December 1971," NARA RG 319, Box 101.

made race an African American problem and constructed black women as "militant" outsiders.

These experiences were part of a broader pattern of racial tension in the Vietnam-era military. Racism boiled over into conflict among WACs in the United States as well. On November 16, 1971, a mixed-race group of enlisted men and women left the Enlisted Men/Enlisted Women's Club at Fort McClellan and approached the buses that would take them back to their barracks. The white military driver of the first bus allegedly refused to allow the black servicemen and women onto the bus, so they boarded the second bus and allegedly insisted that the white enlistees leave. Fighting began, and a group of about sixty African American personnel marched through the base in protest.

The following morning, more than thirty African American WACs gathered at a baseball field in the center of the post and demanded a meeting with the post commander and unit commanders to discuss their grievances. During the meeting, a group of black enlisted women allegedly assaulted a white woman reporter from a local newspaper who had arrived to write an article about the previous night's incident. As a result of the skirmish with the reporter, seven hundred troops arrested one hundred thirty-nine protesters, sixty-eight of whom were African American WACs. The arrested women stayed in the city jail in Anniston, the town where Fort McClellan was located, for two days, until military police created a temporary prison for women on base. Arrested men were held in the stockade on base and jails in surrounding communities. Of the sixty-eight arrested women, the Army discharged nine and transferred forty-six others.[97]

It was not the first incident of racial tension at the WAC headquarters. Earlier in November, about one hundred black enlisted personnel met with the managers of the Hilltop Service Club, where many black servicemen and women gathered in their free time, and asked why the club did not book African American bands or have soul music in the jukebox. They also requested the appointment of a black club manager. Dissatisfied with the club manager's responses, the group took their concerns to Colonel William A. McKean, the post commander, who pledged to investigate the problems. After the November 16 incident, McKean created committees in every unit to deal with racial tensions at Fort McClellan. A committee that investigated the events of November 16 and its aftermath concluded that "black leaders undoubtedly contributed

[97] Morden, 347–48.

to the problem" of racial polarization on base and found no fault in the actions of the post commander. The committee did note, however, that "the need to improve communications upwards as well as down with the young soldiers, and especially the young black soldiers, through the chain of command, is most apparent."[98] Assigning blame to African American demagogues rather than to institutional conditions of racism was typical of the ways in which white military leadership handled racial strife in the 1960s and 1970s. The incidents that occurred at Fort McClellan in 1971 were part of a broader context of racial conflict that happened throughout the Vietnam War, both in Vietnam and on bases in the United States.[99]

The race and gender tensions affected men as well as women, shaping the image of the American soldier and, by extension, U.S. foreign policy. GIs were cast as both the protectors of American civilization embodied in the girl next door and the gentle warrior charged with rescuing the Vietnamese from communism. Military publications and mainstream newspapers featured stories about Army and Marine units providing health care to Vietnamese villagers and bringing gifts to orphanages, and accompanying photographs depicted U.S. troops as father figures hugging children and comforting Vietnamese women. These images of gentle warriors contrasted with the aggressive heterosexual masculinity that defined basic training and was prominent in training manuals, comics, and soldier legends. Faced with contradictory messages about the character of a warrior, some GIs struggled to make sense of their purpose in U.S. relations with South Vietnam, and they responded in ways that highlight the impact of the gender tensions on their experiences in and understanding of the Vietnam War.

---

[98] Morden, 349–50.
[99] Riots erupted in the wake of the assassination of the Rev. Dr. Martin Luther King Jr. on April 4, 1968. A riot at Long Binh Prison in August 1968 resulted in the death of one inmate. Just as home-front urban uprisings revealed the anger and discontent of African Americans living amid poverty and racism, conflicts on bases shed light on the tenuous state of race relations in the military.

4

Gender and America's "Faces of Domination" in Vietnam

A photographer for the *Observer*, the official newspaper of the U.S. Military Assistance Command Vietnam (MACV), captured a shot of Nick Poulos, a paratrooper with the 101st Airborne Division, as he prepared to administer a smallpox vaccination to a Vietnamese toddler. In December 1967, the 101st Airborne dispensed immunizations to children in villages throughout South Vietnam. The picture that ran in the *Observer* was a close-up shot framing the faces of Poulos and the little boy. It portrayed the U.S. soldier as a tender man whose concern for children was instinctive. Poulos's eyes held a look of compassion as he, according to the photo's caption, assured the Vietnamese child that the vaccination would not hurt too much. The picture was one of many photos and articles published in the *Observer* depicting U.S. troops as humanitarian caregivers who healed the sick, fed the hungry, sheltered the homeless, and made children smile with gifts of candy and toys. Summing up the message behind the images, the *Observer* stated that, as a result of military humanitarian projects, the Vietnamese were beginning to see the U.S. serviceman as a "'gentle warrior.' In addition to being a fighter and protector, he is a friend, diplomat, and healer."[1] The article went on to explain that although "traditionally the American paratrooper has been one of the most aggressive, well-trained, and toughest soldiers in the world, the specialization of modern warfare requires that he also be versatile – a 'man of many faces.'"[2] The U.S. soldier could be strong and

---

[1] "Paratroopers 'Gentle Warriors' to Civilians in Da Nang," *Observer.* January 16, 1967, National Archives, Record Group 472 – Records of the United States Forces in Southeast Asia, Headquarters, United States Army Vietnam [hereafter NARA RG 472], Box 1.
[2] Ibid.

gentle, a lover and a fighter, a man for whom providing medical care and wielding weapons were not mutually exclusive responsibilities.

Just as home-front gender ideology defined the roles and experiences of American and Vietnamese women, it also shaped the image of the American serviceman, who was the face of the U.S. mission in Vietnam. In the rhetoric of the Kennedy and Johnson administrations, the purpose of U.S. intervention was to prevent the spread of communism by offering American aid and support as a better alternative to Ho Chi Minh and the Viet Cong (VC).[3] Marines and Army units, such as the 101st Airborne, dispensed that aid, assuming the role of caring father figures to ill, frightened, and orphaned Vietnamese. Even though those gestures of goodwill undoubtedly brought some form of comfort to the recipients, however, they did not alleviate the widespread suffering and destruction that U.S. troops also caused as part of the war. The central contradiction in the gentle warrior as the *Observer* defined him was that he was to be both a fighter and a friend, characteristics that proved irreconcilable in Vietnam.

The gentle warrior, then, was a metaphor for U.S. intervention – policymakers presented it to the American public and the Vietnamese as a benevolent effort to democratize and modernize South Vietnam even as the U.S. presence harmed the ally it was ostensibly meant to save. The picture of a paratrooper hugging a Vietnamese toddler he just vaccinated appears to be a vision of fatherly concern, but beneath the surface were imperialistic beliefs about the rights and responsibilities of the U.S. military to Vietnam, including the notion that the U.S. must tear South Vietnam down first before rebuilding it.[4] Captured with a wider lens, sorrow, destruction, and death filled out the picture around the child and the caring GI. The VC and North Vietnamese Army were also responsible for the devastation the war inflicted on Vietnam, including atrocities committed against civilians, but the United States had positioned itself as the humane option to oppressive communism, making its digressions from that promise all the more sinister.

The gentle warrior was only one face of the American serviceman in Vietnam, part of a larger constellation of images that reflected the

---

[3] See Lloyd Gardner, *Pay Any Price: Lyndon Johnson and the Wars for Vietnam* (Chicago: Ivan R. Dee, 1995); David Halberstam, *The Best and the Brightest* (New York: Random House, 1992); Howard Jones, *Death of a Generation: How the Assassinations of Diem and JFK Prolonged the Vietnam War* (New York: Oxford University Press, 2003).

[4] After the U.S. bombing of the Mekong Delta city Ben Tre in February 1968, an American officer allegedly told journalist Peter Arnett that U.S. forces had to "destroy the village in order to save it," which referred to the fact that the U.S. risked civilian casualties to rid Ben Tre of Viet Cong.

complex ideas about masculinity and sexuality that were embedded in home-front and military culture. In military publications such as the *Observer*, in the rhetoric and culture of basic training, and in soldier folklore, U.S. servicemen encountered three recurring images of the American fighting man. A second key image, that of the gunslinger, derived from the actor John Wayne and the characters he portrayed in movies mythologizing the frontier and World War II. As Tom Engelhardt and Richard Slotkin have shown, the John Wayne persona of the lone gunman on the frontier, stoic and deft with his weapon, was a dominant image in the popular culture of many Vietnam-era soldiers.[5] Sociologist Michael Kimmel has written that Wayne, who, according to polls from the 1950s into the 1970s, was "the American man that other American men most admired," was not a father figure but a "two-fisted loner who would not get tied down by domestic responsibility but always kept moving toward the edges of society, toward the frontier."[6]

According to psychiatrist Robert J. Lifton's discussion of the warrior myth, combat is the ultimate rite of passage from boyhood to manhood. Basic training strips the soldier of emotion, civilian identity, and attachment to personal community to ensure his loyalty to the military.[7] If the gentle warrior were meant to bring aid and comfort to the South Vietnamese as a paternalistic demonstration of benevolent foreign policy, then John Wayne was the gunslinger fighting the VC just as Wayne, playing Davy Crockett, fought Mexicans at the Alamo in a film he also directed and produced. Absolute distinctions between good and evil, right and wrong, defined Wayne's worldview, which included neat divisions between cowboys and Indians, good guys and bad guys.[8] In this morally unambiguous world, the girl next door symbolized all that was good about America, a figure of purity in need of protection. Even though he is a solitary man out on the frontier away from the constraints of domesticity, the gunslinger's actions, however brutal, are justified because he

---

[5] Loren Baritz, *Backfire: A History of How American Culture Led Us Into Vietnam and Made Us Fight the Way We Did* (New York: William Morrow and Co., 1985); Richard Slotkin, *Gunfighter Nation: The Myth of the Frontier in Twentieth-Century America* (Norman, OK: University of Oklahoma Press, 1998), 519–20; Tom Engelhardt, *The End of Victory Culture: Cold War America and the Disillusioning of a Generation* (New York: Basic Books, 1995).

[6] Michael Kimmel, *Manhood in America: A Cultural History* (New York: The Free Press, 1996), 253.

[7] Robert Jay Lifton, *Home from the War: Learning from Vietnam Veterans* (Boston: Beacon Press, 1992), 23–31.

[8] Kimmel, 253.

protects civilization against savages. As did the gentle warrior, the frontier loner practiced paternalism, assuming responsibility for the women and children back on the homestead, as well as for weaker, less masculine men living in the towns and on farms.[9]

Official rhetoric aside, Vietnam did not offer such tidy categories. Conflicting viewpoints, an unclear mission, and the elusive nature of guerrilla warfare created a murky environment for U.S. troops who, as the conflict wore on, increasingly questioned its purpose. In his poem, "Guerrilla War," W. D. Ehrhart, a Pennsylvanian who served in the U.S. Marines for three years, including a thirteen-month tour in Vietnam, wrote that in the war, it was "practically impossible to tell civilians from the Viet Cong."[10] Many wore an outfit Americans called "black pajamas," similar to the clothes ordinary farmers wore, instead of an official military uniform; they spoke the same language as the Vietnamese who were supposedly America's friends; they allegedly hid grenades and other explosive devices under their clothes and in their shopping baskets; and they employed women and children to fight alongside men. All these factors made it difficult for U.S. servicemen to tell friend from foe. "After awhile [*sic*], you quit trying," Ehrhart wrote.[11] In the worst examples of the U.S. mission gone awry, troops used the vagaries of guerrilla warfare to justify their indiscriminate abuse of Vietnamese civilians, which flew in the face of the gentle warrior's comforting aid and the gunslinger's defense of supposedly vulnerable women, children, and weak communities under attack.

A third face of the U.S. serviceman, rarely mentioned directly in official military publications but implied via pinup photos and suggestive cartoons, was that of the sexual aggressor. The daily interactions between GIs and Vietnamese women were at times shaped by perceptions of them as dragon ladies and whores, images that were complicated by the presence of women in the VC. The sexual aggression was fostered during basic training and condoned by policies that supported the creation of areas such as Sin City, an entertainment complex in which brothels were the most popular spots. Although Vietnamese women were primarily victims of troop sexuality, occasionally an entrepreneurial Vietnamese woman

---

[9] The 1960 John Sturges film, *The Magnificent Seven*, portrays these ideas particularly clearly. See also Slotkin, 474–86.
[10] W. D. Ehrhart, "Guerrilla War," in *Unaccustomed Mercy: Soldier-Poets of the Vietnam War*, ed. W. D. Ehrhart (Lubbock, TX: Texas Tech University Press, 1989), 57.
[11] Ibid.

capitalized on military masculinity by establishing herself as a successful brothel owner. At least one such woman ran into trouble with U.S.
Army officials and became the subject of a congressional investigation
into corruption in South Vietnam.[12]

The tensions among the three images were embedded in larger patterns
over which individual GIs had no control. In military media, the gentle
warrior was invoked to soften the gunslinger figure, but it could not mask
the havoc U.S. policies and the war wreaked on Vietnam. Degrading
sexual encounters between American troops and Vietnamese prostitutes
in the brothels of Sin City contradicted the image of the U.S. military
as a benevolent rescuer of a feminized South Vietnam in distress. That
the gentle warrior, the gunslinger, and the sexual aggressor were one
and the same further complicated the situation. The soldier who could
improve life could also take it, trading a syringe for a rifle and returning
to the village to snuff out suspected VC. Marines built homes and
sponsored orphanages, but Vietnamese were homeless and parentless
because U.S. policies generated the suffering that civic action programs
could not possibly alleviate. The war's destruction of the Vietnamese
countryside drove throngs of women into cities in search of work, often
in the sexual service of U.S. troops.[13] To be sure, individual servicemen
did believe they were helping to improve the lives of the Vietnamese, and
some provided real humanitarian assistance to villages, orphanages, and
schools in the midst of war. But their personal convictions could not hide
the war's devastating consequences or counter the misguided policies
that mired American soldiers in Vietnam. Even though some tried to, and
did, mitigate suffering on a local scale, American GIs could not change
the overall situation in which U.S. policymakers had placed them.

The images of the gentle warrior, the gunslinger, and the sexual aggressor comprised what historian Stephen Kantrowitz calls the "faces of
domination." Studying slavery in the U.S. South, Kantrowitz argues that
domination in that context relied on paternalism and its twin powers of
violence and restraint.[14] Similarly, as Cynthia Enloe has shown, in South
Vietnam, the U.S. military relied on "patriarchal family structures" to

---

[12] U.S. Senate Committee on Government Operations, Permanent Subcommittee on Inves-
    tigations, *Fraud and Corruption in Management of Military Club Systems* (Washington,
    DC: U.S Government Printing Office, 1971).

[13] For the war's impact on the Vietnamese countryside, see James Gibson, *The Perfect War:
    Technowar in Vietnam* (New York: Atlantic Monthly Press, 1986).

[14] Stephen Kantrowitz, "The Two Faces of Domination in North Carolina, 1800–1898,"
    in *Democracy Betrayed: The Wilmington Race Riot of 1898 and Its Legacy*, ed. David

assert power and control.[15] During the Vietnam War, U.S. troops articulated the masculine side of patriarchy through fatherly care, the killing of enemies in combat, and the sexual domination of Vietnamese women. In all three forms, American servicemen enforced U.S. power in Vietnam, permeating the social, economic, and political structures of the country well beyond the combat zones. U.S. troops confronted the unavoidable tensions in the three images in different ways; some came to understand that the humanitarian efforts of individual gentle warriors could not mask the war's destruction of Vietnam. Historian Andrew Huebner has detailed how American mainstream media increasingly focused on the image of the Vietnam GI as a victim of bad policies, a depiction that stood in stark contrast to the warrior ideal presented in military publications and diplomatic rhetoric.[16] As expressions of GI disillusionment increased after 1968, some troops began to view themselves as victims specifically of the machismo that undergirded U.S. intervention in Vietnam, and they called for an end to both the war and the era's gender politics.

John Wayne and Cold War Masculinities

As part of the all-encompassing social change that occurred in the decades after World War II, conventional white, middle-class notions of how men should live and work came under increasing pressure. After the war, sociologists and psychiatrists worried about veterans' ability to readjust to civilian life. With the help of advice columnists in women's magazines, they emphasized the importance of establishing home lives in which breadwinning and fatherhood bolstered manhood. Middle-class women who had gone to work outside the home during the war were to return to their kitchens, while their husbands sought careers that would allow them to provide a comfortable, consumer-driven, suburban life. Even as they resumed their expected roles, some men and many women felt disillusioned, anxious, and empty, wondering why they were not happy when they had everything society had told them they should want.

Cecelski and Timothy B. Tyson (Chapel Hill, NC: University of North Carolina Press, 1998), 95–111.

[15] Cynthia Enloe, *Does Khaki Become You? The Militarization of Women's Lives* (London: Pandora, 1988), 188–89.

[16] Andrew Huebner, *The Warrior Image: Soldiers in American Culture from the Second World War to the Vietnam Era* (Chapel Hill, NC: University of North Carolina Press, 2008).

In the 1950s, authors such as J. D. Salinger, Ayn Rand, and C. Wright Mills criticized American conformist culture and created male characters who rejected the role of the faceless "organization man" toiling in an office building so that his wife and children could have the same material possessions that the neighbors had. Rebellion by white men against suburban manhood took several forms. Jack Kerouac immortalized the road-trip male bonding of the Beats. Norman Mailer romanticized African American men as authentically masculine, calling on white men to save themselves by following the "male urban outlaw, living on the edge, searching out sex, using marijuana, appreciating jazz, finding momentary truth in the body." Men's magazines created in the 1950s – *Male, Real: The Exciting Magazine for Men, Impact: Bold True Action for Men,* and *True* – glorified the outdoorsman and the warrior as the antidote to stifling wives and domestic responsibilities. Hugh Hefner's *Playboy* offered the blueprint for a heterosexual bachelor utopia in which neither consumerism nor women were the enemies, but rather were enjoyable pursuits when unconstrained by domesticity.[17]

The emergence of John Wayne – both the actor and the persona his film characters embodied – during this period reflected both an ideal of masculinity and an alternative to the bland Willy Lomans and the men in gray flannel suits.[18] Loren Baritz argues that Wayne represented "the traditional American male" who "performs, delivers the goods, is a loner, has the equipment, usually a six-shooter or a superior rifle, to beat the bad guys, and he knows what he is doing."[19] Throughout the 1950s and into the 1960s, novels, television shows, and films glorified the frontier as the "meeting point between civilization and savagery," in which toughness and a commitment to absolute truths defined real men. Western-themed shows dominated television in the fifties; in 1958 alone, fifty-four Western films were made.[20] Wayne became the ultimate cowboy–hero; in his own life he made it his mission to promote "good, old-fashioned American virtues," which in the Cold War world meant fighting communist

---

[17] Kimmel, 223–58. See also Jack Kerouac, *On the Road* (New York: Viking, 1957); Norman Mailer, "The White Negro: Superficial Reflections on the Hipster," *Dissent,* Summer 1957; Barbara Ehrenreich, *Hearts of Men: American Dreams and the Flight from Commitment* (New York: Anchor, 1987).

[18] See Arthur Miller, *Death of a Salesman* (New York: Penguin, 1949); Sloan Wilson, *The Man in the Grey Flannel Suit* (New York: Da Capo Press, 1955).

[19] Robert Jay Lifton, *Home from the War: Learning from Vietnam Veterans* (Boston: Beacon Press, 1992), 23–31.

[20] Kimmel, 252.

insurrections. In 1966, Wayne toured Vietnam to entertain U.S. troops, and he returned home an outspoken supporter of the war. His experience in Vietnam inspired him to direct and star in *The Green Berets*, a film that critics panned but that grossed $7 million in its first three months.[21] For many of the men who served in Vietnam, cowboys, Indians, and the Wild West shaped the playtime of their youth, and "Indians" stood in for faceless communism in their childhood war games.[22] Noting the international reach of the John Wayne image, Cynthia Enloe characterizes Wayne as "globalized shorthand for militarized masculinity."[23]

The ideas Wayne embodied played out not only on the big and small screens but also in the development of U.S. foreign policy. Cowboy movies enforced the notion that the United States had a noble mission to press ahead into the "new frontier" and tame the "savage" world.[24] Immersed in a culture in which the figure of John Wayne symbolized the masculine ideal, U.S. policymakers were influenced, consciously and unconsciously, by these cultural narratives as they plotted the course of America's international relations. The influence showed up in the language they used to talk about Vietnam.[25] Numerous historians have observed that the boundaries that determined men's and women's roles in domestic society extended overseas wherever the American armed forced deployed advisors or troops. John F. Kennedy won the presidency in 1960 with a vision that U.S.-style democracy would touch all corners of the globe. But the new president feared that suburban comforts had made American young men "soft" and thus unfit to compete in Cold War competitions. Robert Dean argues that, to justify projects such as the expansion of the Army's Green Berets, Kennedy exploited the fear that a "crisis of masculinity" could weaken U.S. global power.[26] The president wrote articles for *Sports Illustrated*; hired Bud Wilkinson, a former University of Oklahoma football coach, to be his physical fitness advisor; and created the President's

[21] Ronald L. Davis, *Duke: The Life and Image of John Wayne* (Norman, OK: University of Oklahoma Press, 1998); Michael Kimmel, *Manhood in America: A Cultural History* (New York: The Free Press, 1996); Jerry Lembcke, *The Spitting Image: Myth, Memory, and the Legacy of Vietnam* (New York: New York University Press, 2000).

[22] Tom Engelhardt, *The End of Victory Culture: Cold War America and the Disillusioning of a Generation* (New York: Basic Books, 1995), 71–72.

[23] Enloe, xxix.

[24] Richard Slotkin provides a detailed analysis of the frontier idea in U.S. history, including the policies related to the Vietnam War. See Slotkin, *Gunfighter Nation*.

[25] Robert D. Dean, *Imperial Brotherhood: Gender and the Making of Cold War Foreign Policy* (Amherst, MA: University of Massachusetts Press, 2001).

[26] Ibid., 169.

Council on Youth Fitness, which set standards for physical education at public schools.[27] Kennedy believed that American men must be "tough" and physically fit to endure "military demands in Europe and the jungles of Asia."[28] As David Halberstam wrote in *The Best and the Brightest*, "Manhood was very much in the minds of the architects" of Kennedy's, and later Lyndon Johnson's, Vietnam War policies. "They wanted to show who had bigger balls."[29]

Lyndon Johnson inherited Vietnam from Kennedy, and John Wayne-like concerns about masculinity also informed his policymaking. He feared that he would appear "less of a man" than Kennedy if he brought U.S. troops home before winning the war.[30] Reflecting the paternalism of American Cold War foreign policy, Johnson believed the United States had an obligation to help alleviate poverty in the decolonizing world. Lloyd Gardner argues that Johnson and advisors such as Walt Rostow viewed economic development as the means to halt the spread of Communism. Initiatives such as the Mekong Project, which was modeled after the New Deal Tennessee Valley Authority, aimed to bring electricity to and improve irrigation in the Mekong River region. To provide a moral justification for U.S. intervention in Vietnam, Johnson sought to extend the "Great Society" into foreign policy by committing money and manpower to modernization and development projects. It reflected his paternalistic conviction that the United States had a duty to aid the development of "backward regions."[31]

The economic gestures were part of a broader United States attempt to influence the Cold War world by reaching out to decolonized regions and offering an American-style alternative to communism. It was because of U.S. financial backing, political support, and military protection that South Vietnam existed. In 1956, then-Senator John F. Kennedy gave a speech to the pro-South Vietnam lobby American Friends of Vietnam that emphasized the paternalistic nature of the relationship between the U.S. and South Vietnam. "If we are not the parents of little Vietnam,

[27] Ibid.
[28] Donald Mrozek, "The Cult and Ritual of Toughness in Cold War America," in *Rituals and Ceremonies in Popular Culture*, ed. Ray B. Browne (Bowling Green, OH: Bowling Green University Popular Press, 1980), 183; John F. Kennedy, "The Vigor We Need," *Sports Illustrated*, July 16, 1962.
[29] Cited in Kimmel, 466, fn 16. See also, David Halberstam, *The Best and the Brightest* (New York: Random House, 1972).
[30] Kimmel, 269.
[31] Lloyd C. Gardner, *Pay Any Price: Lyndon Johnson and the Wars for Vietnam* (Chicago: Ivan R. Dee, 1995); see also Thi Dieu Nguyen, *The Mekong River and the Struggle for Indochina: Water, War, and Peace* (Westport, CT: Praeger Publishers, 1999), 87.

then surely we are the godparents," Kennedy contended. "We presided at its birth, we gave assistance to its life, we have helped to shape its future.... This is our offspring – we cannot abandon it, we cannot ignore its needs."[32] The parent–child image continued into Johnson's presidency. The underlying paternalism of the gentle warrior and gunslinger images was clear in the 1965 propaganda film *Why Vietnam*, narrated by Johnson, which showed U.S. troops taking care of Vietnamese children as a means of presenting the United States as the humane alternative to brutal Communism.[33]

John Wayne, whose personal politics aligned clearly with social conservatism at home and activist policies abroad, was not the model of masculinity for all American men who served in Vietnam, but patriarchal attitudes were pervasive. Leaders of the Black Panther Party articulated a version of manhood based on African Americans' achieving independence and control over their lives and communities. To them, manhood meant rejecting white social, political, economic, and cultural structures that for so long had been used to oppress blacks. Other African Americans saw manhood embodied in the boxer Muhammad Ali, who refused to report for Army duty in 1965 after his petition for conscientious objector status was denied. In 1966, the Student Nonviolent Coordinating Committee (SNCC), a leading organization in the black freedom struggles of the era, issued a statement in support of men who chose to avoid a war that SNCC considered a racist endeavor of white imperialism against the Vietnamese. These constructions of masculinity did not reject sexism or gender stereotypes, though, as women activists have testified, speaking out about their marginalization within organizations such as SNCC and others. Though perhaps not inspired by John Wayne, some Southern black men embraced military service as the best option for escape from the discrimination and brutality of the Jim Crow South, where violence and lack of opportunities for economic advancement emasculated them as part of efforts to maintain the status quo of white supremacy.[34]

Yet another form of masculinity was present in Hispanic communities. Through World War II, Mexican Americans had emphasized military service as an avenue for proving manhood and worthiness of citizenship.

---

[32] Patrick Hagopian, *The Vietnam War in American Memory: Veterans, Memorials, and the Politics of Healing* (Amherst, MA: University of Massachusetts Press, 2009), 311.
[33] Ibid.
[34] A good oral history collection of Southern Vietnam veterans, which provides insights into black Southern veterans' attitudes toward military service, is James R. Wilson, *Landing Zones: Southern Veterans Remember Vietnam* (Durham, NC: Duke University Press, 1990).

The desire to demonstrate loyalty and manhood fostered a "readiness to die" among young Chicanos that, according to George Mariscal, carried over to the Vietnam generation. Some young Chicanos built an antiwar movement around rejecting the imperialistic attitudes that John Wayne represented, however, identifying with Vietnamese resistance. Yet Chicanas have written and spoken about being relegated to positions as secretaries, cooks, and maids within movement organizations. Paternalism and chauvinism affected definitions of manhood in every racial group, reflecting the pervasiveness of Cold War gender ideals. Regarding the men who became soldiers, either voluntarily or through conscription, Robert Jay Lifton wrote that whatever an individual soldier's view of manhood, for those who became soldiers, either voluntarily or through the draft, "a crucial factor was the super-masculinity promoted within the military."[35]

Asian American servicemen faced a particularly complex set of pressures and were sometimes explicitly excluded from following John Wayne's lead. During basic training at Quantico, Virginia, in 1966, a drill instructor told Don Mitsuo, a Japanese American Marine, to don a pair of loose black pants, a black shirt, and a conical straw hat. After he put on the costume, the drill sergeant handed Mitsuo a rifle, directed him to a stage in front of the other Marines, and said, "This is what your enemy looks like. I want you to kill it before it kills you."[36] Like Mitsuo, Don Lau, an Army enlistee, had to play a VC in basic training. The racism followed him to Vietnam when he deployed in 1968 as a war correspondent. Heading out one evening during R&R at Vung Tau, Lau encountered two MPs shortly after he left his hotel. The officers spoke to him in Vietnamese, but Lau explained to them that he was a born-and-raised Brooklynite and a journalist for the U.S. Army. They did not believe him, so they asked him to state who won the 1933 World Series. "I did not know then that it was the Washington Senators, because that was the only World Series that they had ever won, and even the most true-blooded Americans don't know that," Lau said. The MPs continued to harass him, but he convinced them to take him back to the hotel and

35 Curtis J. Austin, *Up Against the Wall: Violence in the Making and Unmaking of the Black Panther Party* (Fayetteville, AR: University of Arkansas Press, 2006), 78–79; James Westheider, *Fighting on Two Fronts: African Americans and the Vietnam War* (New York: NYU Press, 1997), 18, 27, 143; Lorena Oropeza, *Raza Si! Guerra No! Chicano Protest and Patriotism during the Vietnam War Era* (Berkeley, CA: University of California Press, 2005), 111–26; George Mariscal, *Aztlan and Viet Nam: Chicano and Chicana Experiences of the War* (Berkeley, CA: University of California Press, 1999), 203–12; Lifton, 239.
36 Toshio Whelchel, *From Pearl Harbor to Saigon: Japanese American Soldiers and the Vietnam War* (London: Verso, 1999), 13.

up to his captain's room. The captain was familiar with Lau's plight. "He was always getting me out of trouble with whites and blacks who thought I was a Viet Cong," Lau said. With a gun pressed into the small of his back, Lau walked with the officers to his captain's room. When they arrived, the captain told the officers that Lau was "one of us." The MPs released him, but anger over the incident stuck with Lau for a long time afterward. Lau even had to explain himself to the Vietnamese secretaries, nicknamed Cho-Cho and Baby Doll, who worked in his sergeant's office. When they asked him to explain why he was wearing an American uniform, Lau realized that they thought he was Vietnamese because of his Asian heritage, which cast him as the enemy, not John Wayne.[37]

Gentle Warriors

Although the John Wayne image required violence as part of a civilizing mission, U.S. military publications made a conscious attempt to highlight the benefits accruing to the Vietnamese from the American presence. Official U.S. military newspapers such as MACV's *Observer* and the *Army Reporter* carefully constructed and maintained images of U.S. soldiers as tender caregivers. In the pages of military publications, intended primarily for military personnel, the gentle warrior stood for freedom and democracy, for immunizations and water purification systems, for the benevolent sharing of American ideas and ways of life. Sprinkled among articles about battles, troop levels, and personnel changes were stories of Marines throwing birthday parties at orphanages, units of paratroopers delivering pencils and books to schools built by Army engineers, and military doctors staffing rehabilitation centers for wounded Vietnamese civilians. Reinforcing paternalistic images of the Vietnamese as victims in need of the gunslinger's protection, numerous stories highlighted soldiers' work with Vietnamese children and families; many included photographs of GIs playing with babies and comforting worried mothers (Figure 10).

Descriptions of the Marine Corps' Civic Action Program, published by the Department of the Navy in 1967, clearly casts Marines as fatherly gentle warriors, whose humanitarian efforts were a key part of the American pacification program. A pamphlet titled "Marines Care" told the story of six Vietnamese women from a village near Da Nang who rejected VC anti-American propaganda and aided Marines in capturing VC

---

[37] "Asian Viet vets want memorial to honor their own war dead," *East-West*, February 20, 1985, Lily Adams Collection, University of Denver Penrose Library Special Collections, Denver, CO, Box 1.

FIGURE 10. SP4 Mark Ellerbee, 9th Infantry Division Medic, treats a Vietnamese woman in Rach Kein. Army News Features Photo. U.S. Army Aviation Museum Volunteer Archivists Collection, The Vietnam Archive, Texas Tech University.

operatives in the area. Following the story was a question: "Why would these six women risk their lives to help the Marines, when only three months ago they feared Americans?" The rest of the pamphlet explained how Marines won the loyalty of the villagers and other Vietnamese through civic action. Viet Cong operatives had terrorized the village, kidnapping its chief, schoolteacher, and local government officials and beheading them. When the Marines arrived, they, with the help of the local Vietnamese women, captured a VC patrol after winning over some of the villagers with food, medical care, and repaired infrastructure, including a school. The pamphlet described "the battle-scarred hands of a Marine infantryman teaching a small Vietnamese boy to count in English; a smiling face under a camouflaged helmet offering a can of 'C' rations and still another green-clad figure giving a little girl – destined by the fate of guerrilla warfare to spend her youth in an orphanage – her first real doll."

Waging a "war within a war," the Marines, through civic action, were "armed not with guns, but with kindness and understanding." Taken at face value, the story is a touching glimpse of human contact in the midst of a brutal, dehumanizing war. For the individual Marines involved, it was a chance to have an immediate, positive impact on the lives of the children and other villagers. But the fact was that much of the suffering the Marines alleviated was a direct result of the American military presence. As the pamphlet reminded readers, the Marines had two sides: "the cold-blooded courage to storm in battle, then the warm-hearted kindness to comfort the victims – the hungry, naked 'children' caught up in the conflict."[38] Although the article portrays the two personas as compatible, the images revealed one of the central contradictions in U.S. intervention. The purpose ostensibly was to liberate the South Vietnamese from communist oppression and VC terror, but the United States was complicit in a war that orphaned children and visited destruction upon Vietnam. No individual Marine could resolve the irreconcilable contradictions encompassing the image of the gentle warrior.

As the rhetoric of Kennedy, Johnson, and others suggested, images of U.S. troops aiding Vietnamese children were important to American propaganda regarding the U.S. mission in Vietnam. Both the nation of South Vietnam and the South Vietnamese people were cast as children in need of American protection and support, and articles in military publications reflected this notion.[39] The most common humanitarian stories published in the *Observer* and *Army Reporter* featured U.S. troops embarked on humanitarian projects as early as 1961, when the Army's 509th Radio Research Group adopted the Sancta Maria Orphanage in Gia Dinh, a suburb of Saigon; throughout the war, the *Observer* and *Army Reporter* featured stories about U.S. soldiers visiting orphanages with supplies, toys, and candy. An article in the February 27, 1967 *Observer* noted that from the time the 509th adopted the orphanage, a home for about 300 children, the unit donated about $1,000 plus clothes and supplies to it each month. Donations came in from the States and from other military bases throughout the world. Soldiers from the 509th regularly visited the orphanage, usually to deliver gifts and money. To help their fellow servicemen take care of the orphans, a team of medics from the

---

[38] "Marines 'Care': Civic Action, A Study in Humanitarianism," U.S. Department of the Navy, 1967. Douglas Pike Collection: Unit 02 – Military Operations, Folder 14, Box 09, The Vietnam Archive, Texas Tech University.

[39] Hagopian, 312.

16th Medical Dispensary made sick calls to the orphanage to treat the children.[40]

Similar tales concerned units such as the Navy Seabees stationed at Da Nang, who threw parties for the children living at the World Evangelical Crusade Orphanage in the city. The *Observer* reported the "delighted squeals of little girls clutching new dolls and teddy bears, and the shouts of boys as they received basketballs from Chaplain Ferguson." Before the Seabees handed out the gifts, a Vietnamese interpreter told the excited orphans that the American servicemen were happy to host the party. Then, Seaman James Collins "delighted" the children by speaking Vietnamese to them, welcoming them to the party in their native tongue. The article noted that the orphans were well-behaved and "filed by in a well-ordered fashion to receive the gifts." In the end, though, the Seabees were the ones who received the "greatest gift," the article observed. "There could have been no gift greater than to see the eager sparkle in the children's eyes, the joy on their faces as they played with their gifts, and to hear the shrieks of delight as they unwrapped their prizes."[41] Like the friendly uncle in town for a visit, American soldiers arrived at the door of the orphanage bearing gifts and offering piggy-back rides to energetic nieces and nephews.

Some troops built homes, distributed food and clothing, and offered language and technical courses. An article in the *Observer* reported that, in 1966, American soldiers helped build or repair homes for nearly nine thousand families. During the year, they delivered more than 8,500 tons of food, nearly 750 tons of clothing, and almost 300 tons of soap to Vietnamese civilians. Military personnel staffed more than ten thousand English classes and more than five hundred vocational training courses throughout South Vietnam. Rounding out the work of the Civic Action Program were the building of 191 houses of worship, 245 dispensaries, 81 hospitals, 85 orphanages, 447 schools, and 1,108 classrooms. An article describing a Marine engineering project began by announcing that "an investment in the future of a free Vietnam was made recently at the dedication of the Hoa Khan school." The Marines built the school to serve about 500 children from a refugee community just outside Da Nang.[42]

[40] "509th Radio Research Personnel Continue to Support Orphanage," *Observer*, February 27, 1967, 1, NARA RG 472, Box 1.
[41] "Party Delights Viet Children," *Observer*, February 6, 1967, NARA RG 472, Box 1.
[42] "U.S. Marines Build School for Refugees," *Observer*, February 27, 1967, 4, NARA RG 472, Box 1.

Additionally, through the Army's Medical Civic Action Program (MEDCAP), medics treated more than five million Vietnamese civilians.[43] Next to the story was a photograph of an American medic holding a stethoscope to the chest of baby held by a nervous-looking Vietnamese woman. The photo's caption noted that the child had bronchitis and identified the medic as Staff Sergeant Wolfram Bischof of the Special Forces A Team. The school-building article portrayed American military personnel as surrogate fathers investing in their children's education, and the picture showed a man comforting a mother and child with ease. In these contexts, U.S. servicemen were teachers, personal hygiene instructors, and health care providers. No mention was made of the fact that the homes and schools were being built to replace those destroyed by other U.S. forces engaged in war. However sincere the efforts of the gentle warrior, it was impossible to resolve the fundamental, ultimately unsustainable, contradictions in the U.S. mission.

Still, the gentle warrior image appeared in article after article. A photographer for the *Observer* captured the image of a Vietnamese baby grabbing the face of Captain Morris White, a flight surgeon with the 145th Combat Aviation Battalion. White was holding the baby and smiling as a tiny hand reached for his nose. The photo's caption read that the battalion regularly visited a small town called Bien Co, bringing health care supplies and offering medical examinations to residents. The caption noted that town residents "consistently turn out for Captain White against the advice of the local Viet Cong."[44] The front page of the April 3, 1967, issue of the *Observer* featured a photograph of a young Navy medic examining an eleven-month-old Vietnamese girl. The headline of the accompanying article read, "Babies, Disease, Shrapnel: 'It's All in a Day's Work.'" In the story, nineteen-year-old Navy Corpsman Carroll C. Taylor saved the choking baby while her frantic, helpless parents looked on. She was the only daughter among the family's eleven children, and according to the article, her mother was "overjoyed" when Taylor handed the breathing baby to her. Later in the story, the reporter explained that sick Vietnamese villagers went to the aid station Taylor staffed in the coastal village of Tuy Loan, a few miles southwest of Da Nang. Some had toothaches; others suffered from infected sores. Villagers brought

[43] "Impressive Civic Action Statistics Cited," *Observer*, February 27, 1967, 3, NARA RG 472, Box 1.
[44] "Choi Oi, Doc, What a Nose!" *Observer*, January 9, 1967, NARA RG 472, Box 1.

family members and friends with broken bones and more serious injuries inflicted by booby traps and land mines.

Taylor, known as "Doc," attributed many of the minor injuries and illnesses he treated to Vietnamese backwardness, especially poor hygienic practices and sanitary conditions. "These people have customs that don't change easily," Taylor told the *Observer* reporter. "Seabees came out here and built a toilet for these people, but soon it was torn to pieces." Another unit of Seabees went to Tuy Loan and installed two more toilets, a well with a hand pump, and a shower facility, the article reported. Taylor planned to enclose the village's central market with a screen to help stop the spread of diseases carried by insects.[45]

Taylor's words and actions highlight the contradictions inherent to the gentle warrior. Without a doubt, civic action work did much good for the Vietnamese on the receiving end of the projects, but the cultural attitudes that underwrote such programs were inseparable from categories of race and gender used to further American foreign policy. The gentle warrior image relied in part on notions of Vietnamese primitivism. As Ann Laura Stoler has argued, "the management of bodies and dispositions – and racialized thinking about them" often forms the basis of modernization efforts.[46] The U.S. serviceman who provided health care to or built schools for the Vietnamese symbolized ideas about American power and the notion that the U.S. had a duty – and a right – to enter countries and attempt to control them, even if that meant creating many of the problems with which the gentle warriors helped. The image of men as protectors – whether gunslingers or gentle warriors – determined that all Vietnamese would be subject to the protection and instruction of American servicemen.

The Observer's metaphorical account of the 1966 flooding of the Mekong River provides a striking example of the association between images of Vietnamese women, the gentle warriors, and the ideological justification for the U.S. presence in Vietnam. Published beneath the suggestive headline, "Mekong River Does the Twist," the article described "a big, beautiful woman who has had a little too much to drink ... the twisting, curvaceous Mekong River wandered drunkenly into the countryside." Her "decision to roam" wreaked havoc on Vietnamese men, women, and children, flooding their land and destroying their livelihood.

---

[45] "Babies, Disease, Shrapnel: 'It's All in a Day's Work,'" *Observer*, April 3, 1967, 1, NARA RG 472, Box 1.

[46] Stoler, "Intimidations of Empire," 5.

The 5th Special Forces A Team, however, arrived to rescue the soaked villages and control the unruly river. They filled sandbags and stacked them high until the wall seemed tall enough to stave off the flow of the water. The story predicted that, "like a victim of a hangover when the party's over, a tired and weary Mekong will soon return to her banks." With the river restrained, U.S. troops would help rebuild the area so that life could "return to normal" in the delta.[47] In the tale, the river, a woman out of control, was Vietnam. The Vietnamese peasants were passive bystanders too ignorant to take control. The members of the 5th Special Forces A Team were the benevolent, strong men who had the skills to save the day.

Even in coverage of the 1968 Tet offensive, the largest, longest, and deadliest series of battles in the Vietnam War, the *Observer* offered stories of U.S. soldiers as caregivers. One article described a "counteroffensive" launched by members of the Traffic Management Agency Headquarters in Saigon. Their retaliation involved soap and clothing, not bullets and bombs. Sergeant John Giertz, Specialist 5 Charles Ronayne, and Specialist 4 David Frazier collected the items from their churches back home and delivered them to a refugee center for civilians displaced by the Tet offensive. It was not the first time the men had donated goods to Vietnamese civilians. They regularly delivered gifts to children in the neighborhood in which they were stationed. When they arrived at the refugee center, curious children ran to "greet them with salutes and wide smiles." One of the soldiers mentioned that the children didn't seem to mind living in a makeshift refugee camp in a schoolyard. "Most of them looked as if they were enjoying the change in the daily routine of living in the same area," he remarked. "I doubt if many of them realize it was a deadly war which brought them together in a crowded school courtyard to live." To show their gratitude, some of the children surprised the servicemen by saying "thank you" to them in "perfect English."[48] The contrast between rhetoric and reality is stark. Although the individual servicemen of the Traffic Management Agency Headquarters may have viewed their actions as a humane counteroffensive to the Tet attacks, the U.S. military launched a major bombing campaign on South Vietnamese cities in retaliation for Tet, which did much more damage than soap and gifts could repair.

[47] "Mekong River Does the Twist," *Observer*, October 17, 1966, NARA RG 472, Box 1.
[48] "Three Saigon Soldiers Start Small Aid Program," *Observer*, March 6, 1968, NARA RG 472, Box 1.

"All the Way with Negligee"

"You want to know her inside and out, every contour and curve, every need and whim, what makes her tick." Thus began a new edition of the M16A1 rifle operation and maintenance manual, issued on July 1, 1969, by the Department of the Army. By that time, the M16A1 was the main rifle used by U.S. infantry troops in Vietnam. A cartoon of a curvaceous white woman led the reader through instructions on cleaning, reassembling, and storing the weapon – and sexual innuendo, including the proper uses of lubrication when caring for the M16, figured prominently throughout the manual. The section on taking the rifle apart was titled "How to Strip Your Baby." It was followed by a series of tips on ensuring that the weapon remained a soldier's "ever-lovin' sweet 16." The M16's plastic storage bag was a "maxi-skirt" and a "negligee" in a section called "All the Way with Negligee." A drawing depicting the rifle's magazine as a woman, featuring slender legs in stiletto heels, a winking eye, and pouty lips guided troops through a section called "Putting Maggie Together," which gave directions for assembling the magazine (Figure 11). Another cartoon in the segment showed "Maggie" reaching for a GI and saying "Protect me, you big strong guy!" The underlying point was that the soldier who treated his M16 tenderly and took care of it would be rewarded when his rifle operated properly in battle.[49]

Built on images designed to entice young soldiers to pay attention to the importance of proper weapon maintenance, the manual reinforced the heterosexual masculinity that was associated with military service in Vietnam. Sexualized images of weaponry represented an extension of American male virility – the strong dominating the weak, masculine dominating feminine in a metaphorical sexuality. "To some people, carrying a gun constantly was like having a permanent hard-on," said one GI. "It was a pure sexual trip every time you got to pull the trigger."[50] Elton Tylenda, an Army engineer who served with the 542nd Detachment in Vietnam in 1968, had a drill instructor who summed up the connection between sex and war in a simple sentence: "A man who don't fuck, don't kill."[51] Often, GIs were told that Vietnamese women were to be on the

---

[49] *The M16A1 Rifle: Operation and Preventive Maintenance*, DA Pam 750–30 (Washington, DC: U.S. Government Printing Office, 1969).

[50] Loren Baritz, *Backfire: A History of How American Culture Led Us Into Vietnam and Made Us Fight the Way We Did* (New York: William Morrow and Co., 1985), 51. See also Richard Slotkin, *Gunfighter Nation*, 519–20.

[51] Author's interview with Elton Tylenda, April 2007, Madison, WI.

FIGURE 11. The July 1969 edition of the operation and maintenance manual for the M16A1 featured sexualized imagery throughout, including this depiction of "Maggie," the rifle's magazine. U.S. Government Printing Office.

receiving end of their sexual prowess. Veteran Jim Roseberry remembered that Vietnamese women "were [considered] pieces of meat" in the culture of basic training.[52] A veteran who told his story in Mark Baker's oral history 'Nam said this about sexuality and power: "In the 'Nam you realized that you had the power to take a life. You had the power to rape a woman and nobody could say nothing to you. That godlike feeling you had was in the field. It was like I was a god. I could take a life, I could screw a woman. I can beat somebody up and get away with it. It was a godlike feeling that a guy could express in the 'Nam."[53] To be a gunslinger meant to be sexually aggressive, creating a bond between the roles of gunslinger and sexual aggressor, and setting up an irreconcilable tension with the image of the gentle warrior presented in the military press.

Answering the need for sexual outlets for U.S. troops, brothels followed the establishment of military bases in Vietnam. In the summer of 1965, 21,000 troops from the 1st Cavalry landed at An Khe, a village in the Central Highlands between Qui Nhon and Pleiku, and, according to newspaper reports and veterans' accounts, throngs of prostitutes arrived for work. To regulate An Khe's burgeoning sex trade, a group of village leaders suggested building a compound of "boom-boom" parlors to employ prostitutes. The result was a twenty-five-acre complex featuring bars, nightclubs, and brothels, surrounded by barbed wire and patrolled by American military police. Its official name was An Khe Plaza, but U.S. GIs called it "Disneyland" or "Sin City." Teenaged Vietnamese boys served as waiters. Vietnamese women who worked there were subjected to weekly exams at a medical clinic in An Khe to make sure they were free of venereal disease. When asked if the brothel posed a moral dilemma for the U.S. military, one colonel told a *Time* magazine reporter, "We wanted to get the greatest good for our men with the least harm."[54] It appears that the U.S. Armed Forces either destroyed or did not keep official records on places such as Sin City, a pattern scholars have identified as commonplace among militaries. As Cynthia Enloe notes, "to avoid political contradictions and risks, military elite try to minimize risks by a combination of decentralized responsibility, informal decision making, and official acknowledgement only of 'health issues.'"[55]

52 Author's interview with Jim Roseberry, April 2007, Madison, WI.
53 Mark Baker, *'Nam: The Vietnam War in the Words of the Soldiers Who Fought There* (New York: Berkeley Books, 1983), 152.
54 "Disneyland East," *Time*, May 6, 1966, http://www.time.com/time/magazine/article/0,9171,901833,00.html.
55 Enloe, 20.

An area known as Dogpatch, where prostitutes, masseuses, and drug dealers peddled their services, developed near the U.S. Marine base in Da Nang. Vietnamese women flocked to Can Tho, eighty miles north of Saigon, in 1966 when they learned that a large deployment of U.S. troops would be stationed there.[56] Brothels were established near the 1st Infantry Division camp at Lai Khe and the 4th Infantry post at Pleiku. At Lai Khe, the brothel compound was situated on a one-acre plot surrounded by a barbed wire fence and guarded by American MPs. Souvenir shops and hot dog and hamburger joints stood alongside two large buildings that were the reasons the complex existed. Inside each building were a bar, a bandstand, and several cubicles in which Vietnamese women worked as prostitutes. Some lived in their cubicles. The women tended to wear heavy makeup and sport bouffant-style hairdos; some injected their breasts with silicone to make them larger. Most of the women were war refugees who had lost their homes because of the fighting. The U.S. military took care of security and medical examinations of prostitutes, but Vietnamese province chiefs, mayors, and other local civilians handled business operations, from recruitment of sex workers to enforcement of payments.[57] Comparing South Vietnam with the American Old West, a *New York Times* reporter writing in early 1966 gestured to the connection between prostitution and the John Wayne mythology: "In places like Pleiku and An Khe, half-a-dozen saloons open up every week. Bar girls wiggle into town, dressed at midday as for midnight. It is all rather like the set for one of those old-style, clear-cut Westerns. You catch yourself expecting to see John Wayne ride in at any moment."[58]

In 1967, officials in the coastal city of Nha Trang cracked down on prostitution, arresting some three hundred women in two months. An estimate from the city's social welfare office counted approximately one thousand prostitutes, most of whom worked in the 100 brothels serving the 20,000 U.S. troops stationed in and around Nha Trang. Rumors circulated that city leaders and U.S. military officials worked together to regulate and perpetuate the sex trade, which was lucrative for prostitutes. According to one bar owner, sex workers in Nha Trang made an average yearly salary of 30,000 piasters, which was only about 4,000 piasters less than the salary of then-president Nguyen

---

[56] "G.I. Boom is Awaited," *New York Times*, Dec. 3, 1966, 2.
[57] Susan Brownmiller, *Against Our Will: Men, Women, and Rape* (New York: Bantam Books, 1976).
[58] Anthony Carthew, "Vietnam is Like an Oriental Western," *New York Times*, January 23, 1966, 208.

Cao Ky. Truong Thai Xiu, a nineteen-year-old prostitute who was arrested during the city's sweep of vice, stated that most of her customers were U.S troops, whom she charged anywhere from 300 to 500 piasters. South Vietnamese customers received a discounted rate of 200 piasters.[59]

Officials in Pleiku blamed the city's crime, congestion, and decline on the sex trade that catered to American GIs after Pleiku was placed "on limits" to troops in April 1968. U.S. servicemen were allowed to roam the city's streets from noon until six o'clock in the evening; their presence drew an estimated ten thousand bar girls looking for work. Major General Lu Lan, the ARVN commander in II Corps, where Pleiku was located, complained of the tensions generated between the U.S. military and residents of Pleiku when Army truckloads of Vietnamese women, presumed to be either bar girls or prostitutes (a distinction that did not matter in the eyes of many Vietnamese), arrived in the city to work in popular American hangouts such as Maxim's Chinese Restaurant and the Miami Bar. Several incidents of brawling between U.S. and ARVN troops broke out over Vietnamese women, straining relations between the supposed allies. Commenting on the issue, one U.S. official told a reporter: "When you get people from a different race and a different country who appears, because of his size and wealth, to be superior, there's bound to be some resentment." Another American official voiced a common concern throughout the U.S. chain of command: "Some of these girls are Viet Cong and we know that in a group of twenty to thirty prostitutes you'll find one who is working to gather information."[60] To alleviate the tensions between Americans and Vietnamese, some U.S. officials wanted to bring in the national police to remove bar girls and prostitutes. Considering that idea impractical, other American officials suggested moving saloons, massage parlors, and brothels to a ghetto just outside Pleiku. The area, which a reporter described as a "deserted Hollywood movie set," was built by the South Vietnamese for American GIs but stood vacant, for reasons unknown. One American official suggested that it was because no U.S. military commander wanted to be accused of condoning prostitution in Vietnam.[61]

---

[59] Jonathan Randal, "Nhatrang Fights Vice 'Grottoes,'" *New York Times*, April 28, 1967, 17.
[60] Bernard Weinraub, "Pleiku, Open to GIs, is Problem City," *New York Times*, August 12, 1968, 3.
[61] Ibid.

Regardless of official military sanction, the sex trade was a common element in the American GI experience, even for men who did not purchase the services of a prostitute. Elton Tylenda, an Army electrical engineer who was drafted at the end of 1967 when he was twenty-one years old, arrived at An Khe with the 542nd Detachment in May 1968. The Army assigned him to a team of engineers working with an independent contractor on electrical projects in the city. The engineers reported for duty, and a man in a black leather jacket, carrying an AK-47 rifle, pulled up on a motorcycle. He introduced himself as John Henry, their supervisor. He then told them about Sin City, recommended it highly, and explained where they could find his women. He promised that "they're all clean and checked once a week, and it's a safe place to go, and it's where the action is," Tylenda said. The man seemed a bit unbelievable to Tylenda. He was not even sure he believed the guy's name was John Henry, or if he had taken the name in reference to the African American folk hero whose strength and quickness powered him to beat a steam drill in a contest. The story became even more bizarre, however. Henry told the engineers that he had a home in the country outside An Khe and invited them to come by any time and visit. He provided the coordinates so they could find their way.

Curiosity got the best of Tylenda, and a few days later, he joined several other GIs who had stolen a jeep and headed out to find John Henry's house. It was at the end of a remote road, and there were no security fences or guards on the property. So they parked the jeep and knocked on the door. A Vietnamese woman greeted them and summoned John Henry. He emerged, welcomed them in, and told two other Vietnamese women to fetch scotch and amaretto for a round of drinks. As Henry bid the men farewell, he reminded them to visit Sin City. Tylenda suspected he had partnerships with both the U.S. and the VC because he was able to live out in the country unbothered.[62]

John Henry may have been real, or he may be a part of Vietnam veteran folklore, but he symbolizes a rugged masculinity expressed through individualism, detachment from the "establishment," and sexual indulgence. He went to Vietnam as an independent contractor, not a member of a military institution, so he was free to make arrangements to ensure his personal comfort; his only companions were Vietnamese women who served him domestically and sexually. He was a sexualized form of the John Wayne ideal – the individual man on the frontier, outside the reach

---

[62] Author's interview with Elton Tylenda.

of military bureaucracy or government control. It was a modified version of Hugh Hefner's "American Dream" – a house on a remote plot of land, a motorcycle, good bourbon, and Vietnamese women.

When Tylenda visited Sin City, he found U.S. military police guarding the entrance to the complex; visitors had to pass through a gated checkpoint to enter. Inside, there was a series of buildings on both sides of a road. Visitors could find "fine musical instruments, the best entertainment... and lots of women," Tylenda said. "It was like a little oasis in the middle of nowhere." He did not remember seeing any Vietnamese soldiers at Sin City, and he concluded that the operation's primary purpose was serving American men. The only Vietnamese men he encountered in Sin City were a few musicians who worked there. Vietnamese women had to have medical clearance and show an identification card to get in, Tylenda added.[63] Jim Mifflin, an Army helicopter crew chief, corroborated Tylenda's story. Mifflin was stationed at An Khe in 1968. In his experience, platoon sergeants and other leaders gave GIs permission to spend a day in Sin City once a week. He said no one ever forbade him or his friends from visiting the area, which he characterized as "a bunch of bars and whorehouses" and "ramshackle buildings." It was in the center of the city, "just something set up to make money off GIs. They'd have go-go dancers, bars, nightclubs, dancers, prostitutes, that's why you went down there." Although Sin City was within walking distance of the base, he and other GIs took a jeep when they visited. Mifflin had heard that, at one time, medics with the 1st Cavalry, the first U.S. troops to arrive at An Khe, had performed medical exams on prostitutes and treated those with venereal diseases. "It was kind of not talked about," Mifflin said, but the practice stopped after "somebody complained."[64]

Other American veterans remember areas similar to Sin City in different towns. Mike Subkoviak, a statistician who served in the Army in Vietnam in 1971 and was stationed at Long Binh and Binh Thuy in the Mekong Delta, noted that "there were massage parlors and there were brothels always on the periphery of wherever there was a large encampment." He knew that "some of our medical officers used to go check out the women to make sure they didn't have venereal diseases." The medics went to brothels regularly, he said. In Binh Thuy, "there was a recommended brothel because people said the women there were clean

[63] Ibid.
[64] Author's telephone interview with Jim Mifflin, May 2007, Madison, WI.

and our doctors went and tried to make sure they were free of disease," he added.[65] Typically, military authorities took a "boys will be boys" – hormonally charged, heterosexual boys – approach in their behavioral expectations of U.S. troops.

Stationed in Vung Tau and Can Tho in 1968, Bill Davis, an Air Force flight mechanic, noted that Vietnamese authorities also regulated the sex trade. Many cities and villages were off limits to Americans after dark; Vietnamese police patrolled the streets, making sure foreigners followed the law. If they discovered a GI trying to spend the night in a brothel, they arrested him. Some police officers were not above accepting bribes, however, and cigarettes usually did the trick. "You could get through roadblocks at night with cartons of cigarettes," Davis said. "They liked the menthols."[66] Vietnamese proprietors ran the majority of brothels Davis knew about. "Brothels were everywhere," he said. "There were little mom-and-pop operations up to large-scale fancy sort of things for officers." Brothels weren't the only places where soldiers could buy sex. Some barber shops were known for services other than haircuts, he said. Additionally, Davis asserted that the "American military cooperated in a health care sort of thing in some places." The sex industry in Vietnam wasn't developed by Americans, though, Davis said. The French established it when they were in Vietnam, and "it was just a matter of kicking it back into gear with the Americans." A report compiled in June 1971 for the Senate Committee on Foreign Relations concluded that the rise of prostitution was one of the main indicators that the war had caused an "erosion of the social fabric" of Vietnam.[67]

In January 1972, the Army made its relationship with prostitution public when it officially allowed Vietnamese prostitutes onto bases. By then, most cities and villages were off limits to American servicemen, so it was difficult to find places to purchase entertainment, female companionship, and sex. Despite concerns about security risks and drug trafficking, Army officers "said they supported the practice to keep peace within the increasingly disgruntled ranks" of U.S. servicemen remaining in Vietnam. The prostitutes were called "local national guests." To get on base they

---

[65] Author's interview with Mike Subkoviak, May 2007, Madison, WI.

[66] Author's interview with Bill Davis, May 2007, Oak Park, IL.

[67] Bill Davis interview; *Impact of the Vietnam War*, prepared for the use of Committee on Foreign Relations, United States Senate, by the Foreign Affairs Division, Congressional Research Service, Library of Congress (Washington, DC: U.S. Government Printing Office, 1971), 40.

needed a Vietnamese government-issued identification card, and a soldier had to sign them in when they arrived. As long as a serviceman accompanied them, the women were allowed into movie theaters, clubs, and barracks on base. Such open access meant that women could observe the positioning of weapons and the conditions of bases and supplies.[68] Nonetheless, at a time when the United States had all but lost control of the Vietnam War, American ideas about gender and sexuality still controlled relations between American and Vietnamese, and the security risk was largely ignored.

At times, sexual aggression resulted in violence. When combined with racism, the devaluation of Vietnamese women in boot camp sometimes led to rape and murder, as servicemen testified in various venues. Investigations into the My Lai massacre revealed that rape was one of the weapons used that morning in the hamlet. Early on March 16, 1968, a unit of the Army's American Division murdered more than 300 Vietnamese civilians, most of whom were women, children, and the elderly. In a sworn statement, Michael Lee Minor, a member of the unit in question, told of four GIs raping a Vietnamese girl, followed by a fifth soldier who inserted his M-16 into her vagina and pulled the trigger. Another GI, James H. Flynn, testified that "there was a lot of raping going on in the village," and Dennis Bunning, a rifleman, stated that he observed at least seven rapes, including some in which the perpetrators killed the woman after raping her. He testified to seeing one incident in which three servicemen gang-raped a woman. Pointing out that rape did not happen only in My Lai, Bunning added that he had witnessed many rapes during his tour of duty.[69]

A particularly disturbing instance of violence against a Vietnamese woman at the hands of American troops occurred in 1966, when four members of an Army reconnaissance patrol kidnapped an eighteen-year-old South Vietnamese woman named Phan Thi Mao, who was asleep in the house she shared with her parents. Over a twenty-four-hour period,

---

[68] "U.S. Now Admitting Prostitutes to Some of Its Vietnam Bases," *New York Times*, January 25, 1972, 12.

[69] Witness testimony of Michael Lee Minor to Jack P. Byers, United States Army Criminal Investigation Division Agency, Office of the Provost Marshall General, January 19, 1970. My Lai Collection, Folder 47, Box 01, The Vietnam Archive, Texas Tech University, Lubbock, TX; Testimony of Mr. James H. Flynn, February 11, 1970, p. 35, My Lai Collection, Folder 37, Box 01, The Vietnam Archive, Texas Tech University; Testimony of Mr. Dennis M. Bunning, January 16, 1970, pp. 26–36. My Lai Collection, Folder 34, Box 01, The Vietnam Archive, Texas Tech University.

they raped her repeatedly before taking her to a place called Hill 192, stabbing her, and, finally, shooting her to death. The fifth member of the patrol refused to take part in the brutality; when he returned to the post, he described the incident to a chaplain, who then took the initial steps toward a court-martial. The accused men had committed two offenses – kidnapping and rape – that were classified as capital crimes in the Uniform Code of Military Justice.[70] The trial resulted in four convictions, but one serviceman later was acquitted and the remaining three received lesser sentences. The patrol member who turned them in also told his story to *New Yorker* reporter Daniel Lang, who wrote an article for the October 18, 1969, issue called "The Crime on Hill 192," which became the basis for his subsequent book, *Casualties of War*. (In the 1980s, director Brian Di Palma adapted Lang's book for the screen.) In his reporting, Lang called the testifying soldier "Sven Erikkson" to protect his identity. According to Erikkson's testimony, Mao was not a suspected VC, and the only reason the troops abducted her was "for the purpose of boom-boom, or sexual intercourse." The men had intended to murder Mao once they had had their sexual fill.[71]

The atrocity was just one example of the violence bred by the combined dehumanization of Vietnamese women and enforcement of aggressive heterosexuality that started in basic training. The Army's responses to it highlight the morally hollow excuses given for such incidents as cover for the deep-seated military culture that perpetuated the idea that sexual violence was an expected and acceptable part of war. When Eriksson told Harold Reilly, the lieutenant of his platoon, what had happened to Mao, Reilly responded nonchalantly, "What else can you expect in a combat zone?"[72] That type of dispassion characterized the responses of other higher-ups and Eriksson's fellow GIs, and it came out in the four courts-martial proceedings. Those who did express concern, such as Captain Otto Vorst, Reilly's superior, appeared to worry about the Army's image, not Mao's brutal murder. Eriksson testified that he often heard the argument that "the V.C. also kidnapped, raped, murdered," as if to justify Americans' use of the same vile tactics.[73]

---

[70] Daniel Lang, *Casualties of War* (New York: McGraw-Hill, 1969), 26.

[71] "GI denounces another crime of his buddies," *Vietnam Courier*, December 22, 1969, Douglas Pike Collection: Unit 03 – War Atrocities, Folder 03, Box 39, The Vietnam Archive, Texas Tech University; Lang, 26; Appy, 271–72.

[72] Lang, 58.

[73] Ibid., 67.

During the trials, witnesses for the defense attempted to shift the focus away from the crimes by emphasizing the defendants' reputations as good soldiers. In contrast, at one point in the proceedings, a defense witness pointed to Eriksson's quiet demeanor as evidence that he was not like the other typical GIs, who tended to be more light-hearted and find humor in heavy situations. The witness testified that Eriksson was "less than average as far as being one of the guys," thereby calling his masculinity into question.[74] As for the defendants themselves, one of the GIs, Manuel Diaz, used the stale argument that he was just following the orders of his sergeant, Tony Meserve, who had conceived of the plan to kidnap a Vietnamese woman for the patrol members' sexual pleasure. When it was Meserve's turn to take the witness stand, he told the court about a time when he had given mouth-to-mouth resuscitation to a Vietnamese child suffering from smoke inhalation. His point was to show that American troops were not just involved in combat in Vietnam – they helped the Vietnamese, too.[75]

The story of the crime on Hill 192 involves all three images of the American serviceman in Vietnam and shows how the gunslinger and the sexual aggressor fused in Vietnam and negated the gentle warrior. By telling the story of how he saved a choking Vietnamese girl, Meserve demonstrated that he was not simply a robotic killing machine who had raped and killed a Vietnamese woman because he viewed all Vietnamese as inhuman. He revealed himself to be a man who chose to rape and kill a Vietnamese woman because according to the war's culture, he could – because "boom boom" was good "for the morale of the squad."[76] That saving the child and killing Phan Thi Mao did not seem incongruous to Meserve was a metaphor for U.S. intervention in Vietnam.

Responding to the My Lai incident, a congressional investigation report released in July 1970 argued that the massacre was "so wrong and so foreign to the normal character and actions of our military forces as to immediately raise a question as to the legal sanity at the time of those men involved." Pondering it from a different perspective, Senator Daniel Inouye of Hawaii asked whether My Lai was not out of the ordinary but rather a consequence of troops' military education. "Is American training which permits common reference to the Vietnamese as 'Gooks,' 'Dinks,' or 'Slopes' at fault?" Inouye asked on the Senate floor. "Are racist

[74] Ibid., 92–94.
[75] Ibid., 99–102.
[76] Ibid., 26.

overtones at work here?"[77] Inouye's comments pointed to a deeper military culture that spawned My Lai, a culture that harmed GIs mentally and emotionally and destroyed Vietnamese women physically.

Madame Phuong versus the Warriors

Sometimes, an entrepreneurial Vietnamese woman was able to attain a measure of autonomy by exploiting the economic opportunities created by U.S. troops' sexual needs. One of them, Tran Thi Phuong, also known as Madame Phuong, attracted the attention of a U.S. Senate subcommittee investigating corruption in the management of military service clubs. With the help of a cooperative brigadier general, Madame Phuong established a steam bath and massage parlor at Long Binh, the largest U.S. military installation in Vietnam. When military brass accused her of operating a brothel in the parlor, agents of the Army's Criminal Investigation Division (CID) launched an inquiry into Madame Phuong's business. She did not give up easily, nor was she above bribery or enlisting her brother and other allies to intimidate the men who threatened her business. Madame Phuong was not alone in her position as a businesswoman in the sex trade. Going back at least to 1965, Vietnamese women tended to own the bars that catered to GIs, as *New York Times* reporter Jack Langguth discovered.[78] The story of Madame Phuong offers a glimpse at one of the ways sex caused problems for the U.S. military, and it shows how at least one Vietnamese woman tried to capitalize on American men's willingness to pay Vietnamese women who offered their services.

Throughout the fall of 1967, Madame Phuong made several trips to Long Binh in hopes of getting permission to open a steam bath and massage parlor to serve soldiers stationed on the base. The Army considered steam baths and massage parlors legitimate businesses and allowed them to operate as long as the services offered remained nonsexual. However, Major Clement St. Martin, the officer in charge of mess halls at Long Binh

---

[77] Investigation of the My Lai Incident: Report of the Armed Services Investigating Subcommittee of the Committee on Armed Services House of Representatives Ninety-First Congress Second Session, July 15, 1970, p. 53. Douglas Pike Collection, Unit 03 – War Atrocities, Folder 13, Box 38, The Vietnam Archive, Texas Tech University; "Alleged Massacre at My Lai," *Congressional Record – Senate*, December 2, 1969, S15342, Douglas Pike Collection, Unit 03 – War Atrocities, Folder 7, Box 39, The Vietnam Archive, Texas Tech University.

[78] Jack Langguth, "Saigon Tries to Live in a Hurry," *New York Times*, Aug. 8, 1965, SM12.

at the time of Madame Phuong's request, testified to a Senate subcommittee that she intended the parlor to double as a house of prostitution.[79] Madame Phuong invited St. Martin and Sergeant William Higdon, the custodian in charge of buildings and grounds at Long Binh, to her villa in Saigon to plead her case for a contract to open her business on base. St. Martin testified that she looked like the "Dragon Lady" character from the "Terry and the Pirates" comic strip. At the end of the visit, Higdon left on his own, and Madame Phuong told St. Martin that her brother would drive him to a hotel where he could spend the night.[80]

On the drive to the hotel, Madame Phuong's brother, whom St. Martin referred to in his Senate testimony as Mr. Phuong, asked about the chances of his sister winning the desired contract. St. Martin explained that the Army had received ten bids for the project but had not made any decisions yet. He stated in his testimony that Madame Phuong's bid included "a house of prostitution, complete with a self-contained medical inspection facility." When St. Martin refused to affirm that Madame Phuong would win the contract, Mr. Phuong mentioned that his sister was "a very personal friend" of Brigadier General Earl F. Cole, deputy chief of staff for personnel and administration at Long Binh, and that Cole "was going to help her obtain the contract." St. Martin replied simply, "That's what you need friends for." The men arrived at the hotel, where Mr. Phuong took the desk clerk aside for a private conversation. The clerk then summoned a bellhop to show St. Martin to his room. Neither registration nor payment was required.[81]

St. Martin barely had time to take off his jacket before the bellhop returned with a bottle of Canadian Club whisky and a bottle of Coca-Cola, "courtesy of the hotel manager." As he mixed himself a drink, St. Martin heard another knock at the door. When he opened it, standing before him was "a beautiful 23-year-old Vietnamese girl who announced she wished to spend the night" with him. The major was "too tired and not really interested" in sex, but he invited the woman in anyway and offered her a drink. They chatted for a bit, and she explained to him that she worked at a discotheque in Saigon. She then said she would be "in some sort of trouble" if she did not stay the night with St. Martin. So he

[79] United States Senate Committee on Government Operations, Permanent Subcommittee on Investigations, *Fraud and Corruption in Management of Military Club Systems* (Washington, D.C.: U.S Government Printing Office, 1971), 162.
[80] United States Senate Committee on Government Operations, *Fraud and Corruption*, 162.
[81] *Fraud and Corruption*, 163.

told her to lie and promised he would, too, and she left. The next morning when St. Martin checked out, the desk clerk told him he owed nothing. When he met with Higdon later that day, Higdon asked St. Martin if he had been "pleased with the merchandise." "Ding-how," St. Martin replied, which he testified was Chinese for "Number One," the phrase the Vietnamese used to indicate in English that something was the best.[82]

Several weeks went by, and on December 22, 1967, Madame Phuong arrived at St. Martin's office at Long Binh to inquire about the contract for the steam bath and massage parlor. He told her that no decision had been made. Madame Phuong countered that General Cole wanted her to have the contract. St. Martin explained that the decision was up to the Army's club system board of governors, not Cole, and Madame Phuong stormed away, proclaiming that she would "take the matter up with Cole." The next day, St. Martin received a memo announcing that the board of governors had awarded the contract to Madame Phuong. Shortly after, the Army transferred St. Martin out of Long Binh.[83]

In January 1968, the Army assigned Colonel Edmund Castle to be the Long Binh post commander, and he set about trying to reform the corrupt club system. A number of proprietors had received permission to sell their wares or operate small businesses on base without any centralized regulation, so Castle issued an order shutting down independent businesses that were not part of the post exchange (PX) system. Any businesses the PX did not take under its jurisdiction would be driven from the base, among them Madame Phuong's parlor. Castle testified to the Senate subcommittee that he "was certain she intended to turn the parlor into a house of prostitution," and thus he did not understand why the board of governors awarded her the contract. He mentioned in his testimony that his staff said Brigadier General Cole had been involved in the contract negotiations. Castle tried to delay construction of Madame Phuong's parlor but was unsuccessful, and building plans moved forward on the $200,000 edifice that would have room for 400 Vietnamese women – 200 masseuses and 200 "to drink and socialize with GIs in a big, dark, side room of the establishment."[84]

The large number of women employees Madame Phuong intended to hire for the parlor worried Castle, and the statues he saw at the front of the new building shocked him. Two "giant bronze statues of female nudes"

---

[82] Ibid.
[83] Ibid., 175.
[84] Ibid.,184.

stood at the main entrance to the parlor. Immediately, his mind went to possible media reaction. "The first thought that entered my mind was, 'My God, if *Time* or *Life* or somebody comes by here, we have had it,'" Castle told the Senate subcommittee. He gave Madame Phuong two hours to fire 200 of the women employees and remove the statues. In his office, furious, facing the woman who had made his time as Long Binh post commander thus far difficult, if not hellish, Castle told Madame Phuong that if she did not take down the nude statues immediately, "he would have his sergeant major assault them with a sledgehammer." Madame Phuong complied, replacing the nudes with "flying dragons" that Castle considered "pretty."[85]

Castle was not finished with Madame Phuong. He warned her that she could not allow prostitution in the parlor, and "no massage rooms could have doors, curtains, or any other device to conceal prostitution taking place." More than that, if any servicemen contracted venereal disease after visiting her business, Castle would shut the parlor down and turn the building into his headquarters. As if Madame Phuong was not enough, Castle also had to contend with her brother, who played the piano to entertain the visiting troops. Castle found it unacceptable, likely because the musician was his nemesis's brother, and thus had some soldiers "render the piano unplayable." Things escalated to the point at which it seemed that Castle and Madame Phuong were engaged in a full-scale war. Following the piano incident, Madame Phuong installed "a great big canopied bed" in the parlor, to which Castle retorted that "no damn beds" were allowed on the premises. He ordered her to get rid of the bed and placed the parlor under constant CID surveillance to make sure Madame Phuong did not disobey any of his orders. Castle went so far as to assign undercover CID agents to monitor the parlor "from the inside." For her part, Madame Phuong "frequently reminded him he was only a colonel and that she had general officer friends to whom she could turn for support."[86]

It seems likely that Madame Phuong's "friends" were the ones who made the anonymous phone calls to Castle, first attempting to bribe him, then threatening him. Castle testified that he began receiving anonymous calls about six months into his tenure as Long Binh post commander. Initially, the callers offered to make his life "more comfortable" if he left the concessions on base alone. One caller offered Castle a new Cadillac,

[85] Ibid.
[86] Ibid., 185.

and another promised $50,000. By the fall of 1968, bribery had given way to death threats, and the Army assigned bodyguards to Castle.[87] In analyzing the testimony of Castle and others, the members of the Senate subcommittee noted that, although the exchanges between Castle and Madame Phuong were humorous, they indicated a significant problem in Vietnam. As war waged, Long Binh was the largest U.S. military post in Vietnam, and the post commander "was forced to concern himself with two enemies – the Viet Cong and the club system vendors and concessionaires."[88]

As for Madame Phuong, the biggest blow to her following the skirmish with Castle was that she could no longer invest in the black market, which had existed in Vietnam since the French colonial era. Initially, troops paid for services at Madame Phuong's parlor and other on-base concessions in scrip, or military payment certificates (MPCs), that the club system cashier could convert to U.S. dollars. Madame Phuong deposited the money into a bank account in New York City under the name C. F. Hsiao, one of thirteen black market accounts the Senate subcommittee discovered. When subcommittee investigators approached Madame Phuong in Saigon in June of 1969, she told them that C. F. Hsiao was her "lover and sponsor" who loaned her $300,000, "which she converted to diamonds in Bangkok and then smuggled into Vietnam." She sold the jewels to pay for the building of her parlor and began to pay Hsiao back with the money the parlor brought in. But when the PX took control of the on-base businesses, Madame Phuong, because she was Vietnamese, could accept only piasters, the Vietnamese currency, as payment. She could not charge or accept scrip, and she could not exchange piasters for dollars, so she had no legal means of depositing money into Hsiao's bank account. Piasters were of little value because of inflation, and Madame Phuong complained to Senate investigators that she "had assembled some four to five million piasters and had no place to deposit them, except in Vietnamese banks, which were not acceptable to her."[89]

The Senate subcommittee that investigated Madame Phuong concluded that her story was "an almost perfect textbook illustration of how enterprising but illicit black marketeers exploited the Vietnamese war through illegal moneychanging."[90] The subcommittee, however, had no

[87] Ibid., 186.
[88] Ibid., 185.
[89] Ibid., 187–88.
[90] Ibid., 187.

interest in scrutinizing the assumptions made about Madame Phuong or the connection between the U.S. military business in Vietnam and the type of establishment she operated. Even though St. Martin and Castle suspected that Madame Phuong planned to incorporate a brothel into her parlor and allegedly stated her intentions outright in her application for the steam bath and massage parlor, the subcommittee's report indicated no proof that prostitution occurred at the parlor. If it did occur, a substantial part of the blame lay with the Army. Senate testimony made it clear that Brigadier General Earl Cole helped secure the contract for Madame Phuong, and he and other Army personnel accepted hotel rooms, liquor, and the company of young Vietnamese women provided by Madame Phuong's brother. While Madame Phuong was assigned the role of scapegoat, the U.S. military presence in Vietnam and assumptions about the sexuality of Vietnamese women and American servicemen enabled her to go into business in the first place.

"Black Babies" – Living Legacies of the Vietnam War

The contradictions embedded in the triad of the gentle warrior, the gunslinger, and the sexual aggressor came to the surface in the lives of the children of American fathers and Vietnamese mothers. These "Amerasians" were the living consequences of the gendered power relations between the United States and Vietnam, in which the paternalistic desire to protect one's children came into stark conflict with the realities of sexual domination. Byproducts of a social, cultural, and political economy that placed Vietnamese women in the service of American men, the children marked their mothers as women who had engaged in sexual encounters with American men, and they represented an American invasion of Vietnam, figuratively and literally.[91] Known as "black babies," the sons and daughters of African American soldiers wore the clearest badges of heritage – their hair, their skin color – and they signified the limits of American power. Although part American, they had no power. Part black, Vietnamese society shunned them.

Statistics published in 1973, the year the United States pulled all of its remaining combat troops out of Vietnam, reported that there were anywhere from 15,000 to 25,000 mixed-race children of both black and

---

[91] For a recent study of Vietnamese war orphans, see Dana Sachs, *The Life We Were Given: Operation Babylift, International Adoption, and the Children of War in Vietnam* (Boston: Beacon Press, 2010).

white American fathers in Vietnam.[92] Bobbie Nofflet, a home economist for the U.S. Agency for International Development (USAID) who was stationed in Vietnam from 1967 to 1975, worked in orphanages in Saigon and other urban areas during the last two years of her assignment. In those two years, she visited about 135 orphanages in cities and villages throughout South Vietnam to report on conditions and try to get funding from the U.S. government to improve them. Most of the orphanages were overcrowded and understaffed, and many of them lacked beds and adequate amounts of food. The majority of orphans had either lost their parents in the war or were the abandoned children of American fathers and Vietnamese mothers.

In general, the Vietnamese frowned on all Amerasian children. Tran Tuong Nhu, a Vietnamese anthropologist, characterized negative Vietnamese attitudes toward mixed-race children as a political sentiment. "The child with foreign blood serves as a constant reminder of the bitter experience of foreign intervention that still exists."[93] But "black babies" faced especially harsh discrimination and treatment, in orphanages and in Vietnamese society. Throughout her time working with orphans, Nofflet noticed that orphanage staff and other Vietnamese often neglected and sometimes mistreated the children of African American fathers.[94] In 1971, the U.S. embassy in Saigon reported to the State Department its specific concern for the children of black Americans troops and Vietnamese women, stating that "the black child may have a more difficult time growing up in Vietnam than other children, either in Vietnamese homes or orphanages."[95] "It is a traditional prejudice," Sister Sabina, one of the Catholic sisters who managed the Go Vap orphanage in Saigon, told an American reporter. "People here believe that when skins get mixed it sets off some instability. They are ashamed of Negro children, and in some orphanages keep them apart from the other children."[96] Marion Williams, a freelance journalist and volunteer nurse who went to Vietnam in 1967, described the orphaned black babies she observed in Vietnam:

[92] Edward B. Fiske, "Adopting Vietnam's Orphans: Efforts Grow to Make It Easier," *New York Times*, August 21, 1973, 24. See also, Gloria Emerson, "Part Vietnamese, Part Black – and Orphans," *New York Times*, February 7, 1972, 26.

[93] "Children of GIs Shunned in Vietnam," *New York Times*, December 24, 1974, 3.

[94] Author's telephone interview with Bobbie Nofflet, June 15, 2006.

[95] Tad Szulc, "Embassy in Saigon Calls Babies of GIs a 'Serious Concern,'" *New York Times*, July 26, 1971, 1.

[96] "Children of GIs Shunned in Vietnam," *New York Times*, December 24, 1974, 3.

These children are abandoned in the alleys to fend for themselves. They roam the streets day after day in clothing that consists of rags fashioned into a type of pajama. They nourish their fragile little bodies with food they have scrounged from garbage cans. They do not know that mothers, fathers, milk, good food, and a happy life exist. They only know the horror of the streets. If they inherited the curl in a rope hair of their father it usually becomes infested with lice. Huddled in groups of three, five, or six children, not necessarily related, they sleep in the gutters, corners of buildings, or doorways of stores.[97]

The squalid conditions in which black Vietnamese orphans lived reflected the role skin color played in Vietnam's social hierarchy. Although all mixed-race children were legacies of the U.S. war in Vietnam, some Vietnamese privileged light-skinned Amerasians because fair skin indicated the higher social status of those who did not have to work in the fields. In Saigon, Vietnamese women often wore wide-brimmed hats and long sleeves to prevent their skin from tanning.[98] In her study of Amerasian children, Trin Yarborough interviewed Nguyen Ba Chung, a Vietnamese writer, who remarked that "in Vietnamese culture, the concept of beauty is white skin, especially for women."[99] Marion Williams wrote in her memoir that babies sired by white American men sometimes sold for about 42,000 piasters, the equivalent of about 300 U.S. dollars, on the black market. The buyer often was a Vietnamese family that believed "the baby will bring it good luck with the gods," Williams said. "On the other hand, when a Vietnamese woman has the child of a black American, she believes the gods have looked down on her."[100] In addition to the premium placed on fair skin, physical characteristics such as hair allowed some mixed-race children of white American fathers to pass as Vietnamese, whereas black Amerasian children who inherited their fathers' hair had a tougher time concealing their African American heritage.

The societal response to black babies born during the Vietnam War was similar to the experiences of the children conceived by Vietnamese mothers and French African soldiers during the French occupation of Vietnam. Official Vietnamese numbers listed approximately 400 mixed-race children of French African fathers. Suzanne Kpenou, daughter of a decorated

---

97 Williams, *My Tour in Vietnam: A Burlesque Shocker* (New York: Vantage Press, 1970), 35–36.
98 Robert S. McKelvey, *The Dust of Life: America's Children Abandoned in Vietnam* (Seattle: University of Washington Press, 1999), 64.
99 Trin Yarborough, *Surviving Twice: Amerasian Children of the Vietnam War* (Washington, DC: Potomac Books, 2005), 88.
100 Williams, 35.

black French Army veteran and a Vietnamese mother, told a reporter from *Ebony* that other Vietnamese children ridiculed her and her siblings, calling them "black" and "Indian." Although Kpenou's father, Paul, stayed in Vietnam and married her mother, Hai, most French African soldiers left the country when France withdrew in 1954.[101] Because Vietnamese society shunned the children of French African fathers and Vietnamese mothers, some of the daughters of such unions had little choice but to enter the life of a bar girl or prostitute. Ann Bryan Mariano, a white American reporter with *Overseas Weekly* stationed in Saigon, lived in a neighborhood near Trinh Minh The Street, the part of town known as "Soulsville," where bars and brothels catered to African American patrons. Mariano noticed that some of the women who worked in Soulsville were the daughters of Senegalese soldiers in the French colonial army that had fought against Viet Minh nationalists in the First Indochina War.[102] A *Time* magazine article that was read into the *Congressional Record* on May 23, 1967, referred to those mixed-race bar girls as "less costly and usually less comely than their sisters on white-dominated Tu Do Street near by."[103] Like so many other parallels between the French and U.S. occupation of Vietnam, it was a vicious cycle that turned on the intersection of race, sexuality, and imperialism.

The urban economy that catered to American soldiers allowed some Vietnamese women to keep their mixed-race children and continue to work. "Day-nurseries" opened in cities so mothers could drop their children off before starting their shifts.[104] Jobs created by the U.S. presence helped the women afford day care. Some GIs took responsibility for their children, giving money and food to their Vietnamese mothers. For example, twice a month, the Afro American Cultural Association, a group of black GIs, took buses of soldiers to orphanages to deliver food, money, and diapers and to throw parties for the children. As U.S. troops retreated from Vietnam, however, the service economy they had supported crumbled. By the early to mid-1970s, the future of Amerasian children was a topic of high concern among the U.S. government, welfare organizations, and adoption agencies. A Senate Judiciary Committee study estimated

[101] Ibid., 108.
[102] Tad Bartimus, et al., *War Torn: Stories of War from the Women Reporters Who Covered Vietnam* (New York: Random House, 2002), 37.
[103] Long, Clarence Dickinson, "Time Magazine Salutes the Negro GI in Vietnam," May 23, 1967. *Congressional Record*, pp. H6001–H6004.
[104] Harvey H. Smith, et al., *Area Handbook for South Vietnam* (Washington, DC: U.S. Government Printing Office, 1967), 352.

that approximately 5,400 mixed-raced children lived in Vietnam, but it was unclear how many of them were fathered by U.S. servicemen. So as to not draw attention to these children, U.S. authorities in Vietnam did not provide special assistance to them unless they were placed in registered orphanages. However, some private groups, including Holt International Children's Fund (an evangelical Protestant group based in Eugene, Oregon), the U.S. Catholic Conference's Committee for Refugees, and the Southern Christian Leadership Conference (SCLC), focused specifically on the plight of black babies.[105]

Because of bureaucratic red tape and a general disapproval of foreign adoptions on the part of the government of South Vietnam, American families wanting to adopt mixed-race children faced a long, expensive, and often unsuccessful process. Responding to the difficult future black mixed-race children faced, the SCLC's Hosea Williams tried to help. In 1971, he and his wife traveled to Vietnam in hopes of adopting a baby. The poor conditions in which black orphans lived inspired Williams to do more than just take home one child. He convinced the SCLC to sponsor the Martin Luther King Home for Children, an orphanage in Gia Dinh, outside Saigon. An anonymous Vietnamese philanthropist donated a building and the services of some Vietnamese personnel. The Williamses did not get a child, though. The baby they wanted to adopt, a little girl named Lanh, whose father allegedly was an African American soldier, died of malnutrition and inadequate care before her prospective parents could complete the lengthy adoption process.[106]

One African American soldier blamed the neglect of black babies on the U.S. government, contending that "there are more black than white mixed kids over there because it was easier for a white GI to get military permission to marry his girlfriend and easier for him to bring his child home."[107] Like their mixed-race children, the African American fathers of Amerasians represented the limits of American imperial power. Racism removed political clout from their hands and made it difficult for them to take fatherly responsibility for their children. U.S. policy placed the burden of providing for a family on the backs of Vietnamese mothers or orphanages in which mixed-race children, especially black babies, faced

[105] Era Bell Thompson, "The Plight of Black Babies in South Vietnam," *Ebony*, December 1972, 110.
[106] Emerson, "Part Vietnamese, Part Black – and Orphans."
[107] Thompson, 107.

neglect at best and abuse at worst. The intimate encounters of the Vietnam War revealed the racism of Americans *and* of Vietnamese.

Winter Soldiers

Some servicemen who were directly affected by the contradictions in the U.S. mission became aware, and attempted to address, the connections between U.S. foreign policy and the sexual violence they had seen in Vietnam. From January 31 through February 2, 1972, Vietnam Veterans Against the War (VVAW) sponsored the Winter Soldier Investigation, a meeting in Detroit of approximately one hundred Vietnam veterans who testified about atrocities committed by U.S. troops during the war. Several times during the event, the testimony turned to the rape and murder of Vietnamese women, and one panelist described how the Marine Infantry Training Regiment (ITR) taught troops to scrutinize Vietnamese women more closely than men during interrogations. "They stress over and over that a woman has more places to hide things like maps or anything than a male," the veteran said. He went on to place the ITR instructions in the context of the broader gender tensions that shaped the war:

It seems to me that the philosophy over there is like somehow or another we're more afraid of females than we are of males, because, I don't know why, but the female was always like you never know where you stood, so you went overboard in your job with her in all your daily actions. You doubled whatever you would do for a male. Because we always heard these stories that, like, the fiercest fighters were the females over there. You know, we didn't want to be embarrassed by getting our asses kicked by a bunch of females.[108]

In addition to protecting the reputation of U.S. troops, treating Vietnamese women harshly also aimed to keep Vietnamese men from working against the Americans "because it makes a lasting impression on some guy – some 'zip' – that's watching his daughter worked over. So we have a better opportunity of keeping him in line by working her over," the veteran continued.[109] Another panelist, a Marine corporal named Christopher Simpson, stated that sexual atrocities committed against Vietnamese women were "pretty usual over there." It was not that being sexually attracted to Vietnamese woman was a bad thing, but instead

---

[108] "Veterans' Testimony on Vietnam – Need for Investigation," *Congressional Record*, April 6, 1971, p. E2831.
[109] Ibid.

of approaching her in the way of normal courtship, "they might stick
a rifle in a woman's head and say, 'Take off your clothes,'" Simpson
said. "That's the way it's done over there. 'Cause they're not treated as
human beings over there, they're treated as dirt."[110] Linking violence
against Vietnamese women to both sexism and a career in the military,
Marine Sergeant Joe Bangert testified about the disembowelment of a
Vietnamese woman that he observed: "I think the person involved was a
freaked out sexist, if that's what you're trying to get at. I think maybe he
had problems. He had to be – he was in the Army for 20 years."[111]

In the Winter Soldier testimonies, Vietnam veterans exposed the dark
side of the gender ideology at the root of the American presence in Vietnam. Just as the images of the dragon lady and the girl next door broke
down under the realities of the Vietnam War, the roles American men
were expected to play revealed the gender ideology to be unsustainable.
The GIs who testified at the Winter Soldier hearings realized that the roles
of the gentle warrior, gunslinger, and sexual aggressor were fundamentally incompatible. As a result, some GIs and veterans began to speak
out and write against the war, forming an antiwar movement that challenged not only the war but also the gender assumptions that informed
it. Servicemen demanded an end to sexism in the military, and some
even reached out to women's groups, adopting the rhetoric of women's
liberation and applying it to their situations. Resistance to the warrior
ethos became part of a widespread questioning and rejection of Cold War
gender roles.

[110] Ibid.
[111] Ibid.

5

Liberating Men and Women

Antiwar GIs Speak Out against the Warrior Myth

Assigned to an office job in Dau Tieng as a communications liaison for combat units in the 25th Infantry Division, Mike Boehm was not on the front lines during his eighteen-month tour of duty from 1968 to 1969. He believed he had escaped the trauma that combat veterans had experienced, so he was surprised when, after a trip back to Vietnam more than twenty years later, waves of grief and rage washed over him as he struggled to make sense of the war's devastation of Vietnam. Where he eventually found redemption and peace was unexpected – the Quang Ngai Province Women's Union, a group which worked to secure micro-credit loans for women in My Lai. After working with the Vietnam Veterans Restoration Project (VVRP) building health clinics in Vietnam, Boehm, a native of Mauston, Wisconsin, founded the Madison Indochina Support Group to help fund the My Lai project. As he got to know women in My Lai and throughout Quang Ngai province, he saw firsthand the trauma of war. He met women such as Nguyen Thi Lan, who, at the age of fourteen, lost a leg after stepping on a landmine. He spent time with Pham Thi Huong, who still broke down in tears every time she told the story of losing her aunt and two of her children during a U.S. raid on the village of Truong Khanh.

Through the pain and suffering, Boehm saw the women's resilience – and they, not John Wayne or other warrior figures, became his heroes. "Women suffered as much as the men did, but their suffering goes unacknowledged," he said. "In the midst of all the killing, they still made the meals for their family.... I hold their strength in awe, that they were not only able to survive, but also to focus all their energies to moving ahead."

To honor his support of the My Lai project, the Quang Ngai Province Women's Union made Boehm an honorary member.[1]

Like the soldiers who testified at the Winter Soldier hearings in 1972, Boehm was part of a movement that attempted to raise awareness of and change policies based on the gendered ideology that created irreconcilable conflicts for both the women and men in Vietnam. For some GIs, basic training and combat stripped the glorious veneer from the military's version of masculinity and revealed "the mentality that turns human beings into . . . murdering soldiers."[2] Even though African American resistance focused on different issues, black GIs, too, understood the connections between their experience in Vietnam and interrelated forms of racial and gender oppression. For some American men who served in Vietnam, the warrior myth as played out amid the realities of war left them feeling not like men at all, if being a man meant killing a man – or a woman or a child. They were the men psychiatrist Robert Jay Lifton called "antiwar warriors," part of an attempt to redefine the myths that U.S. policymakers employed to enforce existing power structures and justify America's Cold War scramble for global domination.[3] Although most GI antiwar activism took place stateside, some peace demonstrations occurred in Vietnam, in Quang Tri, Da Nang, Long Binh, Chu Lai, and Saigon, coinciding with the 1969 Moratorium movement of civilian protests back home.[4]

GI antiwar activism began in the mid-1960s with individual instances of resistance. In November 1965, Lieutenant Henry Howe, stationed at Fort Bliss in El Paso, Texas, participated in a civilian antiwar march downtown. In 1966, three privates stationed at Fort Hood, Texas, were the first to refuse orders to Vietnam; at Fort Jackson, South Carolina, Army doctor Howard Levy refused to train Special Forces medics headed to Vietnam. As opposition to the war grew nationally and troop morale declined, GIs, veterans, and civilians organized a GI Task Force that planned antiwar demonstrations for troops, several of which were held on Armed Forces Day, May 16, 1970. Protests took place on at least

---

[1] *Long Shadows: Veterans' Paths to Peace*, ed. David Giffey (Madison, WI: Atwood Publishing, 2006), 85–108.

[2] "GIs and Asian Women: The Army's Deadly Game," *Fatigue Press*, May 1971, 7. Wisconsin Historical Society.

[3] Robert Jay Lifton, *Home from the War: Learning from Vietnam Veterans* (Boston: Beacon Press, 1992), 30–31.

[4] David Cortright, *Soldiers in Revolt: GI Resistance During the Vietnam War* (Chicago: Haymarket Books, 1975, 2005), 33–34.

twelve Army, Navy, Air Force, and Marine bases, and GIs and veterans participated in demonstrations off-base as well. Among the largest were a protest in Fayetteville, North Carolina, in which more than 750 soldiers from nearby Fort Bragg and 3,000 civilians participated, and a march of approximately 700 Fort Hood troops through Killeen, Texas. As a result of the GI antiwar activism, twenty-eight military bases had to cancel their Armed Forces Day programs. Hoping to prevent protests from becoming mutiny, the Defense Department in 1969 and 1970 issued guidelines allowing limited forms of GI dissent.[5]

Coffeehouses and antiwar newspapers provided some of the most important support and voices for GIs and veterans who opposed the war. In 1967, civilian antiwar activists Fred Gardner and Donna Mickleson founded the first GI coffeehouse, UFO, in Columbia, South Carolina, near Fort Jackson. By 1971, as many as twenty-six coffeehouses existed, including Mad Anthony Wayne's in Waynesville, Missouri, near Fort Leonard Wood; Shelter Half in Tacoma, Washington, near Fort Lewis; Green Machine in San Diego, near Camp Pendleton; and Oleo Strut in Killeen, Texas, near Fort Hood. At the coffeehouses, GIs could discuss the war, obtain legal counseling on issues such as going AWOL and obtaining conscientious objector status, and learn about ways to protest the war.[6] Many of the coffeehouses published antiwar newspapers aimed specifically at GIs and veterans with exposés on poor conditions in military prisons, articles on GI antiwar activities, and testimonials from disillusioned soldiers. The papers, along with antiwar newspapers published by soldiers on bases, provided a forum for soldiers to speak out against the war. In 1967, only three GI newspapers existed, but by March 1972, the U.S. Defense Department had discovered about 245 papers in circulation. Two of the most popular ones – *Fatigue Press*, published by GIs at Fort Hood, and *Bragg Briefs*, published near Fort Bragg – had circulations of about 5,000 each; almost all of their staffers were GIs and veterans.[7] To raise funds for and support the newspapers, coffeehouses, and other GI and veteran antiwar initiatives, Gardner and Mickleson founded the United States Servicemen's Fund (USSF), which provided legal assistance to servicemen as well as financial aid for antiwar activities.[8]

[5] Ibid., 66–67, 75.
[6] Ibid., 98–99.
[7] Melvin Small, *Give Peace a Chance: Exploring the Vietnam Antiwar Movement* (Syracuse, NY: Syracuse University Press, 1992), 98.
[8] Cortright, 61.

Many of the antiwar GIs were conscious of the gendered ideology underlying the war. The rhetoric of GI antiwar newspapers and the missions of GI coffeehouses – cafes where servicemen and women gathered to discuss their opposition to the war – demonstrate that antiwar soldiers believed both women *and* men had to be liberated from their socially constructed roles to stop war. Antiwar GIs argued that racism and sexism were characteristic of the U.S. armed services that perpetuated war. Bill Davis, who became a prominent member of the Chicago chapter of Vietnam Veterans Against the War (VVAW) when he returned from Vietnam, noted that "GI activism was reacting to socioeconomic problems that stemmed from the U.S. and had translated to the military in Vietnam. The military is a microcosm of our society and embodies some of the worst aspects."[9] Chicano veteran Leroy Quintana, a poet from New Mexico, wrote of how he cried when President George H. W. Bush engaged the U.S. military in the Persian Gulf War, remembering his Vietnam experience and thinking about what that and future wars might do to his children. Quintana also wrote of seeing his comrades break down and sob when the stress of the war became unbearable. Admitting that he and other soldiers cried – a very unmasculine behavior according to the warrior ideology – was part of the process of "demystifying" the warrior image.[10]

Soldiers and veterans who wrote for GI antiwar newspapers called on fellow servicemen to reject sexism – *male chauvinism* was the typical term at the time – and support movements for women's equality and social justice. Black GIs connected the degradation of women with the oppression of African Americans as a whole and called for solidarity between black servicemen and servicewomen against military sexism and racism. On the home front, some female civilian activists – black and white – faced sexism perpetrated by male leaders of both antiwar and civil rights groups. Unity among African American service personnel of both sexes demonstrates an alternative perspective on how men and women could relate to each other as they opposed the Vietnam War. The solidarity is especially compelling when considered in the context of ideas about the military as a bastion of masculinity and male bonding. This awareness of gender contrasts with the ambivalence other social movements of the era frequently showed in regard to sexual equality. In his

[9] Author's interview with Bill Davis, May 2007, Oak Park, IL.
[10] George Mariscal, *Aztlan and Vietnam: Chicano and Chicana Experiences of the War* (Berkeley, CA: University of California, 1999), 210–11.

work on draft resistance, Michael Foley has noted that some male anti-draft activists bought into a chauvinistic group culture. Draft resisters faced the accusation that they were cowards, which in the wartime context meant that they were not real men. Some men in the draft resistance movement adopted a compensatory "swagger" to bolster their courage when confronting a government that wanted to send them to war.[11] Even as they rejected service in Vietnam, they adopted an aggressive heterosexual masculinity. In theory, veterans had already "proved" their manhood through their service in Vietnam so, freed from that burden, they could reach out to women.

The awareness of gender expressed itself differently in various groups. In their antiwar activism, GIs and veterans critiqued the use of stereotypically gendered images to promote war and compel men to fight. African American servicemen and women spoke out against male chauvinism as part of a larger culture of racism that accused black women of failing to raise their sons to become responsible men. Civilian women and WACs, many who participated in the GI antiwar movement's rejection of the military's gender norms, called attention to the ways in which sexism harmed men, women, and families. Antiwar GIs often made specific references to the degradation of Vietnamese women. Not all antiwar GIs called for a complete overhaul of American gender constructions – some of the men veterans Lifton worked with sought not to purge John Wayne from the culture but to remake the Wayne image into a symbol for men who worked "in the service of humane goals."[12] Whatever the specific focus, it was clear that the norms of Cold War gender were being challenged and changed by what was happening in Vietnam.

Gender Liberation

Gender liberation – the liberation not only of women, but of men as well – is a recurring theme in the GI antiwar press, and it was part of a broader questioning of conventional masculinity by American men on the home front.[13] Soldiers wrote articles arguing that gender roles oppressed

---

[11] Michael Foley, "The 'Point of Ultimate Indignity' or a 'Beloved Community'? The Draft Resistance Movement and New Left Gender Dynamics," in *The New Left Revisited*, eds. John Campbell McMillian and Paul Buhle (Philadelphia: Temple University Press, 2003), 182, 186.

[12] Lifton, 251.

[13] For a discussion of men's liberation on the home front, see Michael Kimmel, *Manhood in America: A Cultural History* (New York: The Free Press, 1996), 261–90.

them by equating masculinity with fighting and sexual aggression. The
rejection of the type of masculinity the military promoted was part of a
broader opposition to military authority, to the Vietnam War, and to the
ideology that some GIs believed underwrote it. Articles discussed the need
for men and women to unite rather than view each other as adversaries,
and called on soldiers to resist military imagery and language that
degraded women. The GI antiwar rhetoric denouncing sexism reflects the
influence of the American women's and civil rights movements, and of
international movements against imperialism. In his book on the GI antiwar movement, historian Richard Moser estimates that about 25 percent
of GIs participated regularly in antiwar activism.[14] Certainly, not all antiwar soldiers criticized the military's version of masculinity, but antiwar
newspapers and coffeehouse activities indicate that a significant number
of antiwar GIs specifically opposed the masculinity of the warrior myth.

While on base and at war, some GIs became disillusioned by the military's attempts to connect manhood to violence and the degradation of
women. James Daniel, an ex-GI who attended the University of California at Berkeley after he was discharged, referred to military masculinity
as the "manhood game," criticizing it for its glorification of drunkenness,
fighting, and sexual promiscuity. In a letter to *Ally*, an antiwar newspaper
for GIs in the San Francisco area, Daniel argued that true manhood means
learning "to truly love – a woman, an idea, a place, a time, because they
have had an inner vision which makes these real along with a recognition
that a man will fight if he or his is attacked."[15] Some GIs who wrote
for antiwar newspapers argued that the military actively exploited men
through its criteria for masculinity. Writers for Fort Hood's *Fatigue Press*
maintained that most lonely GIs simply wanted "a meaningful relationship with a member of the opposite sex . . . and someone to talk to and be
with," whereas drill sergeants inundated them with the judgment that the
"sign of manhood is the number of women you've made love to."[16] An
article in the paper noted that GIs were "subject to constant propaganda
on sex" from the moment they entered the military.

Drill sergeants constantly rub in the fact that they "got some last night," tell the
married people that "if the army wanted you to have a wife they'd issue you one,"
and make other cracks such as "who needs a wife when you can get a whore"
and "if all wives acted like prostitutes we'd be a lot better off." The army wants

---

[14] Moser, *The New Winter Soldiers*, 132.
[15] "Letters to the *Ally*," Clark Smith Papers, Box 2, Folder 6, Wisconsin Historical Society.
[16] "G.I. Town Part I," *Fatigue Press*, August 1971, 7, Wisconsin Historical Society.

to alienate you from your loved ones at home by planting the idea into your head that your wife, girl, or fiancée is cheating on you and that all women are whores.[17]

The blatant sexism alienated some GIs from the military establishment and, in some cases, from the military's overall mission. An article in *Fatigue Press* encouraged GIs to avoid referring to women as "broads" and thereby prevent the military from controlling their thinking.[18]

Veterans writing for *The Bond*, the newspaper of the antiwar American Servicemen's Union (ASU), explained that sexism undermined GIs' marriages. They testified that, during basic training, drill sergeants made them sing songs about unfaithful women "to make us feel hostile to and distrustful of our wives or girlfriends." Married GIs faced ridicule from sergeants, who encouraged them to take their frustrations out on their wives, the men added. "The chain of command is simple," they wrote. "The CO [commanding officer] shits on the lifer sergeants, they both shit on you, and you're supposed to go home and 'f – k the shit' out of your wife or girlfriend." The connection between sex and violence appeared in all sorts of places. "At the rifle range, we were told by the range NCO [noncommissioned officer] to 'squeeze the trigger like you squeeze your girl's t – s,'" the veterans explained.[19]

Although servicemen of various ranks used sexist language as part of their inherited language and thought patterns, "anti-woman prejudice" was "a conscious policy of the high-ranking generals who run the military," the veterans wrote. They argued that the armed forces pursued "a deliberate sexist policy, that is, a policy of male superiority, to keep men and women divided. This policy is designed to keep male GIs from uniting with their equally oppressed sisters," both military and civilian. Therefore, the vets called on GIs "to build a trust and unity among brothers and sisters in the military and military dependents" and not "play into the hands of the brass" by buying into its sexist ideology and committing "crimes against women."[20]

The veterans argued that sexist language reflected the ideas that shaped U.S. war policy toward Vietnam. Some GIs did not stop with the call to refuse to speak the language of military sexism. They implored fellow

[17] Ibid.
[18] "Gooks and Broads," *Fatigue Press*, Issue 11 (Date missing), Wisconsin Historical Society.
[19] "Anti-woman Propaganda: How the Brass and Their Flunkies Use It Against Us," *The Bond*, December 24, 1971, 2, Wisconsin Historical Society.
[20] Ibid.

soldiers to rethink the ideology of male superiority and the gender roles on which it relied. A sailor wrote in *Dare to Struggle*, a GI antiwar newspaper published in San Diego, that the military brass used sexism to prevent men and women from joining in protest of military policy, thus keeping them subservient to military regulations. He argued that maltreatment of women was akin to the ways "lifers" – career military personnel – related to draftees or enlisted personnel who looked forward to the time when they were discharged. The only way to throw off the brass, then, was to "demand the liberation of women." Doing so would help defeat "the system that oppresses and robs us all of our humanity," the sailor concluded.[21]

An article in *Broken Arrow*, an antiwar newspaper published at Selfridge Air Base near Detroit, asked GIs why they would allow the brass to control them into thinking that women were nothing more than sex objects. The author of the piece argued that "if the women are free to fight for liberation, we will all be a lot stronger. So we have to start thinking of our sisters as fellow human beings, the way *we* want to be treated."[22] Another article, entitled "Men and Women's Liberation," discussed what men give up when they uphold gender roles that assigned them the role of financial provider while limiting women to that of homemakers. "Some men claim that they would enjoy staying home with the children, but their wives usually can't get jobs that pay as well as their husband's job." By adhering to mainstream gender roles, a man loses out on "the joys of having close relationships with his children. It is a sad society that alienates father and son." In addition to preventing healthy relationships from developing between fathers and children, warrior masculinity burdened men emotionally and physically. The article's author wrote that it was "unnatural" for a man not to cry, express fear, or feel pain. Suppressing such feelings was likely one of the main reasons men suffered "heart attacks, nervous disorders, and cases of high blood pressure."[23] The article implies that men who embraced the role of house husband or stay-at-home dad, far removed from the stoic warrior or organization man of popular culture, would have more emotionally fulfilling, less stressful lives.

[21] "Thoughts on Being Human," *Dare to Struggle*, Vol. 1, Issue 9 (Date missing), 6, Wisconsin Historical Society.
[22] "Freeks [sic] and Our Sisters," *Broken Arrow*, February 28, 1971, 5, Wisconsin Historical Society.
[23] "Men and Women's Liberation," *Broken Arrow*, February 28, 1971, 6, Wisconsin Historical Society.

A writer who identified himself as "a 22-year-old male" maintained that "Women's Lib is working for equal rights of the two sexes." He asked GIs to consider what their lives would be like if society gave men the inferior gender role. The author expressed empathy for women and, like the writers for other GI antiwar newspapers, connected sexism to a larger military program of repression. In addition to offering a general explanation of his opposition to mainstream gender roles, the author discussed the issues military wives faced, including inadequate housing, poor medical services, and lack of jobs for them on or around bases. The author also gave a nod to enlisted women, acknowledging the harassment they faced from military men who did not want them around.[24]

An article in the December 1, 1969, issue of *Duck Power*, a GI antiwar newspaper published in San Diego, condemned the Army's role in sustaining the sex trade in Vietnam. Titled "The Army as PIMP," the article explained that the Army's surgeon general in Vietnam advocated for brothels on military bases in hope of lowering the rate of venereal diseases among troops. Base commanders and medical personnel could control the Vietnamese women who worked at the brothels and ensure that they were free of disease. The article noted that "the good doctor doesn't seem concerned with the fate of the women subjected to this servitude." Protesting the degradation of Vietnamese women, the article also objected to the assumption that servicemen required prostitutes to satisfy their sexual desires.[25]

The Bond condemned the U.S. military's decision in January 1972 to allow prostitutes onto bases in Vietnam. Prior to the ruling, military personnel had to leave the base to find prostitutes or brothels, but the directive allowed "local national guests," including prostitutes, on base as long as they had a Vietnamese government-issued identification card. U.S. officers told a reporter for the *New York Times* that "they supported the practice to keep peace within the increasingly disgruntled ranks" of American troops in Vietnam. Contending that the military brass "have always used the oppression of women" to ensure the submission of troops, Private John Lewis, a reporter for antiwar newspaper *The Bond*, argued that "the brass's crimes show that they have used every low and disgusting tactic to try to keep every GI in a state of a dehumanized beast who is willing at any time to do the bidding of these sexist, racist, fascist

[24] "The 'Fair Force' Fights Back!" *Broken Arrow*, November 17, 1970, 4, Wisconsin Historical Society.
[25] "The Army as PIMP," *Duck Power*, December 1, 1969, 3, Wisconsin Historical Society.

monsters." Lewis reported that the U.S. war in Vietnam forced more than 400,000 Vietnamese women into prostitution because the war destroyed farmland and thus pushed rural people into cities in search of work and as refugees. Calling South Vietnam a "colony" of the U.S. with an economy run by the U.S. military, Lewis maintained that many peasant women had no choice but to become prostitutes, the only job available to them in the military economy.[26] The article's headline read, "Legalized Prostitution – Brass's New Weapon Against GIs and Vietnamese Women," suggesting that assumptions about servicemen's sexual desires were part of the larger U.S. project in Vietnam, and that military authorities used those assumptions to control the behavior of troops.

"Come See Us at the Strut"

In April 1971, the proprietors of the Oleo Strut, a GI coffeehouse near Fort Hood, created a women's office in their upstairs section. The organizers' immediate goal was to mobilize Killeen and Fort Hood women for an antiwar march scheduled for Armed Forces Day, May 16, but they were also aware of a broader range of gender issues, stocking the office with literature about birth control options and abortion. The office eventually evolved into a small health clinic; its staff helped form the Killeen Women's Group, whose members occasionally wrote articles about the women's liberation movement for the GI newspaper *Fatigue Press*. In one article, women demanded equal wages and jobs, free birth control, and free abortions, so women of various income levels could have more control over their health. The article encouraged women to "come see us at the Oleo Strut" to learn more.[27] GI wives from Fort Hood worked with the Strut to plan rallies against the war for military families.[28]

GI coffeehouses, like the Oleo Strut, linked antiwar GIs to various civilian movements, including the growing women's movement. The cafes helped GIs view their struggle against the Vietnam War as part of a larger struggle against the oppression of mainstream American power

---

[26] John Lewis, "Legalized Prostitution: Brass's New Weapon Against GIs and Vietnamese Women," *The Bond*, January 27, 1972, 4, Wisconsin Historical Society.

[27] "Women's Liberation," *Fatigue Press*, Issue 21 (Date missing), 13, Wisconsin Historical Society.

[28] "Strike Back Campaign," *Fatigue Press*, Issue 25 (Date missing), 7, Wisconsin Historical Society.

symbolized by sexist expressions of masculinity. Some antiwar GIs, particularly those involved in the coffeehouses, rejected the military's brand of masculinity by supporting and encouraging women's activism. Jack McClosky, a Vietnam veteran and organizer at an Oakland coffeehouse called the Pentagon, viewed GI coffeehouses as education centers. The goal of the Pentagon was to offer information to counter military-enforced racism and sexism. "Our role was to humanize," McClosky said. "One of our jobs in coffeehouses was saying to them, 'Hey, these are mothers, these are fathers, these are sons, these are daughters; this is who you're going to be shooting at. They're no different than you.'"[29]

GI antiwar newspapers provided space for civilian women – usually GI wives – to vent about the war's impact on their lives and to criticize the military's gender ideology. Wives of GIs complained of poor housing on bases, lack of job opportunities in military towns, and the military's general disregard for families. They spoke about the impact the war had on military families, especially those of enlisted men, and showed how ideas from the women's movement intersected with antiwar sentiment in a critique of both war and sexism. The presence of women's articles in the antiwar papers demonstrates an openness to women's perspectives on the part of the papers' editors, who usually were soldiers or veterans. Although some GIs no doubt skipped past those articles, others read them carefully and took to heart their opinions and grievances, in ways that modified their thinking about gender and sexism.

Some GI wives explained that military ideas about women attempted to produce conflicts between women and men to prevent women from convincing men that the military's sexism oppressed them. "The army brainwashes men against us because they're afraid – afraid that we might do something subversive, like regard a GI as a human being instead of an army-issue robot," one woman wrote in *Fatigue Press*. She argued that the military brass feared women would make GIs "feminine" by encouraging a recruit to do things "like refusing to do push-ups until he vomits, finding bayonet training sickening, or feeling compassion for those he's ordered to kill."[30] The writer complained that, because of the cost of the Vietnam War, the military did not pay its members enough to support a family, and inflation in military towns exacerbated the difficulties military families

---

[29] Richard Stacewicz, *Winter Soldiers: An Oral History of the Vietnam Veterans Against the War* (New York: Twayne Publishers, 1997), 216.
[30] "Women Against the War," *Left Face*, October 1971, 12, Wisconsin Historical Society.

had trying to make ends meet. She explained that a "one bedroom shack" in Killeen cost $70 per month to rent but featured "leaky faucets, broken stairs, and dingy walls." Groceries cost more in Killeen, a military town, than in Austin, the woman wrote, and prices seemed to go up around every payday. The health care the military provided was "awful," but the military salary made purchasing other health insurance cost-prohibitive. The woman concluded her article by warning that military wives would not continue to support the military's overseas missions if the military would not support them. As an example, she referred to an antiwar march in Killeen in May 1970, where nearly half of the 1,000 protesters were women.[31] That same year, the Oleo Strut organized the Strike Back Campaign for GI wives to speak out against the military's disregard for the needs of GIs' families. The organization met weekly in members' homes to discuss issues that military women and children faced.[32]

Writer Nora Sayre, who covered the civil rights movement in the 1950s and 1960s, attended an antiwar meeting at a Fort Bragg coffeehouse. She found GIs speaking out against what they had experienced in Vietnam and the most destructive manifestations of "military machismo." "One huge ... GI, just back from Vietnam, said, 'Macho is still the army's biggest drawing card for enlistment – it's even more powerful than patriotism. . . . The army's still capitalizing on their insecurity. So I think civilians' and women's liberation groups can help GIs a lot by continuing to expose the absurdity of the male role.'"[33] For their part, antiwar women knew that because they were not "draftable," they could not oppose the war by refusing to go. In an editorial published in *Ally*, women antiwar activists jokingly seized the reins of sexual power and threatened to imitate the women of ancient Greece portrayed in the play *Lysistrata*, who had refused to engage in sexual activity with men until the fighting ended. The anti-Vietnam War women decided, though, that the most productive tactic would be to "communicate directly with GIs."[34]

Antiwar GIs and veterans – particularly those involved in the coffeehouse movement – considered women and the women's movement vital allies in the fight against the system that created both the Vietnam War and domestic social ills. Pete Zastrow, a veteran who served a one-year tour in Vietnam beginning in December 1968, said that women helped

[31] Ibid.
[32] "Strike Back Campaign."
[33] Moser, 100.
[34] "Peace Talks," *Ally*, May, 1968, 10, Wisconsin Historical Society.

antiwar servicemen focus on "vital issues that, while they weren't direct veterans' issues, were issues that veterans damn well ought to be interested in – child care, the rights of women."[35] Mike McCain, a Vietnam veteran and member of VVAW, said of women in VVAW: "The women taught us boys a whole lot. They were mostly our girlfriends who ended up being some of the most valuable, the most dedicated, the most active, the most disciplined people in the organization."[36] Some members of VVAW viewed women as worthy members:

We were primarily vets, because we were a vets organization, but we refused to have an auxiliary. Women were absolute full members. We saw the inherent sexist nature of having a group who did not belong to the organization and who did work. They wanted to belong to VVAW. They couldn't stand up and tell about their experiences in Vietnam, but they could get up at a VVAW meeting and say what they thought we should be doing.[37]

Jeanne Friedman, a former civil rights activist and organizer of antiwar veterans, remembered that in VVAW, "women were doing a lot of the work. Women were paying attention to taking care of business."[38]

McCain and Friedman's comments are particularly interesting when considered in the context of the era's other social movements. One of the criticisms that has been levied against the civil rights, black power, and civilian antiwar movements is that women in those organizations often were relegated to clerical and other types of support jobs rather than leadership positions.[39] Based on McCain and Friedman's comments, it is unclear exactly what types of work women did in VVAW or whether they held positions of power, and allowing women members did not necessarily imply that male veterans considered them equals. But given that the GI antiwar press repeatedly indicated that a redefinition of gender roles and a rejection of male chauvinism were required to liberate men from the warrior myth, it seems clear that at least some GIs and veterans approved of women taking active, and even leadership, roles in the movement. At the same time, it is not surprising that even amid demands for change in the gender hierarchy, ambivalence about what such a transformation should look like remained.

---

[35] Stacewicz, 364.
[36] Ibid.
[37] Ibid.
[38] Ibid.
[39] Sara Evans, *Personal Politics: The Roots of Women's Liberation in the Civil Rights Movement & the New Left* (New York: Vintage, 1980).

Antiwar WACs

Some military women joined GI wives and antiwar soldiers to protest
military sexism and the Vietnam War. The GI Alliance, an organization
for antiwar GIs, advocated including more women in the group's activities. At a conference in 1970, members stated that women in the military,
as well as GI wives, could help the GI antiwar movement combat the
male chauvinism that drove the war in Vietnam.[40] At Fort McClellan in
Alabama, men and women organized GIs and WACs Against the War
and published *Left Face*. In 1971, Fort McClellan women also printed the
underground newspaper *WHACK!* In the August 1971 issue of *Fatigue
Press*, a woman who identified herself as an "ex-WAC" wrote an article
titled "Uncle Sam Wants You 'Baby.'" She accused military recruiters
of "pimping" for the armed services and in return living the high life,
complete with expense accounts and travel opportunities. She went on to
explain her perception of the way military men viewed members of the
Women's Army Corps: "if you lay, your [sic] a whore, if you don't you're
a lesbian; and if you have a good argument against both, you're mixed-
up or frigid." Denouncing both sexism and racism, the writer noted that
these were the issues antiwar military personnel hoped to combat, warning that "the GI movement consists of men and women in the military
who will no longer accept the exploitation and oppression that the United
States military perpetuates upon GIs and civilians in all countries of the
world."[41]

By framing her article in terms of sexuality, the author highlighted
the centrality of ideas about sex and gender to the culture of the U.S.
military during the Vietnam War. The military recruiter as pimp conjures
ideas about gender and power in the armed services; those ideas apply
to broader conceptions of American power in the world, and in Vietnam
particularly. Prostitution was a significant aspect of the Vietnam War,
both in fact and in legend. The metaphor of Vietnam as a woman sur-
faced in U.S. media coverage of the war and veterans' anecdotes from
it. The article also addressed gender constructions of military women
as lesbians or whores, attacking the belief on the part of military men,
particularly officers, that women in the military were unnatural and dangerous. Ultimately, the author argued, the military's attitudes toward and

---

[40] Small, *Give Peace a Chance*, 110.
[41] "Uncle Sam Wants You 'Baby,'" *Fatigue Press*, August 1971, 6, Wisconsin Historical
       Society.

treatment of women symbolized the impact the United States had around the world.

The antiwar group American Servicemen's Union (ASU) actively recruited servicewomen to join its ranks alongside antiwar GIs, using the language of the women's movement to attract new members. ASU member Sue Steinman, a civilian, interviewed Kathy Christian, a member of the Women's Air Force and ASU; in an article in *The Bond*, they explained their views of servicewomen's experiences. "Women are told their whole existence depends on being a wife and a mother only," Steinman wrote. "We are discouraged from attaining higher education; we are discriminated against in jobs; we are told we are weak, dumb, and inferior." Because of limitations placed on women, Steinman argued, some joined the military because they hope to "get a better deal, see the world, get an education, and escape from their dull lives." However, Christian continued, the reality for women in the service was little better. "The officers want us to brighten up their little offices," she said. "They give us makeup classes and we're taught how to look pretty. Makeup is a mandatory part of your uniform. The officers are always telling us we're the private property of the AF [Air Force]. They look at us like whores and they teach our enlisted brothers to view us the same way."[42]

Christian and Steinman connected the treatment of women to a larger conflict between military brass and enlisted women and men. Through its degradation of women, the brass tried to pit servicemen against servicewomen, but antiwar WACs and GIs recognized that sexism and crude language oppressed both men and women. Christian argued: "The struggle of servicewomen is the struggle of all lower-ranking EM [enlisted men], too. Our fight is against the Brass and the lifers. If all the EM and EW [enlisted women] team up together to build the ASU, the Brass won't have a fighting chance."[43] Male veterans also called on GIs to reject the attitudes of "lifers" against WACs. "According to the warped officers, a WAC is a woman who 'couldn't make it' with men on the outside," vets writing for *The Bond* contended. "These half-wits viciously slander our sisters in the military. . . . We must reject this trash." Instead of buying in to the military's sexism, GIs should recognize that some women enlisted for the same reasons some men did – they needed to learn job skills, earn

---

[42] "Servicewoman Exposes Recruiter's Lies," *The Bond*, December 24, 1971, 10, Wisconsin Historical Society.
[43] Ibid.

money, or escape a tough home life.[44] Although Christian and Steinman did not discuss the Vietnam War specifically, their grievances addressed the same themes some antiwar GIs expressed in their opposition to the war. Drill instructors' sexist characterizations of women in basic training were expressions of U.S. beliefs about its power and relationship to Vietnam, antiwar soldiers argued. The sexualized sense of power included a virile masculinity that could tame or penetrate femininities. As comic books and congressional reports indicated, Vietnam was the dragon lady to be tamed.

"Asian Women and the Lifer Mind"

Although most discussions of gender focused on the position of American women, some antiwar GIs also called attention to the ways in which the U.S. military's gender ideology affected Vietnamese women. Several writers noted how characterizations of Vietnamese women were tied to American attitudes toward Asians going back to World War II and U.S. relations with Japan. *Dare to Struggle*, a GI antiwar newspaper published by the Movement for a Democratic Military in San Diego, testified that drill instructors began classes with jokes about Asian women they had known while stationed in Japan or other parts of Asia. "The attitude of the Asian woman being a doll, a useful toy, or something to play with usually came out in these jokes, and how they were not quite as human as white women," one reporter, who identified himself in the article as Asian American, wrote. "For instance, a real common example was how the instructor would talk about how Asian women's vaginas weren't like a white woman's, but rather they were slanted, like their eyes." Just like words such as "gook" dehumanized Vietnamese men and women, "the image of a people with slanted eyes and slanted vaginas enhances the feelings that Asians are other than human, and therefore much easier to kill."[45] In the same report, the writer told the story of a drill sergeant who became obsessed with some pictures of another Asian American GI's sister, who reminded him of a prostitute he had known in Japan.

At night after lights-out, the drill sergeant would pull up a chair next to the GI's bed and talk with him about her, saying she shared the soldier's last name. Apparently, the soldier's sister also looked like the drill

---

[44] "Anti-Woman Propaganda."
[45] "Asian Women and the Lifer Mind," *Dare to Struggle*, Vol. 2, Issue 1 (Date missing), Wisconsin Historical Society.

sergeant's Japanese prostitute. The drill sergeant then spent time harass-
ing the soldier, referring to his sister and saying things like "Yeah, that's
her. That's the prostitute I had."[46] The writer of the article recognized
the connection between attitudes concerning race and gender, noting that
"the view that Asian women are less than human helps perpetuate another
myth – that of the white woman 'back home' being placed on a pedestal,"
also an "oppressive situation." The newspaper presented the story of an
Asian American GI who wanted to marry a Vietnamese woman he met
in Vietnam as an example of the racialized aspect of gender. Various
officers in the military chain of command tried to discourage him, telling
him that the Vietnamese were "not civilized." They also told him that
"you think you want to marry her now, but that's because there are no
round-eye chicks around." The reasoning surprised the soldier, for he
was Asian, not "round-eye." "They'd say, 'And once you get back, you'll
see all those blondes and stuff, and you'll look at your wife and she'll be
this old farmer chick – this gook – and you'll want to get rid of her,"
the serviceman said. "You'll be embarrassed when you get back because
she's Vietnamese.'" The soldier eventually dropped the issue and did not
marry the woman.

Reflecting on the GI's experience, the article stated that the U.S. military establishment saw Asian Americans as foreign, or did not see them
at all. In the case of the Asian American soldier who wanted to marry a
Vietnamese woman, "the military, completely insensitive to the fact that
he too was an Asian, talked about the 'round-eyed' women waiting back
home." Yet, when the same GI arrived at basic training, the drill sergeant
made him stand in front of the platoon to demonstrate "what the enemy
looked like."[47] *Dare to Struggle* commented on the racist sexism against
Vietnamese women and called on its readers to "fight the mentality that
keeps Suzy Wong, Madame Butterfly, and gookism alive. The mentality
that turns human beings into racist murdering soldiers also keeps Asian
Americans from being able to live and feel like human beings here at
home."[48]

Black Servicemen and Servicewomen United in Dissent

The relationship between GI resistance and the rejection of the gendered
ideology in the military took particular forms among African Americans.

[46] Ibid.
[47] Ibid.
[48] Ibid.

These forms were linked in complicated ways with the civil rights and black power movements on the home front. Inspired by and making crucial contributions to the domestic struggles against white supremacy, black service personnel were acutely aware of the racism they faced in the military.[49] Although some antiwar GIs recognized the connection between racial and gender oppression, the situation was complicated by what were widely understood as ongoing attacks against black masculinity. The result was a sometimes chaotic mix of political and cultural approaches in which black GIs, asserting their manhood, raised their voices alongside black women in the military and black civilian women who urged their brothers to join in revolutionary action against all forms of oppression.

Black Women Enraged, a Harlem group founded to oppose the draft, criticized not only the Department of Defense and the armed forces, but also their sons, brothers, and husbands for not having the courage to stand up to the military and refuse to fight "Whitey's war." Members of Black Women Enraged demanded that black men ignore the calls to military service, for they were needed to fight the wars in "the black ghetto at home."[50] Black Women's Organization Against War and Racism, a group based in Berkeley, California, also encouraged black men to refuse to go to Vietnam. As stated in one of the group's newsletters: "It takes a man to say 'hell no' to McNamara and a slave to blindly and silently refuse to make the decision as to who or when he should kill innocent people."[51]

For the members of Black Women Enraged and Black Women's Organization Against War and Racism, real men stayed in the community to fight poverty and racism. They did not obey the military, a central part of the system that oppressed them. The Black and Third World Women's Alliance took the argument one step further, calling on black women to assert themselves in the social wars at home just as women in North Vietnam took up arms in the fight against the U.S. and the government

---

[49] On the experiences of African American troops in Vietnam, see Herman Graham, *The Brothers' Vietnam War: Black Power, Manhood, and the Military Experience* (Gainesville, FL: University Press of Florida, 2003); James Westheider, *Fighting on Two Fronts: African Americans and the Vietnam War* (New York: New York University Press, 1999); and Wallace Terry, *Bloods: An Oral History of the Vietnam War by Black Veterans* (New York: Ballantine Books, 1985).

[50] "Black People of Harlem" and "Black Men!!" Fall 1966, Black Women Enraged files, Wisconsin Historical Society, Social Action Collection.

[51] "Black Man Stay Home!" April 1967, Black Women's Organization Against War and Racism Papers, Wisconsin Historical Society, Social Action Collection.

of South Vietnam. The group noted that "black women's liberation is not anti-male – it is pro-human for all peoples."[52] In all three groups, the women's activism exposed the racism and sexism of the Vietnam War, offered alternative social structures, and highlighted the limits and failures of American ideas about masculine power and race.

The discussion of gender and masculinity in African American communities had been shaped by the Moynihan Report, which was released in March 1965 as the war in Vietnam was entering a new phase. It motivated the Defense Department to embark on a special recruiting effort aimed at attracting young black men to the National Guard. Guard units had been deployed to Los Angeles, Detroit, and other cities to quell riots, and the racial composition of the units was nearly all white. Illinois Governor Otto Kerner and New York City Mayor John Lindsay, members of the National Advisory Commission on Civil Disorders, argued that placing white troops on riot duty was sure to alienate African Americans in the neighborhoods they occupied. Therefore, they called for a recruiting drive focused on potential black recruits. Secretary of Defense Robert McNamara authorized recruiters to exceed assigned strength by 10 percent so long as the additional enlistees were black.[53] As inner-city African Americans watched their neighborhoods erupt in flames, the military tried to send black soldiers in to fight the people some considered to be their brothers and sisters.

In March 1965, Assistant Secretary of Labor Daniel Patrick Moynihan published "The Negro Family: The Case for National Action," known commonly as the Moynihan Report. In the study, Moynihan attributed inner city poverty to what he perceived as an absence of strong African American male role models. Sociologist Thomas Pettigrew shared Moynihan's view and declared that black women's willingness to work for financial independence drove black men away, thus leaving their sons without a male role model. Black mothers consequently indulged their sons in overprotective "smother-love," causing boys to grow up to be hypermasculine, power hungry, and sexually aggressive.[54] Moynihan argued that the "abnormal prominence of women" in African American

[52] Maryanne Weathers, "An Argument for Black Women's Liberation as a Revolutionary Force," October 1968, Black and Third World Women's Liberation Alliance Papers, Wisconsin Historical Society, Social Action Collection.

[53] Bernard C. Nalty, *Strength for the Fight: A History of Black Americans in the Military* (New York: The Free Press, 1986), 297.

[54] Daniel Patrick Moynihan, "The Negro Family: The Case for National Action," Office of Policy Planning and Research, United States Department of Labor, March 1965.

families was equally to blame – along with segregation and employment discrimination – for black men's humiliation and submission. Moynihan suggested that the federal government make employing all African American men its top priority so that black families could develop along the traditional male-dominated trajectory and thus break the cycle of poverty and violence that plagued inner cities throughout the United States.[55]

This characterization of African American women, thoroughly rejected by the members of Black Women Enraged and Black Women United Against War and Racism, mirrors the "momism" that denigrated suburban white mothers in the 1950s. Despite the calls to American women to accept the duties of motherhood as the most noble work, critics located the roots of men's perceived faults in their relationships with their mothers. This tension in Cold War gender construction is another illustration of the divergence between ideology and reality during the period, and it demonstrates how deeply gender permeated the decisions and policies behind the Vietnam War. Just as President Kennedy called for greater attention to the physical fitness of middle-class boys so they would be prepared to answer to call to military service, Moynihan created a picture of black women's supposed maternal shortcomings to justify an emphasis on recruiting of African American men into the armed forces at a time when the Johnson administration was escalating the Vietnam War. In both cases, women's failings as mothers provided a justification for sending their sons to fight and possibly die.

Moynihan reasoned that the military was the place in which black men could learn employable skills. In his report, he noted that 56 percent of African American men who took the Armed Forces Qualification Test in 1962 failed it – a failure rate almost four times that of whites and a factor Moynihan called "the ultimate mark of inadequate preparation for life."[56] Furthermore, Moynihan argued that African American men *needed* military service. He believed that only in military service were African Americans treated as equal to their white counterparts, and, more importantly, military training would teach black youth how to be men.

It is an utterly masculine world. Given the strains of the disorganized and matrifocal family life in which so many Negro youth come of age, the Armed Forces are a dramatic and desperately needed change: a world away from women, a world run by strong men of unquestioned authority, where discipline, if harsh,

[55] Paula Giddings, *When and Where I Enter: The Impact of Black Women on Race and Sex in America* (New York: William Morrow and Co., 1984), 325–28.
[56] Giddings, *When and Where I Enter*, 89.

is nonetheless orderly and predictable, and where rewards, if limited, are granted on the basis of performance. The theme of a current Army recruiting message states it as clearly as can be: "In the U.S. Army you get to know what it means to feel like a man." At the recent Civil Rights Commission hearings in Mississippi a witness testified that his Army service was in fact "the only time I ever felt like a man."[57]

In 1966, Secretary of Defense Robert S. McNamara submitted a plan intended to address the problem Moynihan outlined. During a speech in New York City, McNamara announced that the Department of Defense would lower the mental and physical standards for admission into the branches of the U.S. military, in an attempt to "uplift America's subterranean poor and cure them of the idleness, ignorance, and apathy which marked their lives." "Project 100,000," as McNamara's plan came to be called, was designed to enlist or induct 40,000 soldiers by June 1966 and up to 150,000 men per year.[58] At the same time, defense analysts slated an additional 150,000 soldiers for deployment to Vietnam, and President Lyndon Johnson considered calling up reserves, higher draft calls, and an increase in the defense budget. In May 1965, the Defense Department estimated it would need about 50,000 troops in Vietnam, but by January 1966, the number had increased to more than 400,000 soldiers.[59] Between October 1966 and June 1969, 246,000 men were recruited into the military under Project 100,000; 41 percent of them were black. Of those men, 37 percent were assigned to combat, and more than half went to Vietnam.[60]

The lowered standards of Project 100,000 applied to all draftees and enlistees, but McNamara positioned the program as a specific response to what Moynihan had deemed the needs of inner-city African American young men. In a speech to the National Association of Educational Broadcasters in 1967, McNamara stressed that military service would provide African American men with the chance to learn employable skills so they could be productive citizens in an increasingly technological society. Moreover, military accomplishment would provide a sense of personal achievement that would lift black men out of the "ghetto of the human

---

57 Ibid., 42–43.
58 Lisa Hsiao, "Project 100,000: The Great Society's Answer to Military Manpower Needs in Vietnam," *Vietnam Generation*, 1989, 14.
59 Lee Rainwater and William L. Yancey, *The Moynihan Report and the Politics of Controversy* (Cambridge, MA: Massachusetts Institute of Technology Press, 1967).
60 James Westheider, *Fighting on Two Fronts: African Americans and the Vietnam War* (New York: New York University Press, 1999), 35.

spirit" as well as the urban ghetto and allow them to move forward as productive citizens when they returned from service.[61] Theoretically, after black men put in their time in the military, they would return home, find skilled labor jobs, get married, start families, and break the cycle of poverty that decades of discrimination and woman-led households had created. In short, they would be men. At its heart, Project 100,000 was antimaternal, assuming that mothers had failed in making their sons into men, and touting the military as a substitute for absent black fathers.[62]

Some African Americans GIs called on black men to honor and respect black women and to treat them as equals rather than participate in military talk that degraded women. Cold War beliefs about American military power considered the forces a distinctly masculine realm, but race trumped gender and forged solidarity among some African American personnel in the struggle against military racism and sexism. As more and more troops expressed opposition to the war, especially in the years after 1968 and the Tet offensive, black troops united to speak out against racism and sexism in the military, viewing the Vietnam War as an extension of civil rights injustices African Americans fought at home.

The voices of African American military personnel who rejected the military's gender expectations come through in GI antiwar newspapers. *Broken Arrow*, the Selfridge Air Base antiwar newspaper, reported in its October 1969 issue on a stockade mutiny at Ford Ord, California, that protested, among other things, the jailing of three black WACs who allegedly associated with militant black GIs on base.[63] The issue also carried an article about the arrests of four African American members of the Women's Air Force. Prior to the arrest, African American servicewomen and men at Selfridge complained of harassment by police for wearing Afros and gathering in groups. When some black soldiers met in the servicemen's club on base to plan a fundraiser for children in Georgia, the Air Force criminal investigation division accused them of holding Black Power meetings. The arrest of four African American WAFs in August 1969 was the "final straw."[64]

The four Air Force women had just left their barracks to go to the servicemen's club when they saw that someone had sprayed Sergeant

[61] Robert S. McNamara, "Social Inequities: Urban Racial Ills," in *Vital Speeches of the Day*, December 1, 1967, 98.
[62] Moser, 100.
[63] "Selfridge: No More Shit," *Broken Arrow*, October 23, 1969, 1, Wisconsin Historical Society.
[64] Ibid.

Marion Whitfield's car with shaving cream, spelling out "Nigger" and "Quiet Nigger" in the foam. When the women called security, the officer brushed off their complaint and told them to "forget it." The vandalism was only the most recent incident in several months of harassment by a group of white WAFs. Earlier that summer, Whitfield had fought with Nancy Morin, the white WAFs' leader. The black women were not surprised when they saw Morin and another white WAF a few blocks from Whitfield's car. According to the report, the white women appeared to be drunk, and when Evelyn James, a twenty-year-old African American WAF, asked Morin if she knew who vandalized Whitfield's car, Morin replied, "I don't have to tell nothing to no nigger." After a brief exchange, the black WAFs walked away, but Morin rushed to attack James, setting off a fight that lasted until military police arrived and ordered all the WAFs to return to their barracks.[65]

The incident did not end there. James, Whitfield, and two other African American WAFs went back to James's room at the barracks, and after a while they heard pounding on the door. "You black ass nigger, come on out!" screamed Morin and some other white WAFs. The banging on the door and yelling continued until the police, whom Whitfield had called, arrived at the barracks. When James and Whitfield came out of the room to talk with the police, the officers ordered them back in and told them to "stop making trouble." The officers proceeded to ask the white WAFs to explain what was going on. Later that week, police charged James with disorderly conduct for fighting with Morin.[66]

James had had enough. Supported by a group of African American GIs and WAFs, she refused the administrative punishment the police had given her for disorderly conduct and demanded a court-martial so that she would face a trial. The group hired two lawyers and worked with the interracial staff of *Broken Arrow* to encourage sympathetic GIs and WAFs to pack the courtroom. Civilian allies planned to picket outside the base the day of the trial. James and her supporters hoped her court martial, scheduled for October 7, would be a "trial of racism at Selfridge." The theme was the slogan "No Vietnamese Ever Called Me Nigger," a statement attributed to Muhammad Ali and his refusal to fight in the Vietnam War.[67]

On the day of the court martial, about fifty protesters met at the main gate of the base to support James and denounce the Vietnam War

---

[65] Ibid.
[66] Ibid.
[67] Ibid.

and racism in the Air Force. Military police, Air Force intelligence personnel, Macomb County sheriff's deputies, and police from nearby Mt. Clemens arrived to monitor the protestors. In the course of the trial, two African American military policemen who had come to the scene of the fight between James and Morin testified that Morin had been drunk and had attacked James without provocation. The trial revealed that, several months earlier, the Air Force had ordered a full-scale investigation into racial strife at Selfridge, but the investigation never took place. In the end, the judge presiding over the trial ruled in favor of James. Writers for *Broken Arrow* claimed that James's successful trial showed that African American GIs and WACs could make their voices heard if they banded together.[68]

Events at Fort Meade in Maryland, Great Lakes Naval Training Center in Illinois, and Fort McClellan in Alabama further illustrate ways in which black servicemen and servicewomen united against the military established. In June 1971, the Army discharged six African American WACs who had participated in civil rights demonstrations at Fort Meade a month earlier. The women belonged to Brothers and Sisters for Equality, a group of black GIs and WACs that sought to bring attention to military racism. Of the base's 13,000 residents, about 23 percent were African American. Although members of Brothers and Sisters stated that the Army discharged the women to stymie the group's activism, Colonel Arthur Brinson, the deputy commander of Fort Meade, blamed the women, telling a *Washington Post* reporter that they had poor disciplinary records that warranted discharges. The base's public information officer, Joseph Hedley, said the women had refused to wear their uniforms and report for duty, some for three days, others for five days.

The six discharged WACs had been among nearly one hundred servicemen and servicewomen who, a few weeks earlier, had participated in the civil rights march around the base. Private First Class Melvin E. Smith, a spokesperson for Brothers and Sisters for Equality, said the group sought not to change the military system but to ensure equal treatment for blacks and whites. The group hoped to avoid a race riot like the one that had occurred a week earlier at Travis Air Force Base near San Francisco after authorities ignored African American soldiers' demands for racial equality. As a result of the uprising, ten people were injured and ninety-seven were arrested. Despite the Travis incident, the brass at Fort Meade ignored the demands of African American GIs and WAC. "They

[68] Ibid.

only say shut up and be good slaves," Smith explained. "Not even good soldiers. Just good slaves."[69]

The black GIs and WACs were tired of being "good slaves." They organized a march that began at the WAC barracks and passed the building where soldiers who had gone absent without leave (AWOL) were waiting to be processed out. It was there that military police detained the protesters and arrested two men in the group whom they accused of assaulting other soldiers. Some demonstrators drove to the detention station to find out the status of the arrested men, but they dispersed on police orders. Hedley, the public information officer, later told the *Washington Post* that the protestors went to their cars but did not drive away, so police began to arrest them with force. Officers dragged two WACs into the station, and when another WAC, twenty-three-year-old Nora Murphy, tried to help the women, an officer clubbed her on the head. Another officer clubbed a twenty-year-old Linda Arzu, also a WAC, with a sawed-off baseball bat. At the end of the battle, police arrested ten WACs and twelve GIs on charges of disorderly conduct. Murphy and Arzu were two of the six WACs subsequently discharged.[70]

The next day, a group of African American GIs and WACs tried to file a civil rights complaint at headquarters, but the chief of staff, Brigadier General S. M. Marks, told the troopers they had to get an attorney first. Melvin Smith of Brothers and Sisters said Marks "ordered us to 'get the hell off the steps.' It was just like John Wayne."[71] Smith's comparison of Marks to John Wayne reflects the rejection of white masculinity, which united the currents of black GI resistance. White masculinity had oppressed, injured, and killed black men, and Smith, like the antiwar GIs who demanded an end to the gender stereotypes that defined the Vietnam War, viewed Marks and Wayne as symbols of a system that prevented African American GIs and WACs from enjoying their full rights as citizen soldiers.

In July 1970, authorities at Great Lakes Naval Training Center jailed four African American WAVES after they protested the alleged assault of another black WAVE. *The Destroyer*, a GI paper published in Philadelphia for Navy personnel, reported that about seventy-five black sailors surrounded the building in which the WAVES were held in a show of

[69] "Army Tries to Oust 6 WACs in Protest," *Washington Post*, June 1, 1971, A1.
[70] Ibid.
[71] Ibid.

solidarity with them.[72] After the incident occurred, *Dare to Struggle*, a
GI paper published in San Diego, featured an interview with an unnamed
African American woman stationed at Great Lakes. She explained that
white WAVES might have joined in the protest against the jailing of their
black counterparts if the Navy did not seek to enforce racial division
among troops.

The Navy tries to divide blacks and whites, which I can't dig. People are people
no matter what color they are. It's really strange how some white girls fear black
sisters. Like, some black sisters really messed up some lifers. It was out of sight to
see someone screwing up the Navy after it has been screwing up so many people.
But some of the white girls couldn't dig it because they're scared of black sisters.

The interview ended with the tagline: "Brothers and sisters; we got to get
together and smash racism and male chauvinism!!!"[73]

Gender and race were inextricably combined at Fort McClellan. A
November 1971 issue of *The Bond*, the newspaper of the antiwar American Servicemen's Union, reported what the article called a "Gestapo-like
roundup of black GIs and WACs" at Fort McClellan, Alabama, the base
that served as WAC headquarters. The article connected the arrests to
civilian civil rights struggles, arguing that "there is but one difference
between Fort McClellan and Selma, Alabama – the color of the uniform
worn by the cops." According to the article, 138 African American service people, including 68 WACs, were arrested. The arrests followed a
weekend of protests by black GIs and WACs against racism on base. The
article reported that an off-duty white MP had rammed his car into a
group of black GIs and WACs, injuring five women and one man. In
an effort to prevent a riot, the brass granted permission for an on-post
protest march. When the protest continued into the next day, one of the
colonels invited black GIs and WACs to meet with their commanding
officers on the base football field. The gathering turned into a scuffle,
and several black GIs were sent to the stockade at Fort Bragg, North
Carolina.[74] The American Servicemen's Union issued a statement in support of the arrested GIs and WACs, while *Left Face*, the antiwar paper
for service people at Fort McClellan, denounced the treatment of black

[72] "Stormy Waves in Great Lakes," *The Destroyer*, September 18, 1970, 1, Wisconsin
Historical Society.
[73] "Wave Goodbye," *Dare to Struggle*, Vol. 1, Issue 7 (Date missing), 2, Wisconsin Historical Society.
[74] "Brass Order Gestapo-Like Roundup of Black GIs and WACs," *The Bond*, November
26, 1971, 1, Wisconsin Historical Society.

military personnel and accused military police of racism.[75] The large number of African American WACs arrested in the confrontation showcases the collaboration between black military men and women in the face of sexism and racism.

Solidarity with black GIs may have saved nurse Captain Elizabeth Allen's life. Stationed at a base hospital in Pleiku, Allen befriended some of the black soldiers on base. In the weeks leading up to the Tet offensive, the troops intercepted communications indicating that a large-scale attack might occur around the Tet holiday. Some black GIs warned Allen so that she could be prepared. In that experience, she considered her race a benefit, suggesting that the African American troops might not have shared the information with a white nurse. "There were terrible disadvantages of being a black woman in the war, but advantages, too. The black troops seek you."[76]

While some black GIs might have viewed that in chauvinistic terms – as a successful effort to protect one of "their" women – others recognized the need to resist sexism as well as racism. Many recognized the contribution of militarism to various modes of oppression. Forty-three African American soldiers stationed at Fort Hood had refused to go with their units to Chicago to help quell demonstrations following the assassination of Martin Luther King, Jr. in April 1968. Nicknamed the "Fort Hood Forty-Three," the GIs opposed military efforts to stifle protest activity.[77] Subsequently, they were arrested for disobeying orders.[78] Dave Cline, who was drafted into the Army in January 1967 and sent to Vietnam seven months later, defined the GI sentiment: "we just fought the Vietnamese; now they want us to fight the Americans. A lot of blacks looked at it like they were going to fight their own people."[79] Therefore, the GIs devised a plan to help antiwar protesters identify friendly GIs in case a riot occurred. They printed stickers featuring a black hand with fingers raised in a peace sign, and they planned to wear the stickers on their helmets to show support for the protesters.[80]

[75] "McClellan Hassled," *Left Face*, Ft. McClellan, AL, Issue 2 (Date missing), Wisconsin Historical Society.

[76] *We Were There: Voices of African American Veterans from World War II to the War in Iraq*, ed. Yvonne Latty (New York: Amistad, 2004), 91–98.

[77] *Fatigue Press*, July 1970, Wisconsin Historical Society.

[78] Richard R. Moser, *The New Winter Soldiers: GI and Veteran Dissent During the Vietnam Era* (New Brunswick, NJ: Rutgers University Press, 1996), 84.

[79] Stacewicz, 223.

[80] Stacewicz, 223.

Demand for Freedom told readers that "to use terms such as bitch, broad, chic [*sic*], hammer, or whore in recognizing our Black sisters is a failure to be Black. . . . You don't even realize that in using these depressive terms, you are also speaking of your mother, wife, or daughter, because they too are Black sisters."[81] An article in *About Face*, an antiwar newspaper published by black GIs stationed in Heidelberg, Germany, invoked the honor of black women to discourage black men from getting involved with German women. The article equated black manhood with love for "the daughters of Africa."

Brothers, the eyes of our "brown sugar" are upon us! Let's stand up and be men. Put your brothers and sisters ahead of the trampish floozy who has one hand in your pocket and is winking at another brother at the same time. Do they see us as men, or as big, black, dancing, sexy monkeys? The daughters of Africa are the sweetest, and any "down" brother will tell you this, too!![82]

In some cases, the celebration of black women objectified them, but some black GIs demanded full equality for black women at home and on base. An article in *Demand for Freedom* announced:

Brothers, for too long we have challenged our black sisters with male chauvinism and depressive and reactionary terminology of description. The pigs tricked black brothers and sisters into believing that the man is the leader and the woman is to follow. And because the racist, capitalist system drained the black man from so much of his black manhood, the brothers dug heavily upon male chauvinism because it was to be our power of manhood. We actually designated ourselves as masters over our black sisters, and we were and still are trying to hide our weaknesses from our black sisters. Our black sisters have discovered the oppressor to be male chauvinism, and they realize it's a trick to divide the brothers from the sisters. So brothers, if you still possess male chauvinist attitudes, get rid of them, because neither will our black sisters nor our black brothers tolerate this reactionary form of behavior any longer.[83]

Additionally, the writer of the article called for an extension of solidarity to all nonwhite women. Because Kadena Air Force Base, where *Demand for Freedom* was published, is located on Okinawa, the author called on black GIs to respect "our Okinawan sisters who have been forced by American capitalism and imperialism to engage in prostitution as a means of survival. Brothers, for the sake of the People's humanity and

---

[81] "Liberation for Our Black Brothers and Sisters," *Demand for Freedom*, November 16, 1970, 14, Wisconsin Historical Society.

[82] "Liberation for Our Black Brothers and Sisters."

[83] "Liberation for Our Black Brothers and Sisters."

dedicated love and respect, recognize our black sisters and all Third World females."[84]

Such clearly articulated awareness of the connection between racism, male chauvinism, and the gendered images undergirding American foreign policy were not the norm. Black and white civilian women complained of sexism in antiwar and civil rights organizations, from Students for a Democratic Society to the Student Nonviolent Coordinating Committee. African American women activists such as Frances Beale argued that the rise of Black Power contributed to a decline in the number of black women holding leadership positions within civil rights groups. In her essay "Double Jeopardy: Black and Female," Beale reminded black men that

those who are exerting their "manhood" by telling black women to step back into a domestic, submissive role are assuming a counterrevolutionary position. Since the advent of Black Power, the black male has exerted a more prominent leadership role in our struggle in this country. He sees the system for what it really is for the most part. But where he rejects its values and mores on many issues, when it comes to women, he seems to take his guidelines from the pages of the *Ladies Home Journal*.[85]

Adhering to traditional gender roles would prevent both men and women from moving forward and changing an oppressive system.

"The Opposite of Militarism Isn't Pacifism, It's Feminism"

For some GIs, their experiences in Vietnam dispelled the myths of masculinity in ways that led to an open embrace of feminism. Elton Tylenda came to view military service as an act of cowardice. "That's what a soldier is, basically a coward in a very big way, in that you will do the most cowardly things to avoid being called a coward," he remarked, "because of that whole manhood thing, and you don't want to be called a pussy, a pansy, or whatever." By comparison, the Vietnamese whom the United States fought seemed much more courageous to Tylenda. "We had armor," he said. "I had a heavy flak vest, gas mask, drugs, and medications, a whole warehouse on my back. We were facing people in black pajamas, sometimes with no weapons at all, who would confront us. You see the desperation, you see the resolve in their faces... that

---

[84] "Liberation for Our Black Brothers and Sisters."
[85] Ruth Rosen, *The World Split Open: How the Modern Women's Movement Changed America* (New York: Penguin, 2006), 281.

they would face us like that." For Tylenda, the military's gender ideology was "a house of cards. As you start to see through, it all falls apart."[86]

Sometimes it took a member of an older generation to shed light on the realities of gender and war. Vietnam Army veteran Doug Bradley learned from his father-in-law, an officer in World War II. "It's funny, my father-in-law and I used to talk about this, and he used to say, 'The opposite of militarism isn't pacifism, it's feminism,'" Bradley said. "So he was always big into the women's movement because he thought it was a way to stop some of this nonsense."[87] Despite the antagonism between some GIs and the brass during the Vietnam War years, personality clashes were not always generational. The fundamental characteristics of war – bloodshed, killing, disregard for human life – were constant.

Some antiwar GIs and veterans eventually turned their attention to the impact the warrior myth could have on their sons well before the boys were old enough to go to war. In December 1971, the Veterans for Peace chapter in Madison, Wisconsin, sent letters to local toy stores asking them to stop selling "war toys" such as guns and tanks. "Many of our members have seen the horrors of war at very close range and all of us know that there is nothing glorious or wonderful about killing human beings or destroying the land where they live," wrote Vets for Peace member Carl Doersch. The letter went on to blame pop culture expressions of the warrior myth for the Vietnam War. "We can of course blame all of this on our political leaders but how many of us enjoy a good war movie or a 'shoot-em-out western'?" Doersch asked. "These attitudes may have in fact contributed to the early acceptance of what was going on in Vietnam."[88]

A Madison Veterans for Peace pamphlet titled "Buy Your Son a Gun" featured a cartoon drawing of a young boy holding a machine gun superimposed over a photograph of U.S. troops searching a forest in Vietnam. The pamphlet warned that "it's never too early to begin his conditioning. Rocket launchers, hand grenades, jet bombers, and even GI Joe dolls can give your boy the valuable training he will need in order to keep our country #1 in military might. If you don't teach him how to kill kids now, he may never learn!"[89] The parents of the Vietnam generation

---

[86] Author's interview with Elton Tylenda.
[87] Author's interview with Doug Bradley, March 27, 2006, Madison, WI.
[88] Letter to Madison-area store owners from Carl Doersch, December 13, 1971, Madison Veterans for Peace, Madison, WI, Wisconsin Historical Society, Mss 316, Box 1, Folder 3.
[89] "Buy Your Son a Gun," Madison Veterans for Peace, Mss 316, Box 1, Folder 6

may have bought their boys toy guns, but some of the fathers of the next generation had seen a side of war that made it impossible for them to pass on the notion that war could be child's play.

At the opposite end of the cultural and political spectrum from John Wayne, John Lennon provided a model for some antiwar GIs who hoped to reject military machismo in their daily lives. In August 1971, *Left Face*, an antiwar newspaper published in Anniston, Alabama (near Fort McClellan) ran an interview with Lennon and Yoko Ono, in which the couple discussed gender politics and women's liberation. Lennon noted that "we can't have a revolution that doesn't involve and liberate women. You can't talk power to the people unless you realize that people is both sexes."[90] By that time, Lennon was a househusband who viewed his Asian wife as his equal, if not his intellectual superior. A far cry from John Wayne, Lennon represented a shift in American ideas about masculinity, and antiwar GIs and veterans had contributed significantly to that redefinition.

Psychiatrist Robert Jay Lifton spent several years working with Vietnam veterans as they struggled to come to terms with the war and their roles in it. After hearing countless stories of how the reality of the Vietnam War did not match up to the glorious tales of warfare on which he had been raised, he imagined a scenario between a father and child. The child might ask: "Daddy, what did you do in the war?" Instead of replying with a glamorous battle story, the father would respond proudly, "I fought in it, rejected it, and then did my best to reveal the truth about it."[91] Telling the truth about the war could involve explaining the effects of the warrior myth on women, men, soldiers, families, Vietnamese, and Americans. Antiwar GIs did just that.

Opposition to the Vietnam War – and, more important, to the gender ideals that shaped the experiences of the Americans who served – contributed to a fundamental shift in the U.S. military's image. The war had discredited the notion that military service was the ultimate expression of male citizenship, and it challenged the belief that women and men had neatly separated wartime roles and experiences. With the end of the unpopular draft in 1973, the armed services had to rebrand themselves to fill their ranks. Responding not only to changes within military culture but also to demands for gender equality in the civilian world, recruiting campaigns targeted women, offering education and career advancement.

[90] "Working Class Hero: An Interview with John and Yoko," *Left Face*, Anniston, AL, August 1971, 8, Wisconsin Historical Society.
[91] Lifton, 375.

Real changes occurred on official levels as jobs opened up to women and military publications touted the advances female personnel were making in the forces, yet attitudes among some servicemen were ambivalent toward their women counterparts. As the changes in the post-Vietnam military showed, the transformations in gender relations envisioned by the antiwar GIs were far from complete.

Conclusion

"You've Come a Long Way ... Maybe": Gender after Vietnam

Sergeant Whittington and Captain Corley never imagined they would be "firsts." Both had made careers in the Army, and for the most part, their experiences had been no different from those of their comrades. In 1976, they received promotions – Whittington became conductor of the 14th Army Band, an all-female ensemble, and Corley was named commander of a Women's Army Corps basic training company. Their transitions to positions of authority went relatively smooth; other than Corley getting teased as a "flat-chested WAC," neither received any trouble from the recruits. In the wake of the Vietnam War, as the Army transitioned to an all-volunteer force, the changes opened up positions for personnel who might have been considered unconventional in the past. That was how Otis Whittington and Larry Corley became the first men to hold their respective jobs.[1]

The Vietnam War and its aftermath coincided with several events that together stimulated changes in gender roles and relations in the United States. The idea of extending equal rights to women echoed the beliefs of antiwar GIs who, along with feminist activists, argued for a gender liberation that would free both women and men from social constrictions. Some vets who had grown up playing John Wayne in neighborhood cowboys-and-Indians games found a new role model in John Lennon, who pulled back from the music scene in the mid-1970s to raise his son,

---

[1] Pat Guy, "Men entering all-women strongholds at fort," *Anniston (AL) Star*, Sept. 2, 1976.

Sean.[2] Veteran Doug Bradley, who was drafted into the Army in 1970 and served as a journalist at U.S. Army Republic of Vietnam (USARV) headquarters in Long Binh, swapped a full-time job for part-time work in the early 1980s so he could stay home and bond with his daughter, Summer. He was part of a neighborhood babysitting co-op in Madison, Wisconsin, and although he was one of few dads in the group, the presence of men as caregivers led one neighborhood boy to remark that Bradley's block was the street where "the dads don't work."[3] The child's assessment illustrates the gender ambiguities of the immediate post-Vietnam years, when a rejection of militarized gender relations intersected with changes brought by a deindustrializing economy. GI and veteran resistance to the warrior persona at times allied with struggles against racism and sexism on the home front, and economic changes forced more women into the workforce, even those who might have preferred to stay home.

Rather than a clear resolution of the contradictory wartime ideology that incorporated the dragon lady, the gentle warrior, and the girl next door, the end of the Vietnam War gave rise to a new set of tensions. Some aspects of the ideology were absorbed and reshaped into refurbished belief systems that would guide U.S. foreign and domestic policies in the Reagan years and beyond. There was a movement away from the images of American women as the girl next door in need of protection, which the donut dollies had been meant to symbolize to U.S. troops fighting in Vietnam. The entry of more women, especially married women and mothers, into the workforce, owing in part to economic changes caused by deindustrialization, counteracted the image of women needing protection and rendered the patriarchal image of men as protectors and breadwinners no longer economically practical.[4] Adjusting to the reality of this transformation in American society, the military launched recruitment campaigns

---

[2] "Working Class Hero: An Interview with John and Yoko," *Left Face*, Anniston, AL, August 1971, 8, Wisconsin Historical Society.

[3] Author's interview with Doug Bradley, April 2008, Madison, WI.

[4] For detailed studies of the women's movement of the 1960s and 1970s, and the struggle for economic equality between men and women, see Alice Echols, *Daring to Be Bad: Radical Feminism in America, 1967–1975* (Minneapolis: University of Minnesota Press, 1989); Ruth Rosen, *The World Split Open: How the Modern Women's Movement Changed America* (New York: Penguin Books, 2000); Alice Kessler-Harris, *In Pursuit of Equity: Women, Men, and the Quest for Economic Citizenship in 20th-Century America* (New York: Oxford University Press, 2003); and Dorothy Sue Cobble, *The Other Women's Movement: Workplace Justice and Social Rights in Modern America* (Princeton, NJ: Princeton University Press, 2005). For a social and cultural history of 1970s America, see Bruce J. Schulman, *The Seventies: The Great Shift in American Culture, Society, and Politics* (Cambridge, MA: Da Capo Press, 2001).

aimed at women, and women responded, largely because they needed jobs and money for education.[5] At the same time, both individual men and American policymakers demonstrated a disturbing tendency to return to the old structures, fostering not resolution of the gender tensions that the war made starkly visible, but more contradictions. Deeply ingrained in the American psyche, the meanings embedded in the images of the male warrior, the girl next door, and the abstract foreign woman lingered in U.S. relations with the world. They also continued to influence Americans' understandings of the armed services and which roles women and men should hold in them.

After the draft ended in 1973, the U.S. armed services set out to remarket themselves in response to the movement for women's equality and the unpopularity of the Vietnam War. Once held up as an exclusively masculine institution and a bastion of manhood, in the mid-1970s, the armed forces recreated themselves as institutions in which women as well as men could get an education and learn job skills.[6] In an all-volunteer force that was reaching out to recruit women, John Wayne could no longer serve as the central image of military life. This was partly because of concerns about filling the ranks, but it also represented an implicit acknowledgment that the Vietnam War had discredited the military's John Wayne image. Shifting attention away from combat prowess, Army publications showcased opportunities for women and the advancement of women within the ranks, and they issued statements of support for political measures aimed at gender equality.

The August 1975 issue of the Army magazine *Soldiers* published an article backing the Equal Rights Amendment, arguing that "in the civilian world, more and more women feel that being a housewife is not enough. They are looking for fulfillment in other areas. The purpose of the ERA isn't to push women into non-traditional occupations, but to eliminate discrimination based on sex. The Army, on its own, has made a great head start toward that same goal."[7] As evidence, the article noted that the number of women on active duty in the Army had tripled over the

---

[5] Jeanne Holm, *Women in the Military: An Unfinished Revolution* (Novato, CA: Presidio Press, 1982), 260–88; Beth Bailey, *America's Army: Making the All-Volunteer Force* (Cambridge, MA: The Belknap Press of Harvard University, 2009).

[6] Holm, *Women in the Military: An Unfinished Revolution*; Bailey, *America's Army: Making the All-Volunteer Force*.

[7] "Women: Moving Up," *Soldiers*, August 1975, 11, Record Group 319 – Records of the Army Staff, Women's Army Corps, 1945–1978 [hereafter NARA RG 319], Box 94, Folder 791.

past three years. Simultaneously, the Army eased restrictions on which professions women could enter, allowing them to serve in almost every field except combat. The article also affirmed the League of Women Voters, statement on the ERA: "If a law restricts rights, it will no longer be valid; if it protects rights, it will be extended to both men and women."[8] The expectation that the ERA would pass spurred the branches of the service to become "models of equal opportunity," Congress's General Accounting Office reported in 1976.[9] Legislation aimed at bringing gender equality to the armed services included granting women entry into military academies in 1976 and dissolving the Women's Army Corps and fully integrating women into the Army in 1978. The number of women in the U.S. armed forces increased significantly during the 1970s, from 1.3 percent of the enlisted ranks in 1971 to 7.6 percent in 1979. The Army saw an even larger increase, in which women personnel jumped from 1.2 percent to 8.4 percent.[10]

The changes in women's roles in the military were intertwined intricately with changes in America's racial landscape. Within the increase in women joining the military, by 1987, African American women composed more than 44 percent of all enlisted women in the Army. The number was four times black women's proportion of the civilian female population in the United States. In the total armed forces, black women made up more than 25 percent of all enlisted women. For some young African American women in the Reagan years, the military seemed to be a rare institution that would provide them with education, job training, health benefits, and pay.[11]

As the Defense Department envisioned an all-volunteer military, some white Pentagon officials and white Congressional leaders expressed concerns that an all-volunteer military might come to rely heavily on African American male enlistees to do more than fill infantry positions. When it came to women, though, Defense Department officials ignored race and viewed women in general as "the means to *dilute* black males' potential dominance of the rank and file in the post-Vietnam volunteer army," Enloe wrote (emphasis Enloe's). When Pentagon officials envisioned national security risks, they did not imagine African American

[8] Ibid.
[9] "Military women are not liberated!" *Overseas Weekly*, June 28, 1976.
[10] Holm, *Women in the Military: An Unfinished Revolution*; Bailey, *America's Army: Making the All-Volunteer Force*.
[11] Cynthia Enloe, *Does Khaki Become You? The Militarization of Women's Lives* (London: Pandora, 1988), 136–37.

women in uniform, but black soldiers with guns.[12] It is possible that the trepidation about armed black men also reflected the racial turmoil of the late 1960s and early 1970s, especially specific fears about groups such as the Black Panthers and the Black Liberation Army. At a time when John Wayne-style masculinity had lost credibility in the wake of the Vietnam War, race, not gender, represented the biggest threat to the white male-dominated military. Military publications and public relations campaigns lauded the increases in women military personnel, but within the ranks, male troops attitudes' toward their female counterparts remained ambivalent, if not hostile.

Gender and a Changing Military

In the inaugural issue of *Ms.* magazine, published in the spring of 1972, Daniel Ellsberg reflected on his career as a Defense Department advisor. Best known for exposing U.S. government deceit regarding the Vietnam War in the *Pentagon Papers*, Ellsberg told the editors of *Ms.* about a conversation he had with the commander of U.S. Armed Forces in Japan during a 1960 visit to American military bases in the Pacific. Discussing Japanese resentment of U.S. security forces, the commander told Ellsberg that the Japanese could easily force American troops out. "They could just take away the maids," the commander said. Ellsberg used the anecdote to illustrate his belief that women could "impede the war machine at every level," whether by boycotting companies that profit from war or organizing a Pentagon secretaries' strike. According to Ellsberg, the policymakers responsible for the Vietnam War – all of them men – were blinded by the "masculine mystique" that linked "machismo and violence" and defined manhood through military maneuvers while prohibiting exhibitions of weakness or admissions of defeat. Thus, Ellsberg implored *Ms.* readers and all women to oppose not only war but also the gender ideologies that informed war.[13]

Ellsberg was speaking to a feminist publication, but his statements regarding women's power to stop wars were grounded in traditional notions of femininity and women as inherently peaceful in contrast with naturally aggressive men. In reality, such simplistic gender categories did not account for the increase in the numbers of women who entered the armed services in the 1970s or women who supported belligerent

---

[12] Ibid.
[13] "Daniel Ellsberg Talks About Women and War," *Ms.*, Spring 1972, 39.

U.S. foreign policies.[14] Despite the continued existence of conventional gender beliefs echoing those embedded in Ellsberg's comments, women's actual roles had changed substantially since President Kennedy called on Americans to go out into the world and spread the ideals of democracy and capitalism. With the Equal Rights Amendment up for debate in Congress in the 1970s, the demands of the women's movement were at the forefront of American life. In addition, economic decline and the struggle for gay rights converged with the GI antiwar movement, the memory of the Vietnam War and its draft, and the subsequent shift to an all-volunteer military to encourage a rethinking of gender beliefs. For the U.S. armed services, this meant recruitment campaigns aimed at women, but despite official pronouncements about opportunities for women in the armed services, military culture indicated that new policies did not necessarily stimulate changes in mindset.

Although the services recognized the need to open their ranks to women to fill an all-volunteer force, military culture remained defined by gender difference, sexuality, and narrow ideas about appropriate roles for women in the armed forces. Statistics tell the story of Defense Department authorities responding to needs for personnel by reaching out to women, but newspaper and magazine articles reveal the complexity of trying to modify the military's long-standing image and the ambivalence of servicemen and women to the changes. Some servicewomen spoke out against the harassment and sexism they experienced by male GIs and officers who made assumptions about their sexuality and motives. Others reflected on their service in Vietnam as evidence of already having achieved the independence and professional advancement the women's movement called for.

Military publications reflected the rhetoric of women's opportunities in the all-volunteer forces. The cover of the November 1975 issue of *Translog: The Journal of Military Transportation Management* featured a drawing of four women's faces, each meant to represent a different ethnicity. Inside, articles expressed support for the United Nations' designation of 1975, the year that the Vietnam War ended, as International Women's Year (IWY), "an historic opportunity for the whole world to focus its attention on the situation of women, and on the means to improve it." The theme of IWY was "equality, development, and peace," suggesting

14 For a discussion of conservative women's political activism, see Ronnee Schreiber, *Righting Feminism: Conservative Women and American Politics* (New York: Oxford University Press, 2008).

a link between a leveling of the gender playing field and an end to war. Its emblem incorporated a dove, the mathematical equals sign, and the symbol for woman.

Planning for IWY in the United States had begun as early as 1973, when the State Department gave a grant to Meridian House International, a private foundation in Washington, DC, to establish the U.S. Center for International Women's Year. On January 30, 1974, President Richard Nixon issued a proclamation calling on Americans to observe IWY in 1975 and "to encourage practical and constructive measures to advance the status of women." A year later, President Gerald Ford created the National Commission for International Women's Year, stating that "opening up new doors to approximately half the world's population is vital to solving many of our international problems."[15] In addition, the Defense Department's IWY commission acknowledged the achievements and sacrifices of women who had served the Defense Department in both military and civilian capacities. The Army conducted a study titled "The Utilization of Civilian Women Employees Within the Department of the Army," which investigated gender imbalances in the military and civilian personnel rosters. The editors of *Translog* wrote that, in keeping with the celebration of IWY, their November 1975 issue aimed to show the advancements of women in the fields of Army transportation and traffic management, and also to highlight that more still needed to be done to achieve equality between women and men in the services. "It is the law of eternal justice that man cannot degrade women without himself falling into degradation; and he cannot raise them without himself becoming better," the article observed.[16]

Soldiers, an Army magazine, highlighted IWY with an article titled "Women: Moving Up," featuring the IWY logo, in its August 1975 issue. The piece described Army women entering fields typically thought of as men's occupations, including "military policewomen, women truck drivers, mechanics, equipment repairpersons, parachute riggers, and women in many other nontraditional roles." Army leaders were optimistic about the continued opening of opportunities for women. "You've got to realize we've made a lot of advances in the last thirty-three years,"

---

[15] Virginia R. Allan, "A Challenge for a Changing World," *Civil Service Journal,* April/June 1975, 15–16.
[16] Myrtle Mero, "The Year of the Woman," *Translog: The Official Magazine of Military Traffic Management Command,* November 1975, Vol. VI, No. 11, 2–3, NARA RG 319, Box 94, Folder 791.

said Colonel Georgia Hill, commanding officer of Cameron Station military reservation in Alexandria, Virginia. "In another five or ten years, who knows how many women generals there may be?"[17]

Despite the positive tone, articles about IWY and the opening of opportunities for women in the armed services reveal the contradictions in attempts to address gender inequality in post-Vietnam military and foreign relations. One of the main goals of IWY was to address discrimination against women and come up with ways to incorporate women into international decision-making regarding politics and economics, but the argument for the inclusion of women was based on the gendered connection between femininity and peace. Writing about IWY, Virginia Allan, State Department deputy assistant secretary for public affairs, explained that "the full and complete development of a country, the welfare of the world, and the cause of peace require the maximum participation of women as well as men in all fields." Allan also wrote that "women will help to institutionalize détente" and "to insist that governments march to the mandate of a stable world order." The official objectives of IWY included recognizing "the importance of women's increasing contribution to friendly relations and cooperation among countries and to the strengthening of world peace."[18]

Whereas advocates for IWY linked women with an end to global conflicts, debates about opening combat positions for women in the U.S. Armed Forces highlighted both a desire to shift away from the image of woman as peacemaker and girl next door in need of protection and an interest in preserving combat as a male domain. Rejecting the idea that American society was not prepared to handle women being maimed or killed in war, one WAC told the writer for *Soldiers*: "We say we don't want our girls to get hurt, but who wants our boys to get hurt, either?" As the Vietnam War showed, military and civilian women could and did get hurt and killed in war despite being barred from infantry units. Other WACs interviewed for the article in *Soldiers* said that even though they did not want to fight, the option to participate in combat should be officially available to women. Lieutenant Colonel Sherman Ragland, Walter Reed Army Medical Center's human resources officer, tried to explain the cultural imagery that was part of the dilemma: "A woman in most people's minds is symbolic of motherhood, so when you give a woman a gun, it's the same thing as giving your mother a gun and sending her off to fight." Peggy Paige, an instructor for the 883oth Military Police

---

[17] "Women: Moving Up," *Soldiers*, August 1975, 11–15.
[18] Allan, 16.

Brigade in Gaithersburg, Maryland, also drew on gendered imagery to explain her opposition to serving in combat: "Women are equal brainwise, but not physically. I'm a delicate creature and I want to be treated that way."[19]

As the armed services transitioned to an all-volunteer force and stepped up the recruitment of women, combat remained the chief point of contention in debates about women's roles in the military. The perspectives of both women and men were mixed. In 1976, a Washington Post reporter interviewed cadets and officers at the U.S. military academies, and they provided a variety of perspectives on the subject. Beth Lundquist, a midshipman at the U.S. Naval Academy in Annapolis, wanted the opportunity to serve in combat because she believed it was a waste of time to go through the academy's rigorous training to take a desk job when it was over. Cheryl Spohnholtz, a fellow midshipman, also favored opening combat roles to women and said that her male counterparts resented women's exemption from them. Reginald Bassa and Todd Worthington, Air Force Academy cadets, complained that women got "all the bennies [benefits] but they're not doing the same as the guys. They spend all this money on training the girls and then send them to the adjutant corps."

Those who opposed offering women combat positions provided relatively vague reasons for their opinions. Air Force cadet June Van Horn Glidden "learned this summer that women are just as physically able as men, there's no two ways about that. They're as intelligent, they could take leadership roles, but they couldn't take combat roles." The article offered no further explanation of Glidden's opinion. Lieutenant General Sidney Berry, the superintendent of West Point at the time, hoped women would not be assigned to combat units because he believed that "would tend to reduce the effectiveness of those combat units." Brigadier General Stanley Beck, the Air Force Academy's commandant of cadets, provided the most specific reason for wanting to keep combat roles closed to women. "The fact is the American people don't want women in combat, and I doubt that they will change," he said. "No country in the world wants women in combat. When you get right down to the heart of why not . . . one of the main factors is the effect of women being captured and becoming POWs. They would be subject to greater abuse than their male counterparts."[20]

[19] "Women: Moving Up," 12–14.
[20] Phil McCombs, "Women Cadets See Combat Roles as Key to Equality," *Washington Post*, December 23, 1976.

The responses of the personnel who opposed women in combat illustrate how deeply gendered beliefs about military service were entrenched in the collective American mind. Having understood combat for so long as an exclusively male realm, they could not articulate why women should be banned from fighting other than to argue that the American public would not support it. Beck's comment that women POWs would be treated more brutally than men possibly speaks to the wartime convention of using sexual violence against women. Even if the U.S. military provided full equal opportunity to men and women, that did not guarantee that militaries the United States fought would view women soldiers in the same light as men. Cadets and officers from the U.S. military academies interviewed for a *Philadelphia Inquirer* article emphasized the psychological impact of women in infantry units as overshadowing the physical ability of women to serve. The article described women cadets at West Point who had mastered the use of weapons including M16 rifles, M60 machine guns, and M79 grenade launchers, as well as various combat techniques. Major Zig Roebuck argued that some women cadets "could perform just as men could in combat." But despite female cadets' physical readiness for combat, Roebuck feared that male cadets were not psychologically prepared to fight side by side with women. The sight of a woman being injured or killed might be too much to bear. Roebuck referred to the coed Israeli army, noting that when women troops got hurt, men responded with "extreme shock . . . much more than seeing men injured."

Captain Douglas Murray, chairman of the Navy Reserve Officers Training Corps (ROTC) at the University of Michigan, saw the debate over women in combat as part of a larger conversation about changing gender relations. "I'm of the generation that still holds chairs and opens doors," he said. "So my apprehensions are that men might do very foolish things in the name of gallantry. Like run into open fire to save her the risk." Murray went on to wonder what the demand for women in combat might mean about a transformation of gender relations in broader society. "Are these people a reflection of American womanhood? When will men stop opening doors? Where is this all headed?"[21]

Lieutenant Colonel Richard Parker, chairman of the University of Michigan's Army ROTC program, acknowledged that women recruits could compete on the same level physically as men, but because of Americans' perceptions of soldiering as a man's field, neither women nor men

---

[21] Emily Fisher, "Women mastering combat, but men lag in acceptance," *Philadelphia Inquirer*, November 25, 1976.

could truly envision women in combat roles. Psychologists attributed the attitude to "threatened male pride, a pride based on his superior strength, on an inherited image of himself as hunter, defender, warrior, breadwinner, on the honor that decries his abandoning the sinking ship." John Teahan, a psychology professor at Wayne State University, added that "naturally the male inclination toward protectiveness is at work here; it's ingrained in our culture." Teahan went on to state that "male soldiers resent having to feel protective. It makes them feel more vulnerable because deep down they do not believe the women to be as competent. They fear women cannot back them up well on the battlefield, cannot qualify as a trustworthy member of the team."[22] Cultural changes in the way Americans viewed war and soldiering would have to come before legislation could successfully open combat to women.

Besides the combat issue, concerns arose that women in an integrated force would "lose their identity" – or, in other words, become masculine. As the services worked to increase the numbers of female personnel, they also enacted practices to maintain mainstream femininity. Reflecting on the Air Force Academy going coed, Colonel James P. McCarthy worried that women, who would be outnumbered about twenty-eight to one by men, would adopt "lower voices, athletic walks, and profane language" to blend in. "We want to graduate the most feminine women officers we can," McCarthy said.[23] The experiences of women Marines provide the starkest image of the tension in recruiting women. Basic training for women Marines at Parris Island, South Carolina, followed that of men's basic in style and substance, with drill instructors hurling orders and insults at women recruits and pushing them beyond their physical limits. Yet the one area in which women Marines spent the most time after physical training was a course called "image development." In the classroom where the course was held, desks turned into vanity tables, and recruits learned techniques for applying makeup, including appropriate shades of lipstick that did not clash with the red braid on the Marine cap.[24] The reality of having a coed force was acceptable as long as the image of difference between men and women, representing mainstream gender roles, remained intact.

This was largely the result of concerns about sexuality, which were not new to the post-Vietnam era but took on increased significance as

---

[22] Ibid.
[23] "Air Force Academy, Going Coed, Ponders Pockets and Calories," *Wall Street Journal*, February 18, 1976, 1–2.
[24] "Leathernecks with Lipstick," *Washington Post*, March 7, 1976.

women were integrated into the regular forces. Some men viewed their female counterparts as either "hopeless nymphomaniacs" or "a hopeless loser or a lesbian." Detailing some of these attitudes, *Family: The Magazine of Army/Navy/Air Force Times* published an article titled "You've Come a Long Way...Maybe," a play on the slogan of Virginia Slims cigarettes. The article acknowledged the advances women in the military had made, including an expected increase in the number of women in the armed services due to heightened recruitment efforts, the removal of the cap on the percentage of women allowed to make up the forces, the ending of salary caps for women, and equalization of retirement regulations. By the time of the article's publication in 1972, the armed forces had seen five women generals. Hester Turner, one-time chair of the Defense Advisory Committee on Women in the Services, observed, "The women now in military service are beginning to fade that image of a bench-warmer and are becoming full and active members of the Armed Forces team."[25] But individual attitudes suggested a less than friendly opinion of servicewomen. Air Force Captain John Prince complained that too many members of the Women's Air Force "fit into the truck driver mold." An Army captain argued that "the proximity of women to men in combat would cause problems. People don't react normally under combat. Sex is one of the outlets in a stress situation, and people have personality changes sometimes in combat."[26] Even after Vietnam, sexuality was central to some servicemen's views both of women's roles and of the military itself.

As the gay rights movement continued to mobilize in the 1970s, some gay men and lesbians in the services challenged military regulations banning gay Americans from the forces. The Army law prohibiting homosexuality stated: "Personnel who voluntarily engage in homosexual acts, irrespective of sex, will not be permitted to serve in the Armed Forces in any capacity, and their prompt separation is mandatory." It also read: "Members who engage in homosexual acts...are considered unfit for military service because their presence impairs the morale and discipline of the Army."[27] In the summer of 1975, Private First Class Barbara Randolph and Private Deborah Watson, both WACs, threatened to plead

---

[25] Margaret Eastman, "The Woman in Uniform: How Liberated Can She Be?" *Family: The Magazine of Army/Navy/Air Force Times*, March 15, 1972, 7, NARA RG 319, Box 94, Folder 792.

[26] Ibid., 8.

[27] Viola Osgood, "2 WACs to fight probable homosexual discharges," *Boston Globe*, June 4, 1975.

their cases all the way to the U.S. Supreme Court after they faced discharge from the Army for admitting that they were lesbians. Neither Randolph nor Watson had prior records of misconduct, and Randolph had been named "WAC of the Month" and "Soldier of the Month." Both had been training for the WAC Security Division, which required special clearance, and the Army's persecution of them because of their sexuality reflects the prominent Cold War notion that gay people were security risks because they could be blackmailed by those who threatened to out them.[28]

Sergeant Leonard Matlovich, a decorated Vietnam veteran who served three tours in the war, also challenged discharge proceedings filed against him in March 1975 after he told his supervising officer that he was gay. Arguing that he was "fully qualified for further military service," Matlovich wrote in a letter to his supervisor: "My almost twelve years of unblemished service supports this position." Matlovich later explained that he decided to come out partly for himself but also because he hoped to pave the way for other gays in the military to be able to serve openly.[29] The experiences of Randolph, Watson, and Matlovich were just a few examples of how homosexuality remained forbidden in the military despite demands for a rethinking of the gender ideology that had shaped the American experience in Vietnam. The issue reflected Cynthia Enloe's questions about what type of woman is most acceptable to the male military establishment: "Is it safer to have women who will . . . taint the masculine force with their traces of lipstick? Are lesbian soldiers more threatening to the military's sense of its masculinity?"[30] It also suggested a concern about the military's image of masculinity. They were questions and concerns that would not be answered despite the growth of the gay and women's liberation movements, and the challenges to military masculinity.

Despite the recurring assumptions about women's reasons for joining the military in the post-Vietnam era, one of the most common motivations was the need for employment. As Enloe has noted, military recruitment strategies in the late 1970s and early 1980s played on women's desire for economic independence and security.[31] When the Air Force

---

[28] Ibid.
[29] Lesley Oelsner, "Sergeant Challenges Air Force's Right to Discharge Him for Admitted Homosexuality," *New York Times*, May 26, 1975.
[30] Enloe, 141.
[31] Enloe, 99, 135–36.

Academy opened its doors to women, the guarantee of a job – graduates had to serve in the Air Force for five years – was the most popular reason for applying.[32] An article about Army enlistees from the Detroit area explained that "far from being a collection of steely-souled adventuresses, the young women who are entering the service today range from working wives to teenagers." Viewing the Army as insurance of a steady income, women with children and wives whose husbands were unemployed enlisted as a way to weather the rough economy of the post-Vietnam era.[33]

A report on Kansas and Missouri recruiting efforts revealed similar motivations. Carol Halsted, a twenty-five-year-old from Wichita, Kansas, enlisted in the Army so she could get GI Bill benefits to go to college. "I figured I had a future," she said. "I was divorced and there was the opportunity to find a job and get an education." Nineteen-year-old Paula Wagley, of Leavenworth, Kansas, joined the Navy two years after graduating from high school. She had worked behind a butcher's counter and for a carpet cleaning business, but they were dead-end jobs that did not pay enough so she could save for college. Susie Ann Busby, who was from Independence, Kansas, signed up for the Air Force at the age of twenty-one, something she had wanted to do since she was a child. After graduating from high school, Busby worked factory jobs including machine operator, saw operator, and forklift driver. She planned to attend college after serving her time in the Air Force.[34] In the Denver area in 1975, local recruiters were overwhelmed with women wanting to enlist, and enlistees had to wait several months to start basic training because camps were at capacity. Like many other enlistees at the time, Denver women sought jobs and money for college. "I can't afford to feed, clothe, and educate myself all at the same time," said Bobbi Renner, a twenty-one-year-old who enlisted in the Navy. "My recruiter said girls go in for the education and guys go in because they don't have anything else to do." Ann Davies, also twenty-one, enlisted in the Army because she was in the process of getting divorced and needed income.[35]

In many ways, military and civilian women who had served in Vietnam were models of the women's movement's demands. They had left home, delayed marriage and childrearing, learned employable skills, and worked

---

[32] "Air Force Academy," 2.
[33] Doris Scharfenberg, "This is the Army, Ms. Jones," *Detroit News*, November 7, 1976.
[34] Brenda Fisher, "GI Josephine: The New Army," *Kansas City Times*, April 10, 1975, 4B.
[35] Carol Bell, "Military popular with women," *Denver Post*, May 24, 1975.

in the presumably male environment of war. However, they did not necessarily identify with the movement or its ideals. WAC Staff Sergeant
Susan Franklin had always considered herself independent, so she did not
think about the women's movement when she returned from Vietnam.
"I've always done pretty well what I wanted, and I did things that a
lot of people didn't even consider doing," she said. Franklin's main concern on coming home was readjustment. Like Franklin, Army nurse Lola
McGourty considered herself "a lone wolf" who usually did not follow
agendas other than her own. Growing up with a strict father who instilled
conservative values about gender and sexuality in her, Judy Davis, also an
Army nurse, perceived the women's movement as something that did not
represent her. "I'm not a bra burner, and I'm not a libber at all," Davis
said. "I'm very traditional." Reflecting on her Vietnam service, though,
Davis realized that she lived some of the ideals of the women's movement
"without believing in it" and considered herself a pioneer.

When Marj Graves served with the Army Nurse Corps in Vietnam, she
did not think about the women's movement because she never felt her
authority threatened. "I felt very safe with my position of authority in
the military," Graves said. "I was given a lot of responsibility at a young
age, and I know I did a very good job with that. I was very respected
in the military and not only by the people who worked for me but also
by my superiors and my patients." Although she found respect in the
military, Graves was much more constricted in her personal life. "I was
in a marriage where I was very controlled, and to even think that there
was a possibility that I could have a voice in women's rights was totally
outside my scope of reality," she added.[36]

Just as Graves felt that she had achieved the goals of the women's
movement on her own, donut dollies Marj Dutilly and Patty Wooldridge
set out on their own. Dutilly came from a family in which women had
built careers. Her mother was a syndicated newspaper columnist, and her
sisters were a Navy nurse, a college professor, and the managing editor
of a newspaper, so it seemed natural to Dutilly that she, too, would
establish her own independent sense of self. "I didn't need to connect
with the women's movement because to me, the women's movement was
trying to make a place for women, to give them some identity," she said.
"In my mind, women didn't need to be facilitated or helped to be able to
do things because we were already doing things. The women's movement
helped women to get a place an identity for themselves, but going to war

[36] Author's interviews with Judy Davis, Susan Franklin, Marj Graves, and Lola McGourty.

was mine. I didn't find the women's movement relevant to me. From my perspective, there had always been a place where women could serve." On returning from Vietnam, Patty Wooldridge went to night school to get a degree in engineering and moved to Los Angeles alone. Regarding the women's movement, she said, "I felt like I was living it already, and I didn't need any sort of movement to be a part of. I just needed to do it and so I did."[37]

Some women did not see the link between their experiences and the women's movement until after they returned home; others, looking back in hindsight, sometimes several decades later, noticed connections. While serving in Vietnam, Army nurse Paula Quindlen did not think of herself as part of the women's movement, but after her tour of duty, she realized that by virtue of her service, she actually had been living out those ideals. Having served in the military, what she had viewed as a traditionally male institution, made her wonder "why can't we do anything we want to do? Yes, I was in a traditional role because I was a nurse, but being a military nurse was not traditional," Quindlen said. "I really felt that we needed to work to assure that women had all the choices that men had."

Joyce Denke, a donut dolly, figured that the women's movement had influenced her unconsciously, but she credited her mother, a school cafeteria worker, with an even greater role in shaping her independent spirit. "My mother was one to very much encourage us to do things and try things that were out of the ordinary, so I guess my mother had more influence on me than any kind of movement did," Denke said. Born in 1913 in rural Alabama, her mother had to quit school after the tenth grade even though she had hoped to go on to business school. "She had always wanted to do things in her life but was never given the opportunity," Denke said. When Dorris Heaston returned from serving in Vietnam with SRAO, she got married, had children, and did not work outside the home, so she did not relate to the women's movement at that time. Looking back, though, she believes that donut dollies and other women who served in Vietnam paved the way for the advances women have made since, and she expressed frustration with younger women who seem to take their rights for granted. "You don't get it, you don't realize how hard a lot of women worked," she said. "It (the women's movement) did not appeal to me, it was not what I was looking for when I came back. But I look now, and the ones [women] that are so conservative now do

[37] Author's interviews with Marj Dutilly and Patty Wooldridge.

not realize how they have benefited, how they have the ability to think like they do because of what these women did for them."[38]

Serving with the Red Cross in both Korea and Vietnam, Shirley Hines recognized that her generation of SRAO women was on the cusp of something new because "we were a group of women who spoke out." She herself did so regarding the regulation tights the Red Cross required SRAO workers to wear. The guidelines said "flesh colored tights," but when Hines went to the store, she found that "flesh" meant a color that matched the skin of most white women, but not black women. "I wasn't going to buy them," she said. "I was of a different generation of black women where women were more vocal. I don't know whether it was the women's movement or a generational change, but starting in 1969 and 1970, I think the girls were a lot more vocal. So I guess the women's movement had some influence on that part." The Red Cross eventually allowed women to choose black or navy tights in addition to "flesh."[39]

Although some perceived the movement as anathema to their personal values and others did not see any potential connection between it and their lives, military and civilian women found at least a temporary escape from Cold War domesticity through their wartime service. Interestingly, women such as Davis, who considered herself to be "traditional," played important roles in the breakdown of long-standing images of how men and women experience and participate in war. For women as well as men, military service was the ultimate form of traditional patriotism, whereas social movements such as the struggle for women's equality were viewed with suspicion and contempt as examples of radical influences threatening to disrupt the American way of life. The women who served in Vietnam made fundamental moves away from the roles expected of them, however, even when their jobs required them to act according to the rules of Cold War domesticity. Not only did they establish their economic and social independence, but they also did so within the boundaries of one of the most patriarchal institutions in American life.

Reflecting on their service in Vietnam, some women saw irony in the military changes that, though providing more opportunities for women, likely rendered the specific roles and ideological functions they had served irrelevant. ANC nurse Sylvia Lutz Holland interacted with some servicemen in ways that were similar to the function donut dollies served, filling

---

[38] Author's interviews with Joyce Denke, Dorris Heaston, and Paula Quindlen.
[39] Author's interviews with Joyce Denke, Dorris Heaston, Shirley Hines, and Paula Quindlen.

in for mothers, wives, and girlfriends during quiet times on the hospital wards. They would talk about home, friends and family, and what they wanted to do when they got back. In those moments, Holland felt appreciated specifically because she was a woman. In the post-Vietnam military, though, where women were integrated and more of them filled the ranks, she speculated that the type of relationship between men and women she experienced would no longer exist "because of women's lib and everyone being equal." Given the changes in gender roles and the increase in military women, donut dolly Nancy Smoyer believes there would not be a place for the SRAO program, which assumed that all troops were straight men whose morale would be boosted by the girl next door, in the twenty-first century armed forces.[40]

"What Vietnam Did to Us"

In December 1981, *Newsweek* ran a fifty-page article chronicling the Vietnam War and postwar experiences of the members of Charlie Company of the Second Battalion, Twenty-Eighth Infantry Regiment of the First Infantry Division, stationed in Vietnam from 1968 to 1969. Reporters interviewed survivors and their families, as well as the loved ones of those who had died; the resulting piece told the stories of veterans struggling to make sense of the death and destruction they observed and participated in, to understand why their government had sent them to Vietnam, and to reconcile the justifications for the war with the realities of what actually happened. Some of the men had found a way to settle into civilian life and make peace with the war relatively quickly, whereas others fought it longer, turning to alcohol and drugs to deaden the pain and distancing themselves from others to avoid bringing their emotions about the war to the surface. Recurring throughout the article was the notion that the veterans had gone to Vietnam as boys and had come home as men – but not the John Wayne model of a man. They came home as broken men, men for whom war had not provided a sense of masculine power and men who found it very difficult to establish lives according to traditional domestic patterns.[41] Charlie Company was just one group of

---

[40] Christian Appy, *Patriots: The Vietnam War Remembered from All Sides* (New York: Viking, 2003), 172, 189.

[41] Tom Fuller, Richard Manning, Stryker McGuire, Vern E. Smith, and Ron Moreau, "What Vietnam Did to Us: Survivors of Charlie Company relive the war and the decade since," *Newsweek*, December 14, 1981, 46–97.

servicemen who fought in Vietnam, but the stories captured by the *Newsweek* reporters are examples of how the warrior myth failed many of the men who fought according to it.

Titled "What Vietnam Did to Us," the *Newsweek* article on Charlie Company is laced with references, both overt and veiled, to gender, the warrior myth, and domesticity. The image of the warrior going off to battle, leaving his woman on the home front, is evident early on, beginning with the stories of the young men shipping out to Vietnam. Taras Popel, a Chicagoan whose parents were Ukrainian immigrants, saw war as a romantic adventure for tough men like him. Growing up middle class in a suburb of New York City, Skip Sommer believed it was his patriotic duty to serve in the war. Richard Garcia was "a macho type," said his wife, Sharlene, who refused her offer to help him escape to Canada or Mexico when he got drafted. Although Captain Richard Rogers had considered getting out of the Army when his first stint was up, he stayed to go to Vietnam. He wanted to find out whether he was man enough to handle it.[42]

Under the extreme pressure of combat, some of the men of Charlie Company realized the irreconcilable tension between the warrior image and the realities of soldiering. When the first man under Rogers's command was killed, Rogers, overwhelmed with sadness, refused to speak at the fallen man's memorial service because he feared the troops would see tears as a sign of weakness, as he did himself. Killing women and children stripped the veneer off war for Skip Sommer. He was part of an ambush on a Viet Cong trail on Christmas Eve 1968; when the smoke cleared after the fight, Sommer and the other troops discovered that the Viet Cong had used women and children as a human shield. Three women and three children, two boys and a girl who all appeared to be about nine years old, were dead. After the fight, a colonel congratulated the members of Charlie Company, and they were rewarded with extra sodas back at firebase Cantigny. But when Sommer saw that the women and children were included in the battle's body count, he lost his last shred of faith in the U.S. mission in Vietnam.[43] Unable to play either the stoic John Wayne or the gentle warrior, Rogers, Sommer, and other servicemen like them embodied the irreconcilable tensions between those images and the actual lives of servicemen in Vietnam. The gendered myths that were deeply engrained in American culture cracked under the weight of war,

---

[42] Ibid., 50–51, 96.
[43] Ibid., 52, 64.

when soldiers faced events and tasks that left them feeling neither stoic nor gentle.

Back home, some Charlie Company survivors struggled to settle into a domestic routine that involved marriage, children, and breadwinning. Divorced after five years of marriage, Greg Skeels found it tough to make a lifelong commitment after Vietnam. Like other veterans, Lloyd Collins's struggle with alcohol eventually destroyed his marriage. Jim Soike married his girlfriend, Nancy, a few years after returning from Vietnam, but the union fell apart after two years because it was difficult for Soike to communicate. "I don't believe in pinning everything on Vietnam, but it does make you hard," he said. "It does make you independent. You do think you have to pull things out all by yourself." Those whose marriages or long-term relationships with women lasted often credited their wives with saving the partnerships – and the men. Joe Boxx believed that were it not for his wife, Nancy, he would have become a "real mess." Nancy Boxx stayed with her husband through repeated bourbon and Budweiser binges, believing that the war forced him to do things that were not in his nature – probably not in most humans' nature. "You've got to understand," she said. "It wasn't like him – killing people. I mean. It bothered him a lot. Still does." Boxx was part of Charlie Company's Christmas Eve ambush, and he and another soldier shot the nine-year-old boy. He had struggled with the memory of that moment ever since, but his wife's support kept him together. Although Greg Skeels and his girlfriend eventually broke up, he believed that she saved him during a time when he battled fits of rage. When he had a breakdown, she would "put her arms around me at the end and tell me it was all right."[44]

In some ways, these stories reveal not resolution of the gender tensions that the war made starkly visible, but more contradictions. Even as members of Charlie Company rejected the flag-waving John Wayne image that had been shorthand for America's good intentions in Vietnam and elsewhere during the Cold War, they adopted other aspects of the Wayne persona. Never a sex symbol, Wayne's film characters spent most of their time with other men, either fighting or bonding.[45] Jim Stoike's comment that Vietnam had made him self-reliant, and the challenge of settling into a home life that seemed especially difficult for some veterans, spoke to the very essence of John Wayne. Don Stagnaro made a telling observation to this point during a 1981 reunion of thirty members of

[44] Ibid., 72, 81, 82, 84.
[45] Ronald L. Davis, *Duke: The Life and Image of John Wayne* (Norman, OK: University of Oklahoma Press, 1998), xi.

Charlie Company. Reflecting on the emotional camaraderie among the veterans, some of whom had not been in contact with each other since Vietnam, Stagnaro ventured that the war had forged a love among the men that was stronger than the love they felt for their wives.[46]

Wives, girlfriends, and ex-wives played the age-old wartime female role of caregiver, but like the nurses and donut dollies who served in Vietnam, their domestic duty was messier than popular culture portrayed it. Sometimes they became protectors of husbands hunted by nightmares, alcoholism, and guilt, reversing the roles of the warrior and the woman waiting back home. But the comfort and safety they provided in the domestic sphere was exactly what Cold War domesticity had called for, the home as a shelter – literally and figuratively – from an uncertain, nuclear-charged world, as Elaine Tyler May has written. For some Vietnam veterans, the home was a sanctuary from all that Cold War culture had elevated as honorable and normal – the warrior myth, the unquestioning fight against communism, and the duty of the United States to spread its brand of democracy and freedom throughout the world.

Although the impact of the war on all those servicemen was as diverse as the individuals themselves, the stories of Charlie Company reflect themes – loss of innocence; the destruction of young men, both those who had died in Vietnam and those who returned home to live with the horrors of war; and the collapse of the values that had undergirded U.S. policy in Vietnam. These themes ran through other post-Vietnam news reports that attempted to assess effect of the war on Americans. On May 5, 1975, five days after the North Vietnamese Army captured Saigon, *Pacific Stars & Stripes* ran an article titled "What the Vietnam War Did to America," in which Associated Press reporter John Barbour assessed the war's impact on the United States. Though not overt, gender floated just below the surface. Barbour wrote about the murder of women and children at My Lai and the destruction of Vietnamese cities and towns by the troops who had been there ostensibly to rescue them. He described young men refusing to heed their draft notices and National Guardsmen killing two women, along with two men, during an antiwar protest at Kent State University in Ohio. The article concluded with a quote from Harvard historian and Kennedy adviser Arthur Schlesinger, Jr.: "The collapse of our pretensions both at home and abroad has struck our young men and women with devastating impact."[47]

[46] Fuller, 97.
[47] John Barbour, "What Vietnam War Did to America," *Pacific Stars & Stripes*, May 5, 1975, 11.

Those pretensions included the notion that U.S. military strength could transform the affairs of Vietnam, using the bodies of American young men to implement the deadly policy and images of innocent American and conniving Vietnamese women as rallying points. In the July 1978 issue of *Harper's*, Jeffrey Jay, a clinical psychologist who worked with veterans, wrote that the troops who served in Vietnam "never became the men they hoped to be when, as adolescent recruits, they believed themselves and America invincible. Marked as losers, they feel constantly challenged to prove their manhood." They should not have had to shoulder that burden, Jay argued, because the United States as a whole waged the Vietnam War on their backs.[48] The *Washington Post* chronicled Jay's work with Vietnam veterans in an article that ran on May 4, 1979. In it, a veteran identified only as "Bob" explained that to survive war, "you have to forget how to love people."[49] Contradicting the image of the caring father figure that was the gentle warrior, Bob's reality required that he reject his humanity to stay alive in Vietnam. In all of these accounts, the veterans' experiences revealed the irreconcilable contradictions between American gender ideology and what actually happened in Vietnam.

The story of Roman Metcalf, a Vietnam veteran from Chicago, profiled in a 1971 *Ebony* magazine article about the plight of African American veterans, shows how the combined circumstances of Vietnam and the economic climate of the 1970s sometimes forced an alternative family structure to the one envisioned in the ideology of Cold War domesticity. At the age of eighteen, Metcalf enlisted in the Marines because he had run out of money for college. Sent to Vietnam with the Third Battalion, Third Marine Division, he developed a reputation as a troublemaker, which Metcalf attributed to racism. Believing that whites in the unit received preferential treatment for R&R requests and that blacks were placed in the worst of the jobs in-country, Metcalf asked to meet with the battalion commander. It was unclear what exactly happened next, but Metcalf was court-martialed for fighting with an officer and received a "bad conduct" discharge, a blemish on his record that, though not as damaging as a dishonorable discharge, still hurt Metcalf's employment chances.

The *Ebony* reporter also interviewed Barry Wright, leader of Concerned Veterans from Viet Nam, a Chicago organization that addressed the issues black vets faced on their return back into civilian life after

---

[48] Jeffrey A. Jay, "After Vietnam: I. In Pursuit of Scapegoats," *Harper's*, July 1978.

[49] Sandy Rovner, "Since Vietnam: Years of Quiet Desperation," *The Washington Post*, May 4, 1979.

service in Vietnam. Wright, himself a Vietnam veteran who served with the Navy Seabees, met hundreds of African American men whose record of service in Vietnam was tainted by a bad discharge. "The more we listened to the guy on the street, the more we became aware of this discharge situation," Wright said. "It seemed that one out of every four veterans we talked to had a bad-paper discharge and couldn't find work." At the time the *Ebony* article was published, Metcalf had not found work, so he took on the domestic responsibilities while his wife, Verna, went to work as a nurse's aide at a nursing home. After walking his wife to the bus stop, he returned home to wash the breakfast dishes, mop, iron, and take care of his two-year-old son. He tried to have dinner started before Verna got home, and in free moments, he looked for work.[50]

Considered in the context of Project 100,000 and contemporary concerns about the stability of urban black families, Metcalf's story reveals another side to the notion that military service could alleviate inner-city poverty by teaching black troops about respectable manhood. In early 1973, *The Nation* reported that unemployment among young African American veterans was at 25 percent. Alluding to the Moynihan thesis that after serving in the military, a black veteran would return to home with the skills necessary to get a job and take care of his family, a veteran interviewed for the article said, "The biggest single problem monster for the black veteran is the growing frequency with which he has returned to his family with other than honorable or 'bad paper' discharges."[51] The *Ebony* article noted that many black men found greater opportunities for education and career advancement in the military than they had in the civilian world. It also reported that some African American troops had served with distinction despite facing racial bias.[52] But it was racial bias that prevented black vets from using their military experience to help them advance in their postwar worlds. Certainly, misbehavior warranted some less-than-honorable discharges. Given the racial tensions that simmered and eventually exploded on occasion in Vietnam, however, it is not unlikely that race played a part in determining punishment in some cases.

Turned down again and again by potential employers, veterans such as Metcalf found themselves taking care of the home while their wives

[50] Hamilton Bims, "The Black Veteran: Battle on the Home Front," *Ebony*, November 1971, 35–43.
[51] John Grady, "The 'Less Than Honorable' Solution," *The Nation*, February 19, 1973, 233–36.
[52] Bims, 38.

238   *Beyond Combat*

earned wages. Though not a new social structure, it came out of a time
period that emphasized a wife-as-homemaker, husband-as-breadwinner
model of the American Dream and used the ideas embedded in that model
to classify Americans by race, income, and sexuality. Those home-front
convictions also defined U.S. troops and the women who provided overseas support. Thus, a soldier-turned-househusband challenged the sus-
tainability of the domestic image, regardless of the couple's intensions.
Roman Metcalf made clear in the *Ebony* article that he wanted to find
work outside the home and had applied for many jobs, but the racial
climate in Vietnam played a hand in barring him from answering the call
of fatherly responsibility to take care of his family financially. The stories
of Vietnam veterans' lives after the war provide evidence toward answering the question of what Vietnam did to us, and they reveal how deeply
gender was embedded in American identity. What Vietnam did was challenge accepted images of masculinity, while not completely overturning
them.

"The Remasculinization of America"

The end of the Vietnam War provided a window of opportunity for a
wide-reaching reassessment of gender roles in America. Antiwar GIs and
veterans, along with their supporters, had exposed the destructive consequences of using the warrior myth to explain U.S. military endeavors. The
experiences of American women and images of Vietnamese women also
revealed the damaging effects of the war's gender hierarchy, as well as the
contradictions in the U.S. mission. The combination of the war's unpopularity, the end of the draft, and the growth of the women's movement
motivated the armed services to reinvent themselves as institutions that
would educate and employ Americans as well as protect the nation and
its interests. Although official military recruitment efforts reached out to
women, however, the culture among recruits suggested a reluctance to
let go of the gender hierarchy of the Cold War era. In 1981, the Army
stopped recruiting women, evidence that change in military culture would
not come quickly.[53]

It was not just military culture that resisted change. Susan Jeffords
writes of the "remasculinization of America" – the rebirth of warrior
masculinity as a dominant force in U.S. culture, influencing both domestic
and foreign policies. Beginning in the late 1970s and continuing into

[53] Bailey, 171–72.

the 1980s, films, novels, and television shows repeatedly portrayed male characters, often Vietnam veterans, working against corrupt, inefficient governments and other bureaucracies, sometimes outside legal channels, to help society at large. If "masculinity had gone out of fashion" in the wake of the Vietnam War and home-front social movements, it came back in vogue through the culture of the 1980s. Jeffords explains that television shows such as "My Two Dads," "Full House," "Highway to Heaven," and "The A Team" portrayed men in control of both the home and public spheres, not only excluding women but also erasing their functions.[54]

On an individual level, however, the war led some military and civilian personnel to challenge – and, in some cases, reject – the gender hierarchy. When those individuals came together, as in the GI antiwar movement, their resistance had a profound impact on military culture. The stories of those women and men who did not join social movements provide important insight on the transformative impact of the Vietnam War. Despite the demands of Cold War domesticity as deployed in Vietnam, American women used service in Vietnam as a way to escape or delay marriage and motherhood, thereby participating in a far-reaching challenge to societal expectations. Consciously or not, they paved the way for women's expanded participation in the armed services and in war.

The twenty-first-century wars in Iraq and Afghanistan have seen a significant expansion of military women's roles in war since Vietnam. More and more women have moved up in the ranks, and the number of women commanding all-male units has increased. As of August 2009, about 11 percent of U.S. forces that have served in Iraq and Afghanistan since 2001 have been women. The war in Iraq "has advanced the cause of women in the Army by leaps and bounds," said retired Army colonel Peter Mansoor, who served as an adviser to General David Petraeus while Petraeus commanded U.S. forces in Iraq. "They have earned the confidence and respect of male colleagues." Women remain barred from combat, but the realities of Iraq and Afghanistan – neither have defined battlefields, and absent a draft, the forces need personnel – have allowed women to enter into most positions that are not specifically designated as combat. In Iraq and Afghanistan, servicewomen provide the necessary service of interacting with local women, something that the dictates of local culture prohibit American men from doing. The Marine Corps' "lionesses" are devoted to that work. Some who study military trends argue that America's commitments in western Asia and the Middle East

[54] Jeffords, 168–69.

will require women to be fully integrated into the forces to meet their needs.[55]

Despite the acknowledged need for women personnel and the numbers of them working in Iraq and Afghanistan, there are limits to their advancement. A *New York Times* article reported that sexual assault counselors and rape kits are commonplace in combat zones, clear demonstrations of the intersection of sexuality, gender, and power in military identity. Even the act of taking up arms does not fully place women in the category of soldier, and in some cases, women's attempts to access certain levels of military service have caused a backlash that could threaten their lives.[56] Beyond the status of American women's wartime roles, the notion of U.S. military endeavors being based on protecting women have played out again, this time in the image of veiled Muslim women and Taliban oppression of women. Taken at face value, liberating oppressed peoples appears to be a worthy cause, and media reports of Afghan girls going to school and women owning businesses without fear of Taliban violence conformed to the notion that U.S. intervention is benevolent and uplifting. Some Afghan women undoubtedly would agree, as would U.S. service personnel who developed meaningful relationships with local civilians and troops. But when the idea that a Muslim woman needs to be liberated from her veil becomes a justification for a U.S. military action that involves broader issues of global power, control, and economics, the United States risks falling back into the trap of undermining the freedom and democracy it purports to stand for. Similarly, the continuing controversies over gays in the military and "don't ask, don't tell" suggest that Cold War notions of gender are not entirely a thing of the past.

Although American women have become increasingly more visible in the armed forces in the years since Vietnam, attitudes toward women soldiers still are in flux among Americans and the military. The story of Private Jessica Lynch, whose unit was attacked early in the Iraq War, is an example of the ambivalence toward women in the military. As journalist Susan Faludi has written, the media portrayed Lynch's ordeal as "a tale of a maiden in need of rescue," even though she was only one casualty of the ambush. Another female member of the unit, Lori Piestewa, a Navajo, was killed during the ambush, along with eight male troops.[57]

---

[55] Lizette Alvarez, "G.I. Jane Breaks the Combat Barrier," *New York Times*, August 15, 2009, http://www.nytimes.com/2009/08/16/us/16women.html?pagewanted=1&_r=1.

[56] Ibid.

[57] Susan Faludi, *The Terror Dream* (New York: Metropolitan Books, 2007), 169.

The focus on Lynch shows her to be at once a soldier as close to combat as women can legally be and a white American woman in need of rescue by male U.S. troops. Even though U.S. Army women now wear combat fatigues and carry heavy equipment, gender stereotypes still hold firm to the American public mind. The rescue of the girl next door, even if she is now a soldier, remains an emotional touchstone for Americans who have not heard the cautionary tales echoed in the story of women, gender, and the Vietnam War.

Bibliography

Archival Sources

Lily Adams Collection, University of Denver Penrose Library, Special Collections, Denver, CO.

American Friends of Vietnam Papers, The Vietnam Archive, Texas Tech University, Lubbock, TX.

Anonymous Collection (#5), The Vietnam Archive, Texas Tech University, Lubbock, TX.

William Bruce Bartow Collection, The Vietnam Archive, Texas Tech University, Lubbock, TX.

Viola W. Bernard Papers, Archives and Special Collections, Augustus C. Long Library, Columbia University, New York, NY.

Black Women Enraged files, Social Action Collection, Wisconsin Historical Society, Madison, WI.

Black Women's Organization Against War and Racism Papers, Social Action Collection, Wisconsin Historical Society, Madison, WI.

Black and Third World Women's Liberation Alliance Papers, Social Action Collection, Wisconsin Historical Society, Madison, WI.

Jackson Bosley Collection, The Vietnam Archive, Texas Tech University, Lubbock, TX.

Calvin Chapman Collection, The Vietnam Archive, Texas Tech University, Lubbock, TX.

John Cheney Collection, The Vietnam Archive, Texas Tech University, Lubbock, TX.

Jeanne Christie Collection, University of Denver Penrose Library, Special Collections, Denver, CO.

John Donnell Collection, The Vietnam Archive, Texas Tech University, Lubbock, TX.

GI Antiwar Newspapers, Social Action Collection, Wisconsin Historical Society, Madison, WI.

Donald F. Harrison Collection, The Vietnam Archive, Texas Tech University, Lubbock, TX.

Glenn Helm Collection, The Vietnam Archive, Texas Tech University, Lubbock, TX.

Marguerite Higgins Papers, Syracuse University, Syracuse, NY.

Garth H. Holms Collection, The Vietnam Archive, Texas Tech University, Lubbock, TX.

Don Kilgore Collection (Americal Division Veterans Association), The Vietnam Archive, Texas Tech University, Lubbock, TX.

Madison Veterans for Peace, Wisconsin Historical Society, Madison, WI.

My Lai Collection, The Vietnam Archive, Texas Tech University, Lubbock, TX.

National Archives, Record Group 200 – Records of the American National Red Cross, 1965–1979, Archives II, College Park, MD.

National Archives, Record Group 319 – Records of the Army Staff, Women's Army Corps, 1945–1978, Archives II, College Park, MD.

National Archives, Record Group 472 – Records of the United States Forces in Southeast Asia, Headquarters, United States Army Vietnam. Archives II, College Park, MD.

Oral History Collections, The Vietnam Archive, Texas Tech University, Lubbock, TX.

Douglas Pike Collection, The Vietnam Archive, Texas Tech University, Lubbock, TX.

Clark Smith Papers, Wisconsin Historical Society, Madison, WI.

Social Movements Collection, The Vietnam Archive, Texas Tech University, Lubbock, TX.

U.S. Army Aviation Museum Volunteer Archivists Collection, The Vietnam Archive, Texas Tech University, Lubbock, TX.

Elwin C. Vanderland Collection, The Vietnam Archive, Texas Tech University, Lubbock, TX.

Veteran Members of the 109th Quartermaster Company (Air Delivery) Collection, The Vietnam Archive, Texas Tech University, Lubbock, TX.

Sally Vineyard Collection, University of Denver Penrose Library, Special Collections, Denver, CO.

Jennifer Young Collection, The Vietnam Archive, Texas Tech University, Lubbock, TX.

Government Publications

Army Civilian Employment: Living and Working in Vietnam (Washington, DC: U.S. Government Printing Office, 1969).

Headquarters, Department of the Army, "*Helpful Hints for Personnel Ordered to Vietnam,*" pamphlet no. 608–16 (Washington, DC: U.S. Government Printing Office, 1968).

Harvey H. Smith, et al., *Area Handbook for South Vietnam* (Washington, DC: U.S. Government Printing Office, 1967).

Investigation of the My Lai Incident: Report of the Armed Services Investigating Subcommittee of the Committee on Armed Services House of Representatives Ninety-First Congress Second Session, July 15, 1970.

The M16A1 Rifle: Operations and Preventive Maintenance (Washington, DC: U.S. Government Printing Office, 1969).

Daniel Patrick Moynihan, "The Negro Family: The Case for National Action," Office of Policy Planning and Research, United States Department of Labor, March 1965.

A Pocket Guide to Vietnam (Washington, DC: U.S. Government Printing Office, 1966).

U.S. Senate Committee on Government Operations, Permanent Subcommittee on Investigations. *Fraud and Corruption in Management of Military Club Systems: Illegal Currency Manipulations Affecting South Vietnam* (Washington, DC: U.S. Government Printing Office, 1971).

U.S. Department of State. *Foreign Relations of the United States, 1961–1963 Volume 1. Vietnam.* (Washington, DC: U.S. Government Printing Office, 1988) [hereafter *FRUS*].

———. *FRUS, 1961–1963. Volume 2. Vietnam.* (Washington, DC: U.S. Government Printing Office, 1990).

———. *FRUS, 1961–1963. Volume 3. Vietnam.* (Washington, DC: U.S. Government Printing Office, 1991).

———. *FRUS, 1961–1963. Volume 4. Vietnam.* (Washington, DC: U.S. Government Printing Office, 1991).

———. *FRUS, 1964–1968. Volume 1. Vietnam.* (Washington, DC: U.S. Government Printing Office, 1992).

———. *FRUS, 1964–1968. Volume 2. Vietnam.* (Washington, DC: U.S. Government Printing Office, 1996).

———. *FRUS, 1964–1968. Volume 4. Vietnam.* (Washington, DC: U.S. Government Printing Office, 1998).

———. *FRUS, 1964–1968. Volume 5. Vietnam.* (Washington, DC: U.S. Government Printing Office, 2002).

GI Antiwar Newspapers

About Face
About Face Germany
About Face USSF
Aboveground
Act
All Ready on the Left
Ally
Attitude Check
Broken Arrow
Counter Attack
Cry Out
Dare to Struggle

Demand for Freedom
Do It Loud
Duck Power
Dull Brass
Exile Report
Eyes Right
Fall in at Ease
Fatigue Press
Final Flight
First Amendment
GI News and Discussion Bulletin
Left Face
Left Flank
Liberated Barracks
Liberty Call
Navy Times Are Changin'
Omega Press
Short Times
The Bond
The Destroyer
The Logistic
Travisty

Newspapers and Periodicals

Anniston (AL) Star
Army Digest
Army Times
Asian Week
Boston Globe
Chicago Tribune
Civil Service Journal
Denver Post
Detroit News
East-West
Ebony
Family: The Magazine of Army/Navy/Air Force Times
Harper's
Independent Journal
Kansas City Times
Life
Life in Vietnam
Los Angeles Herald Examiner
MACV Observer
Mekong Features
Ms.
Muhammad Speaks

Newsweek
New York Times
Overseas Weekly
Pacific Stars and Stripes
Philadelphia Inquirer
Pipeline
Ramparts
Rice
Soldiers
Sports Illustrated
The Hurricane
The Nation
The New Republic
Time
Times of Vietnam
Translog: The Official Magazine of Military Traffic Management Command
Uptight
Vietnam Courier
Vietnam Magazine
Vietnam Observer
Vital Speeches of the Day
Wall Street Journal
Washington Post

Author's Interviews

Lynda Alexander
Doris "Lucki" Allen
Joan Barco
Doug Bradley
Nancy Calcese
Jeanne Christie
Bill Davis
Judy Davis
Joyce Denke
Marj Dutilly
Susan Franklin
Marj Graves
Dorris Heaston
Shirley Hines
Kathleen Huckabay
Kay Johnson
Rene Johnson
Ann Kelsey
Martha Maron
Linda McClenahan
Lola McGourty

Susan McLean
Jim Mifflin
Janie Miller
Bobbie Nofflet
Eileen O'Neill
Sandra Pang
Dorothy Patterson
Linda Pugsley
Paula Quindlen
Kathy Reed
Mary Robeck
Jim Roseberry
Emily Strange
Mike Subkoviak
Elton Tylenda
Nancy Warner
J. Holley Watts
Linda Wilson
Patty Wooldridge
Jennifer Young

Other Primary Sources

Ken Melvin, *Sorry 'Bout That: Cartoons, Limericks, and Other Diversions of GI Vietnam* (Tokyo: The Wayward Press, 1966).
_____, *Be Nice: More Cartoons and Capers of GI Vietnam* (Tokyo: The Wayward Press, 1967).
Tim O'Brien, *The Things They Carried* (New York: Penguin Books, 1990).
Winnie Smith, *American Daughter Gone to War* (New York: Pocket Books, 1994).
Unaccustomed Mercy: Soldier-Poets of the Vietnam War, ed. by W.D. Ehrhart (Lubbock, TX: Texas Tech University Press, 1989).

Secondary Sources and Published Memoirs

Nina S. Adams, "The Women Who Left Them Behind," in *Give Peace a Chance: Exploring the Vietnam Antiwar Movement*, ed. Melvin Small and William D. Hoover, (Syracuse, NY: Syracuse University Press, 1992).
Patrick Allitt, *Catholic Intellectuals and Conservative Politics in America, 1950–1985* (Ithaca, NY: Cornell University Press, 1993).
David L. Anderson, *The Columbia Guide to the Vietnam War* (New York: Columbia University Press, 2002).
Terry H. Anderson, *The Movement and the Sixties: Protest in America from Greensboro to Wounded Knee* (Oxford: Oxford University Press, 1995).
Christian Appy, *Working Class War: American Combat Soldiers and Vietnam* (Chapel Hill, NC: University of North Carolina Press, 1993).

Christian G. Appy, *Patriots: The Vietnam War Remembered from All Sides* (New York: Viking, 2003.

Curtis J. Austin, *Up Against the Wall: Violence in the Making and Unmaking of the Black Panther Party* (Fayetteville, AR: University of Arkansas Press, 2006).

Beth Bailey, *America's Army: Making the All-Volunteer Force* (Cambridge, MA: The Belknap Press of Harvard University Press, 2009).

Mark Baker, *'Nam: The Vietnam War in the Words of the Men and Women Who Fought There* (New York: Berkley Books, 1981).

Loren Baritz, *Backfire: A History of How American Culture Led Us Into Vietnam and Made Us Fight the Way We Did* (New York: William Morrow and Co., 1985).

Tad Bartimus, et al., *War Torn: Stories of War from the Women Reporters Who Covered Vietnam* (New York: Random House, 2002).

Milton J. Bates, *The Wars We Took to Vietnam: Cultural Conflict and Storytelling* (Berkeley, CA: University of California Press, 1996).

Gail Bederman, *Manliness and Civilization: A Cultural History of Gender and Race in the United States, 1880–1917* (Chicago: University of Chicago Press, 1995).

Behind the Lines: Gender and the Two World Wars, ed. Margaret Randolph Higonnet, et al. (New Haven, CT: Yale University Press, 1987).

Thomas Borstelmann, *The Cold War and the Color Line: American Race Relations in the Global Arena* (Cambridge, MA: Harvard University Press, 2003).

Mark Bradley, *Imagining Vietnam and America: The Making of Postcolonial Vietnam, 1910–1950* (Chapel Hill, NC: University of North Carolina Press, 2000).

Mark Philip Bradley, *Vietnam at War* (Oxford: Oxford University Press, 2009).

Wini Breines, *Young, White, and Miserable: Growing Up Female in the Fifties* (Chicago, University of Chicago Press, 1992).

Susan Brownmiller, *Against Our Will: Men, Women, and Rape* (New York: Bantam Books, 1976).

Robert Buzzanco, *Vietnam and the Transformation of American Life* (Malden, MA: Blackwell Publishers, 1999).

Dorothy Sue Cobble, *The Other Women's Movement: Workplace Justice and Social Rights in Modern America* (Princeton, NJ: Princeton University Press, 2005).

Matthew Connelly, *A Diplomatic Revolution: Algeria's Fight for Independence and the Origins of the Post-Cold War Era* (Oxford: Oxford University Press, 2002).

Robert J. Corber, *Homosexuality in Cold War America: Resistance and the Crisis of Masculinity* (Durham, NC: Duke University Press, 1997).

David Cortwright's *Soldiers in Revolt: GI Resistance During the Vietnam War* (Chicago, IL: Haymarket Books, 1975).

K.A. Cuordileone, *Manhood and American Political Culture in the Cold War* (New York: Routledge, 2005).

Ronald L. Davis, *Duke: The Life and Image of John Wayne* (Norman, OK: University of Oklahoma Press, 1998).

Robert Dean, *Imperial Brotherhood: Gender and the Making of Cold War Foreign Policy*. (Amherst, MA: University of Massachusetts Press, 2001).

John D'Emilio, *Sexual Politics, Sexual Communities: The Making of a Homosexual Minority in the United States, 1940–1970* (Chicago: University of Chicago Press, 1983).

Jane Sherron De Hart, "Containment at Home: Gender, Sexuality, and National Identity in Cold War America," in *Rethinking Cold War Culture*, ed. Peter J. Kuznick and James Gilbert (Washington, DC: Smithsonian Institution Press, 2001).

Susan J. Douglas, *Where the Girls Are: Growing Up Female with the Mass Media* (New York: Times Books, 1994).

Mary L. Dudziak, *Cold War Civil Rights: Race and the Image of American Democracy* (Princeton, NJ: Princeton University Press, 2002).

Alice Echols, *Daring to Be Bad: Radical Feminism in America, 1967–1975* (Minneapolis: University of Minnesota Press, 1989).

_____, *Shaky Ground: The Sixties and Its Aftershocks* (New York: Columbia University Press, 2002).

_____, "Women's Liberation and Sixties Radicalism," in *Major Problems in American History Since 1945*, eds. Robert Griffith and Paula Baker (Boston: Houghton Mifflin Company, 2001).

_____, "'Women Power' and Women's Liberation: Exploring the Relationship Between the Antiwar Movement and the Women's Liberation Movement," in *Give Peace a Chance: Exploring the Vietnam Antiwar Movement*, ed. Melvin Small and William D. Hoover (Syracuse, NY: Syracuse University Press, 1992).

Bernard Edelman, *Dear America: Letters Home from Vietnam* (New York: W.W. Norton & Co., 1985).

Barbara Ehrenreich, *Hearts of Men: American Dreams and the Flight from Commitment* (Garden City, NY: Anchor Press/Doubleday, 1983).

David Ekbladh, *The Great American Mission: Modernization and the Construction of an American World Order* (Princeton, NJ: Princeton University Press, 2009).

Tom Engelhardt, *The End of Victory Culture: Cold War America and the Disillusioning of a Generation* (New York: Basic Books, 1995).

Cynthia Enloe, *Bananas, Beaches, and Bases: Making Feminist Sense of International Politics*, (Berkeley, CA: University of California Press, 2000).

_____, *Does Khaki Become You? The Militarization of Women's Lives* (London: Pandora, 1988).

_____, *The Morning After: Sexual Politics at the End of the Cold War* (Berkeley, CA: University of California Press, 1993).

Sara Evans, *Personal Politics: The Roots of Women's Liberation in the Civil Rights Movement and the New Left* (New York: Vintage Books, 1980).

Susan Faludi, *The Terror Dream* (New York: Metropolitan Books, 2007).

Ruth Feldstein, *Motherhood in Black and White: Race and Sex in American Liberalism, 1930–1965*. (Ithaca, NY: Cornell University Press, 2000).

Michael Foley, *Confronting the War Machine: Draft Resistance during the Vietnam War* (Chapel Hill, NC: University of North Carolina Press, 2003).

———, "'The Point of Ultimate Indignity' or a 'Beloved Community'? The Draft Resistance Movement and New Left Gender Dynamics," in *The New Left Revisited*, ed. John McMillian and Paul Buhle, (Philadelphia: Temple University Press, 2003), 178–98.

Gillian Frank, "Discophobia: Antigay Prejudice and the 1979 Backlash Against Disco," *Journal of the History of Sexuality*, Vol. 16, No. 2, May 2007, 276–306.

Lloyd Gardner, *Pay Any Price: Lyndon Johnson and the Wars for Vietnam* (Chicago: Ivan R. Dee, 1995).

Gender and War: Australians at War in the Twentieth Century, ed. Joy Damousi and Marilyn Lake (Cambridge: Cambridge University Press, 1995).

James Gibson, *The Perfect War: Technowar in Vietnam* (New York: Atlantic Monthly Press, 1986).

Paula Giddings, *When and Where I Enter: The Impact of Black Women on Race and Sex in America* (New York: William Morrow and Co., Inc., 1984).

Gerald Gill, "From Maternal Pacifism to Revolutionary Solidarity: African American Women's Opposition to the Vietnam War," in *Sights on the Sixties*, ed. Barbara Tischler (New Brunswick, NJ: Rutgers University Press, 1992).

Nils Gilman, *Mandarins of the Future: Modernization Theory in Cold War America* (Baltimore: Johns Hopkins University Press, 2007).

Todd Gitlin, *The Sixties: Years of Hope, Days of Rage* (New York: Bantam Books, 1987).

Susan H. Godson, *Serving Proudly: A History of Women in the U.S. Navy* (Annapolis, MD: Naval Institute Press, 2001).

Joshua S. Goldstein, *War and Gender: How Gender Shapes the War System and Vice Versa* (Cambridge: Cambridge University Press, 2001).

Van Gosse, *Where the Boys Are: Cuba, Cold War America, and the Making of a New Left* (London: Verso, 1993).

Herman Graham, *The Brothers, Vietnam War: Black Power, Manhood, and the Military Experience* (Gainesville, FL: University Press of Florida, 2003).

Olga Gruhzit-Hoyt, *A Time Remembered: American Women in the Vietnam War* (Novato, CA; Presidio Press, 1999).

Monte Gulzow and Carol Mitchell, "'Vagina Dentata' and 'Incurable Venereal Disease': Legends from the Vietnam War." *Western Folklore*, Vol. 39, No. 4 (Oct. 1980).

Patrick Hagopian, *The Vietnam War in American Memory: Veterans, Memorials, and the Politics of Healing* (Amherst, MA: University of Massachusetts Press, 2009).

David Halberstam, *The Best and the Brightest* (New York: Modern Library, 2001).

Susan M. Hartmann, *From Margin to Mainstream: American Women and Politics since 1960* (New York: Alfred A. Knopf, 1989).

———, "Women's Employment and the Domestic Ideal in the Early Cold War Years," in *Not June Cleaver: Women and Gender in Postwar America, 1945–1960*, ed. Joanne Meyerowitz (Philadelphia: Temple University Press, 1994).

Le Ly Hayslip, *When Heaven and Earth Changed Places: A Vietnamese Woman's Journey from War to Peace* (New York: Plume, 1990).

George C. Herring, *America's Longest War: The United States and Vietnam, 1950–1975* (New York: Knopf, 1979).

Marguerite Higgins, *Our Vietnam Nightmare* (New York: Harper and Row, 1965).

Kristin Hoganson, *Fighting for American Manhood: How Gender Politics Provoked the Spanish-American and Philippine-American Wars* (New Haven, CT: Yale University Press, 1998).

Jeanne Holm, *Women in the Military: An Unfinished Revolution* (Novato, CA: Presidio Press, 1982).

Jan Hornung, *Angels in Vietnam: Women Who Served* (San Jose, CA: Writers Club Press).

Lisa Hsiao, "Project 100,000: The Great Society's Answer to Military Manpower Needs in Vietnam," *Vietnam Generation*, 1989.

Andrew J. Huebner, *The Warrior Image: Soldiers in American Culture from the Second World War to the Vietnam Era* (Chapel Hill, NC: University of North Carolina Press, 2008).

Andrew Hunt, *The Turning: A History of Vietnam Veterans Against the War* (New York: New York University Press, 1999).

Michael Hunt, "East Asia in Henry Luce's 'American Century'," *Diplomatic History*, Vol. 23, No. 2 (Spring 1999).

_____, *Lyndon Johnson's War: America's Cold War Crusade in Vietnam, 1945–1968* (New York: Hill and Wang, 1996).

Michael Hunt, *Ideology and U.S. Foreign Policy* (New Haven, CT: Yale University Press, 1987).

Seth Jacobs, *America's Miracle Man in Vietnam: Ngo Dinh Diem, Religion, Race, and U.S. Intervention in Southeast Asia* (Durham, NC: Duke University Press, 2005).

Susan Jeffords, *The Remasculinization of America: Gender and the Vietnam War* (Bloomington, IN: Indiana University Press, 1989).

Kimberly Jensen, *Mobilizing Minerva: American Women in the First World War* (Urbana, IL: University of Illinois Press, 2008).

Howard Jones, *Death of a Generation: How the Assassinations of Diem and JFK Prolonged the Vietnam War* (Oxford: Oxford University Press, 2003).

Stephen Kantrowitz, "The Two Faces of Domination in North Carolina, 1800–1898," in *Democracy Betrayed: The Wilmington Race Riot of 1898 and Its Legacy*, ed. David Cecelski and Timothy B. Tyson (Chapel Hill, NC: University of North Carolina Press, 1998).

Stanley Karnow, *Vietnam: A History* (New York: Viking, 1991).

Alexander Kendrick, *The Wound Within: America in the Vietnam Years, 1945–1974* (Boston: Little, Brown, and Co., 1974).

Alice Kessler-Harris, *In Pursuit of Equity: Women, Men, and the Quest for Economic Citizenship in 20th-Century America* (New York: Oxford University Press, 2003).

Christina Klein, *Cold War Orientalism: Asia in the Middlebrow Imagination, 1945–1961* (Berkeley, CA; University of California Press, 2003).

Michael Kimmel, *Manhood in America: A Cultural History* (New York: The Free Press, 1996).

Yusef Komunyakaa, *Dien Cai Dau* (Hanover, NH: Wesleyan University Press, 1988).

Daniel Lang, *Casualties of War* (New York: McGraw-Hill, 1969).

Michael E. Latham, *Modernization as Ideology: American Social Science and "Nation Building" in the Kennedy Era* (Chapel Hill, NC: University of North Carolina Press, 2000).

Jacqueline Lawson, "'She's a Pretty Woman... for a Gook': The Misogyny of the Vietnam War," in *Fourteen Landing Zones: Approaches to Vietnam War Literature*, ed. Philip K. Jason (Iowa City, IA: University of Iowa Press, 1991).

Christopher J. Lee, *Making a World After Empire: The Bandung Moment and Its Political Afterlives* (Ohio University Press, 2010).

Steven M. Lee, "'All the Best Cowboys Have Chinese Eyes': The Utilization of the Cowboy-Hero Image in Contemporary Asian-American Literature," in *Across the Great Divide: Cultures of Manhood in the American West*, ed. Matthew Basso (New York: Routledge, 2001).

Robert G. Lee, *Orientals: Asian Americans in Popular Culture* (Philadelphia: Temple University Press, 1999).

Jerry Lembcke, *The Spitting Image: Myth, Memory, and the Legacy of Vietnam* (New York: New York University Press, 2000).

Laura Tyson Li, *Madame Chiang Kai-Shek: China's Eternal First Lady* (New York: Atlantic Monthly Press, 2006).

Robert Jay Lifton, *Home from the War: Learning from Vietnam Veterans* (Boston: Beacon Press, 1992).

Long Shadows: Veterans' Paths to Peace, ed. David Giffey (Madison, WI: Atwood Publishing, 2006).

George Mariscal, *Aztlan and Viet Nam: Chicano and Chicana Experiences of the War* (Berkeley, CA: University of California Press, 1999).

Kathryn Marshall, *In the Combat Zone: An Oral History of American Women in Vietnam, 1966–1975* (Boston: Little, Brown, 1987).

Antoinette May, *Witness to War: A Biography of Marguerite Higgins* (New York: Penguin Books, 1983).

Elaine Tyler May, *Homeward Bound: American Families in the Cold War Era* (New York: Basic Books, 1999).

Melani McAlister, *Epic Encounters: Culture, Media, and U.S. Interests in the Middle East Since 1945* (Berkeley, CA: University of California Press, 2005).

Robert S. McKelvey, *The Dust of Life: America's Children Abandoned in Vietnam* (Seattle: University of Washington Press, 1999).

John Mecklin, *Mission in Torment: An Intimate Account of the U.S. Role in Vietnam* (Garden City, New York: Double Day, 1965).

James H. Meriwether, *Proudly We Can Be Africans: Black Americans and Africa, 1935–1961* (Chapel Hill, NC: University of North Carolina Press, 2001).

Leisa D. Meyer, *Creating G.I. Jane: Sexuality and Power in the Women's Army Corps During World War II* (New York: Columbia University Press, 1996).

Joanne Meyerowitz, *Not June Cleaver: Women and Gender in Postwar America, 1945–1960* (Philadelphia: Temple University Press, 1994).

Yanek Mieczkowski, *Gerald Ford and the Challenges of the 1970s* (Lexington, KY: University of Kentucky Press, 2005).

Jennifer Milliken and David Sylvan, "Soft Bodies, Hard Targets, and Chic Theories: U.S. Bombing Policy in Indochina," *Journal of International Studies*, 1996, 25(2): 321–59.

Milton Caniff: Conversations, ed. Robert C. Harvey (Jackson, MS: University Press of Mississippi, 2002).

Bettie J. Morden, *The Women's Army Corps, 1945–1978* (Washington, DC: Center of Military History, 1990).

Joseph G. Morgan, *The Vietnam Lobby: The American Friends of Vietnam, 1955–1975* (Chapel Hill, NC: University of North Carolina Press, 1997).

Richard R. Moser, *The New Winter Soldiers: GI and Veteran Dissent During the Vietnam Era.* (New Brunswick, NJ: Rutgers University Press, 1996).

Donald Mrozek, "The Cult and Ritual of Toughness in Cold War America," in *Rituals and Ceremonies in Popular Culture*, ed. Ray B. Browne (Bowling Green, OH: Bowling Green University Popular Press, 1980).

Bernard C. Nalty, *Strength for the Fight: A History of Black Americans in the Military* (New York: The Free Press, 1986).

Jonathan Nashel, *Edward Lansdale's Cold War* (Amherst, MA: University of Massachusetts Press, 2005).

Jonathan Nashel, "The Road to Vietnam: Modernization Theory in Fact and Fiction," in *Cold War Constructions: The Political Culture of United States Imperialism, 1945–1966*, ed. Christian G. Appy (Amherst, MA: University of Massachusetts Press, 2000).

Nathalie Huynh Chau Nguyen, *Memory is Another Country: Women of the Vietnamese Diaspora* (Santa Barbara, CA: ABC-CLIO, 2009).

Thi Dieu Nguyen, *The Mekong River and the Struggle for Indochina: Water, War, and Peace* (Westport, CT: Praeger Publishers, 1999).

Gerald Nicosia, *Home to War: A History of the Vietnam Veterans Movement* (New York: Carroll & Graf, 2004).

Frank Ninkovich, *The U.S. and Imperialism* (Malden, MA: Blackwell Publishing, 2001).

Elizabeth M. Norman, *Women at War: The Story of Fifty Military Nurses who Served in Vietnam* (Philadelphia: University of Pennsylvania Press, 1990).

Joseph Nye, *Soft Power: The Means to Success in World Politics* (Cambridge, MA: PublicAffairs, 2004).

James S. Olson and Randy Roberts, *Where the Domino Fell: America and Vietnam, 1945–2006* (Maplecrest, NY: Brandywine Press, 2006).

Lorena Oropeza, *Raza Si! Guerra No! Chicano Protest and Patriotism during the Vietnam War Era* (Berkeley, CA: University of California Press, 2005).

Ann Pfau, *Miss Yourlovin: GIs, Gender, and Domesticity during World War II* (New York: Columbia University Press, 2008), via Gutenberg-e, www.gutenberg-e.org/pfau/.

Donna Penn, "The Meanings of Lesbianism in Postwar America," in *Gender and American History Since 1890*, ed. Barbara Melosh (London: Routledge, 1993).

Brenda Gayle Plummer, *Rising Wind: Black Americans and U.S. Foreign Affairs, 1935–1960* (Chapel Hill, NC: University of North Carolina Press, 1996).

Lee Rainwater and William L. Yancey, *The Moynihan Report and the Politics of Controversy* (Cambridge, MA: Massachusetts Institute of Technology Press, 1967).

Mary Renda, *Taking Haiti: Military Occupation and the Culture of U.S. Imperialism, 1915–1940* (Chapel Hill, NC: University of North Carolina Press, 2002).

Ruth Rosen, *The World Split Open: How the Modern Women's Movement Changed America* (New York: Penguin, 2006).

Emily S. Rosenberg, "Gender," *Journal of American History*, 77 (June 1990), 116–24.

———, "Walking the Borders," *Diplomatic History*, 14 (Fall 1990), 565–73.

———, "Foreign Affairs After World War II: Connecting Sexual and International Politics," *Diplomatic History*, Winter 1994.

Andrew Rotter, *Comrades at Odds: The United States and India, 1947–1964* (Ithaca, NY: Cornell University Press, 2000).

———, "Gender Relations, Foreign Relations: The United States and South Asia, 1947–1964, *Journal of American History*, Vol. 81, No. 2 (Sept. 1994), 518–42.

Dana Sachs, *The Life We Were Given: Operation Babylift, International Adoption, and the Children of War in Vietnam* (Boston: Beacon Press, 2010).

Al Santoli, *Everything We Had: An Oral History of the Vietnam War By Thirty-Three American Soldiers Who Fought It* (New York: Random House, 1981).

David F. Schmitz, *The United States and Right-Wing Dictatorships* (Cambridge: Cambridge University Press, 2006).

———, *Thank God They're on Our Side: The United States and Right-Wing Dictatorships, 1921–1965* (Chapel Hill, NC: University of North Carolina Press, 1999).

Ronnee Schreiber, *Righting Feminism: Conservative Women and American Politics* (New York: Oxford University Press, 2008).

Bruce J. Schulman, *The Seventies: The Great Shift in American Culture, Society, and Politics* (Cambridge, MA: Da Capo Press, 2001).

Joan W. Scott, *Gender and the Politics of History* (New York: Columbia University Press, 1988).

Nayan Shah, *Contagious Divides: Epidemics and Race in San Francisco's Chinatown* (Berkeley, CA: University of California Press, 2001).

Neil Sheehan, *A Bright Shining Lie: John Paul Vann and America in Vietnam* (New York: Vintage Books, 1988).

Naoko Shibusawa, *America's Geisha Ally: Reimagining the Japanese Enemy* (Cambridge, MA: Harvard University Press, 2006).

Sights on the Sixties, ed. Barbara L. Tischler (New Brunswick, NJ: Rutgers University Press, 1992).

Caroline Chung Simpson, *An Absent Presence: Japanese Americans in Postwar American Culture, 1945–1960* (Durham, NC: Duke University Press, 2001).

Richard Slotkin, *Gunfighter Nation: The Myth of the Frontier in Twentieth-Century America* (Norman, OK: University of Oklahoma Press, 1998).

Melvin Small, *Give Peace a Chance: Exploring the Vietnam Antiwar Movement* (Syracuse, NY: Syracuse University Press, 1992).

Winnie Smith, *American Daughter Gone to War: On the Front Lines with an Army Nurse in Vietnam* (New York: Morrow, 1992).

Richard Stacewicz, *Winter Soldiers: An Oral History of the Vietnam Veterans Against the War* (New York: Twayne Publishers, 1997).

Ron Steinman, *Women in Vietnam* (New York: TV Books, 2000).

Ann Laura Stoler, *Carnal Knowledge and Imperial Power: Race and the Intimate in Colonial Rule* (Berkeley, CA: University of California Press, 2002).

_____, *Haunted By Empire: Geographies of Intimacy in North American History* (Durham, NC: Duke University Press, 2006).

_____, "Intimidations of Empire: Predicaments of the Tactile and Unseen," in *Haunted By Empire: Geographies of Intimacy in North American History*, ed. Stoler, (Durham, NC: Duke University Press, 2006).

_____, *Race and the Education of Desire: Foucault's History of Sexuality and the Colonial Order of Things* (Durham, NC: Duke University Press, 1995).

Col. Mary V. Stremlow, *A History of the Women Marines, 1946–1977* (Washington, DC: History and Museums Division Headquarters, U.S. Marine Corps, 1986).

Jeremi Suri, *Power and Protest: Global Revolution and the Rise of Détente* (Cambridge, MA: Harvard University Press, 2003).

Amy Swerdlow, *Women Strike for Peace: Traditional Motherhood and Radical Politics in the 1960s* (Chicago: University of Chicago Press, 1993).

Sandra C. Taylor, *Vietnamese Women at War: Fighting for Ho Chi Minh and the Revolution* (Lawrence, KS: University Press of Kansas, 1999).

Wallace Terry, *Bloods: An Oral History of the Vietnam War by Black Veterans* (New York: Random House, 1984).

Charley Trujillo, *Soldados: Chicanos in Viet Nam* (San Jose, CA: Chusma House Publications, 1990).

Karen Gottschang Turner, *Even the Women Must Fight: Memories of War from North Vietnam* (New York: John Wiley and Sons, Inc., 1998).

Vietnam and America: A Documented History, ed. Marvin E. Gettleman, et al. (New York: Grove Press, 1995).

Lynda Van Devanter, *Home Before Morning: The Story of an Army Nurse in Vietnam* (Amherst, MA: University of Massachusetts Press, 2001).

Penny Von Eschen, *Race Against Empire: Black Americans and Anticolonialism, 1937–1957* (Ithaca, NY: Cornell University Press, 1997).

Kara Dixon Vuic, *Officer, Nurse, Woman: The Army Nurse Corps in the Vietnam War* (Baltimore: The Johns Hopkins University Press, 2010).

Keith Walker, *A Piece of My Heart: The Stories of Twenty-Six American Women Who Served in Vietnam* (New York: Ballantine Books, 1985).

We Were There: Voices of African American Veterans From World War II to the War in Iraq, ed. Yvonne Latty (New York: Amistad, 2004).

Odd Arne Westad, *The Global Cold War* (Cambridge: Cambridge University Press, 2005).

Robert Westbrook, "'I Want a Girl, Just Like the Girl That Married Harry James': American Women and the Problem of Political Obligation in World War Two," *American Quarterly* Vol. 2, No. 4, December 1990, 592.

James Westheider, *Fighting on Two Fronts: African Americans and the Vietnam War* (New York: New York University Press, 1999).

Toshio Whelchel, *From Pearl Harbor to Saigon: Japanese American Soldiers and the Vietnam War* (London: Verso, 1999).

Laura Wexler, *Tender Violence: Domestic Visions in an Age of U.S. Imperialism* (Chapel Hill, NC: University of North Carolina Press, 2000).

Andrew Wiest, *Vietnam's Forgotten Army: Heroism and Betrayal in the ARVN* (New York: New York University Press, 2007).

Marion L. Williams, *My Tour in Vietnam: A Burlesque Shocker* (New York: Vantage Press, 1970).

Window on Freedom: Race, Civil Rights, and Foreign Affairs, 1945–1988, ed. Brenda Gayle Plummer (Chapel Hill, NC: University of North Carolina Press, 2003).

Trin Yarborough, *Surviving Twice: Amerasian Children of the Vietnam War* (Washington, DC: Potomac Books, 2005).

Marilyn Young, *The Vietnam Wars, 1945–1990* (New York: Harper Perennial, 1991).

Index

Made in United States
Orlando, FL
13 April 2022